ANDREA ROBINSON'S

2007 WINE BUYING GUIDE

for Everyone

ANDREA ROBINSON'S

2007 WINE BUYING GUIDE

for Everyone

**FEATURING MORE THAN 700 TOP WINES
AVAILABLE IN STORES AND RESTAURANTS**

Andrea Robinson

Broadway Books / New York

BROADWAY

PUBLISHED BY BROADWAY BOOKS

Copyright © 2007 by Andrea Robinson

First edition published 2002

Published in the United States by Broadway Books, an imprint of The Doubleday Broadway Publishing Group, a division of Random House, Inc., New York

www.broadwaybooks.com

BROADWAY BOOKS and its logo, a letter B bisected on the diagonal, are trademarks of Random House, Inc.

The Library of Congress has cataloged the first edition as follows:
Immer, Andrea
[Wine buying guide for everyone]
Andrea Immer's wine buying guide for everyone /
Andrea Immer; edited by Anthony Giglio.—1st ed.
p. cm.
Includes index.
1. Wine and wine making. I. Title: Wine buying guide
for everyone. II. Giglio, Anthony. III. Title.

   TP548 .I4624 2002
   641.2'2—dc21   2002023077

ISBN-13: 978-0-7679-1985-2
ISBN-10: 0-7679-1985-8

PRINTED IN THE UNITED STATES OF AMERICA

10 9 8 7 6 5 4 3 2 1

CONTENTS

ANDREA ROBINSON'S

2007 WINE BUYING GUIDE

for Everyone

INTRODUCTION

Although enjoying a good glass of wine is easy, all the types, costs, and confusing labels can make *shopping* for a bottle pretty hard. For the typical wine consumer, buying guidance—in the form of critics' 100-point scores and elaborate tasting reports of rare and exclusive bottlings—isn't much help. That is why I wrote *Andrea Robinson's Wine Buying Guide for Everyone.* It is your road map to the *real* world of wine buying— from restaurants and hotels to supermarkets, price clubs, wine shops, and Web sites. Here is what you'll find inside:

Real-World Wines
This guide showcases more than 700 of the most popular and available wines on the market. That includes everything from supermarket stalwarts to trade-up labels to superpremium "restaurant" brands (with plenty of boutique pedigree but without the you-can't-get-it frustration). Putting it plainly, if the wine is in your favorite neighborhood shops and eateries, at your supermarket or Costco, Olive Garden or Walt Disney World, Marriott or Carnival Cruises, JetBlue airlines or wine.com, it's probably in this book.

Wine Reviews from the Trenches
I am indebted to the many consumers and wine pros who helped assess, for each of the wines in this book, what really matters to buyers at the point of purchase—taste and value for the money. For each wine, you'll also see their real-world reactions, as well as my impressions of how the wine stacks up in its grape or style category and in the marketplace overall. My tasters also contributed write-in candidates to the list of wines, and I've included those that received the highest number of positive mentions and have decent availability. There's also space in each listing for your notes, so you can keep track of the wines you

try. (I hope you'll share your impressions with me for the next edition—read on to see how.)

Other Helpful Buying Tools in the Guide

Throughout the *Guide,* I've included simple tools to address just about every major wine buying question I've ever been asked. They are

Most Popular Lists—A quick reference to the top-performing wines in each grape or style category.

Andrea's Kitchen Fridge Survivor™ and Kitchen Countertop Survivor™ grades—"How long will a wine keep after it's opened?" Having heard this question more than any other from my restaurant customers and wine students, I decided several years ago that it was time to find out, so I started putting every wine I taste professionally to the "fridge/countertop test." The resulting report card should help both home wine drinkers and restaurateurs who pour wine by the glass make the most of the leftovers, by simply recorking and storing red wine on the kitchen countertop and storing recorked sparkling, white, and pink wines in the fridge.

Andrea's Best Bets—This is the book's "search engine" of instant recommendations for every common wine occasion and buying dilemma, from Thanksgiving wines to restaurant wine list best bets, party-crowd pleasers, blue chip bottles to impress the client, and more.

Wine List Decoder—This handy cross-reference chart will help you crack the code of different wine list terms, so you can quickly and easily find the styles you like.

Great Wine Made Simple **Mini-Course**—Mini-lessons covering wine styles, label terms, glassware, buying wine in stores and restaurants, and other housekeeping details to simplify buying and serving wine, so you can focus on enjoying it.

I had been in the restaurant wine business for more than a decade before I wrote my first book, *Great Wine Made Simple*. Having studied like crazy to pass the Master Sommelier exam (the hardest wine test you can imagine), I knew there were lots of great books out there. So why another? Because as I worked training waiters and budding sommeliers, I began to see that in practice those books weren't much help. Wine, like food, golf, the saxophone, and so many other sensory pursuits, is something you learn not by studying but by doing. So *Great Wine Made Simple* teaches wine not through memorization but the way I learned it—through tasting. It works, and it's fun, whether you are just a dabbler or a committed wine geek.

Similarly, I intend this guide to fill a gap. Most people around the country buy wine based on price and convenience. And whether it's restaurant guests, viewers of my *Simply Wine* and *Pairings* shows on Fine Living network, or visitors to www.andreawine.com, they all have the same questions: What are the good, cheap wines? And which wines are really worth the splurge? This buying guide is the first to answer those questions realistically, featuring wines and tastes in the broad marketplace, along with plenty of shrewd pro advice to help you make the most of every wine purchase. Food is one major way to do that, so as a professionally trained cook I've also included lots of pairing pointers.

What's New in This Year's Guide

First, lots more wines! My Web site's (www.andreawine. com) Tasting Panel has now rated literally thousands of wines, and culling that list for really worthy selections to include in the *Guide* resulted in hundreds of new additions with impressive taste and value reviews. One note: The new additions are not included in the Most Popular rankings because they're so new to the book (but they'll be eligible next year if they continue to perform well with the panel). I hope you'll log on to www.andreawine.com, join the Tasting Panel, and contribute *your* reviews—it's free, and a great way to keep track of your tasting notes. While you're there you can check out my new interactive wine-tasting DVD, *Andrea's Complete Wine Course for Everyone*, and my new wine club of rare but great-value wines, the A-List™.

Another new feature in this year's *Guide* is what's *not* included. Specifically, I decided not to waste space on wine reviews for big-selling wines that are underperforming in terms of quality versus the competition. Consequently, I had to delete quite a few entries from several well-known wine brands, including Beringer Founders' Estate, Meridian, Robert Mondavi Private Selection, Woodbridge, and Yellow Tail, among others. I taste the wines in this important value category all the time and have observed quality declines in many of the varietals to the point at which I cannot recommend them, especially because there are so many more worthy alternatives at the same price. Now for the trends.

Sauvignon Blanc and Riesling Rising
Wow! These two wonderful white grapes were already on the upswing in last year's *Guide* but now they are just on fire. I couldn't be happier, because they both have such distinctive characters and great acidity, making them super food partners. If you check out the Most Popular table rankings, you will see that in particular Rieslings from Germany and Sauvignon Blancs from New Zealand have really caught the public's attention.

The Critter Craze Continues . . . and Morphs
In the last two years, so-called critter labels, with a cute or funky animal on the label and often a story, came on strong with big marketing budgets to capture some of the excitement (and market share) around the Aussie Yellow Tail brand. A few of them were successful, but many lacked the quality and flavor needed to create brand loyalty. Those that I think are worthy of your attention—namely Monkey Bay, HRM Rex Goliath, The Little Penguin, and Three Blind Moose, made the *Guide*. Otherwise I didn't bother, and you shouldn't either. A few wineries evolved the critter phenomenon into a hip and unusual (but not animal) label design, again with a story or a marketing aura designed to position the wine as a lifestyle statement. The brand Twin Fin is the best of these and most of their varietals made the book because they're excellent for the price.

Prices Are Dropping

Yay! Competition has put downward pressure on prices across the board and depending on the market, many wineries are programming extra discounts to try to get your attention. As such I encourage you to shop around for your favorite wines. I think global competition and some large crops in recent harvests will continue to keep prices in check.

How to Use This Buying Guide

Here is everything you need to know to get instant buying power from the *Guide*.

Looking Up Wine Recommendations— by Wine Category or Winery Name

Wine Category—Grape, Region, or Type

The wine reviews are grouped by major grape variety, region, or type. For example:

Review section headings look like this

> # WHITE WINES
> ## *Sparkling/Champagne*

You'll probably recognize some of the main grape and style categories, because they lead the wine market in both quality and sales. These include what I call the "Big Six" grapes (the white grapes Riesling, Sauvignon Blanc, and Chardonnay; and the reds Pinot Noir, Merlot, and Cabernet Sauvignon), plus Pinot Grigio, Italian reds, Syrah/Shiraz, and some other popular categories. This is also the way most wine lists and many shops are set up. The "Other Whites" and "Other Reds" sections are used for less common grapes and proprietary blends.

Helpful to Know: I've arranged all the wine categories from lightest to fullest in body, as a quick reference for when you are shopping or perusing a wine list. More and more, restaurant wine lists are being arranged by body style, too, because it helps both the guest and the server quickly determine which wines are lightest or heaviest, so they can match their personal preference or food choice if they wish.

Winery Name—Alphabetical Wine Listings
The wines in each category are in alphabetical order by
winery name, so you can easily find the specific wine
you're looking for. For example:

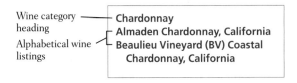

Wine category
heading

Alphabetical wine
listings

Chardonnay
Almaden Chardonnay, California
Beaulieu Vineyard (BV) Coastal
Chardonnay, California

Helpful to Know: If you are looking for a specific winery
name rather than a grape or style category, the Winery
Index at the back of the book will show you which
producers' wines were reviewed for the guide and the
page number for each wine review.

Key to the Ratings and Symbols in Each Wine Entry

This sample entry identifies the components of each
wine listing.

1. Wine name and provenance (country or state)
2. Price category
3. Taste and value ratings
4. Symbols: These identify wines rated as
   ✓ best-of (rated most popular in their
     category) or
   ✗ worthy write-ins in their respective
     categories.
   ☺ An Andrea personal favorite

			❷		❸
❶	**Chateau Andrea Rose**		PC	T	V
	New York		$$	26	28

❹ ✗ Tasters marvel at its "amazing quality for a
❺ bag-in-the-box." Pro buyers (including me) find
it "every bit as good as the finest Cold Duck . . .
and sometimes better!"
❻ *Kitchen Fridge Survivor™ or Countertop Sur-*
vivor™ Grade: A
❼ Your notes: _____

5. Reviewers' commentary, in quotation marks, along with my notes on the wine
6. My Kitchen Fridge Survivor™ or Kitchen Countertop Survivor™ Grade
7. Space for your wine notes.

Price Category

Prices for the same wine can vary widely across the country. Here's why: Individual states regulate the sale and taxation of wine within their borders, and sometimes local municipalities have further regulations and taxes. That means the price for any particular wine depends very much on where you live and shop. In general, wines are cheapest in large urban areas, where there's lots of retail competition. They are usually most expensive in so-called control states, where there is zero competition because the state acts as the sole retailer (Pennsylvania is one example). In addition, some of the wines in the survey are available in a different size or in more than one size (e.g., half bottles, standard 750-ml bottles, magnums, jugs, and larger). The price categories here, based on a standard 750-ml bottle, are intended as a guideline to help you compare relative prices of the different wines in the survey:

$ = up to $12
$$ = $12.01 to $20
$$$ = $20.01 to $35
$$$$ = above $35

NA indicates a wine not available in 750-ml bottles (sold only in jugs or bag-in-box format; prices for these are quite low).

Note: These are retail store prices, not restaurant wine list prices.

Taste and Value Ratings

Tasters (no pro credentials necessary, just an opinion) were asked to assess any of the listed wines that they'd tried in the past year on the following criteria:

• *Taste*—What did you think of the wine's taste?
• *Value for the Money*—Were you happy with what you got for the price you paid?

I kept the rating criteria simple, with scores listed on a scale of 0 to 30:

> 0–9 = Poor
> 10–15 = Fair
> 16–19 = Good
> 20–25 = Very good
> 26–30 = Outstanding
> X = No data available (applies to write-in wines)

Certainly everyone has an opinion based on his or her own preferences and experience, and that is precisely what I sought to capture with this simple scale. I have also learned, from my years in the restaurant business and teaching wine classes, that most consumers can recognize inherent wine quality, regardless of their level of wine sophistication. I am pleased to say that the responses bore that out. Specifically, the wines that are consistently recognized by experts as quality and value leaders in their category were standouts among my tasters, too. Similarly, wines that have slipped, or whose price has risen unduly, were for the most part assessed accordingly. Other provocative attributes that influenced commentary and ratings included extreme prices (either high or low), an extreme reputation (either good or bad), and substantial inconsistency in the taste from one year to the next.

Symbols

Best-of (✓) —Identifies the top-rated wines in each category. (Rated "most popular" in the category—an average of the taste and value scores.)

Worthy write-in (X) —Denotes that a wine was added to the book listings by popular demand (as noted earlier, only those write-ins with decent availability were included). Because most tasters gave their write-ins verbal endorsements rather than scores, I haven't included scores here but will do so in future editions of the *Guide*.

Andrea personal favorite (☺) — Not always those with the highest scores!

Reviewers' Commentary and My Notes

Along with their taste and value assessments, reviewers were asked to include comments on the wines—not tasting descriptions per se but "buyers' notes," reflecting their gut reactions to the wine. If they felt a wine was overrated, underappreciated, delicious, awful, in a beautiful (or ugly) bottle, or whatever, I asked them to say so and have passed along those impressions; here you'll find my own thoughts based on working every day with myriad wines, wine servers, and wine drinkers.

Andrea's Kitchen Fridge Survivor™ and Kitchen Countertop Survivor™ Grades

I think a great many people hesitate to open wine for everyday meals because they won't know what to do with leftovers. No wonder! It's wildly expensive to pour out unfinished wine. And the frustration of wondering and worrying whether your wine's over the hill, *after* the intimidation of shopping for the wine, is more than most of us can be bothered with.

Because I couldn't stand the idea of people pretty much giving up on wine with dinner, and "How long will it keep after I open it?" is one of the most common wine questions I'm asked, I decided it was time to give some real answers.

I'm a bit embarrassed to admit that I began to test how long wines hold up in the everyday kitchen not because I was on a quest to answer these big-picture questions but because I kept tasting some impressive leftovers. In my sommelier and writing duties, I taste multiple wines often, and rarely with enough company to finish them the day they're opened, or even the next. In going back to the leftovers—to see if they were as good (or as disappointing) as I'd remembered—I got some amazing surprises. Far more often than you'd think, the good wines stayed that way for days. Even more astonishing, some of the wines that were initially underwhelming actually came around and started tasting better after being open for a while (in the same way that some cheeses need to sit out at room temperature to show their best flavor or a pot of chili can taste better after a day or two in the fridge).

And thus were born the Kitchen Fridge Survivor™ and Kitchen Countertop Survivor™ experiments. I hope the grades will give you confidence to enjoy wine with dinner more often, or even multiple wines with one meal (I frequently do), knowing that you can have tastes or just a glass of many wines, over several days, without the wines going "bad."

To test the wines' open-bottle longevity, I handled them as follows:

Whites—Recorked with the original cork (whether natural or synthetic). Placed in the fridge.

Reds—Recorked with the original cork. Placed on the kitchen counter.

Sparkling wines—Opened carefully without popping (popping depletes carbonation faster). Closed with a "clamshell" stopper designed for sparkling wines—sold in housewares departments and sometimes wine stores. Placed in the fridge.

Bag-in-box wines—These were not tested, because the airtight bag inside keeps the wine from oxidizing as it's consumed—one of the major virtues of this type of packaging.

The same process was repeated after each daily retaste, until the wine's taste declined noticeably. As I said, some wines actually taste better after a day or two. They were handled the same way.

There's no science to this. My kitchen is just a regular kitchen, probably much like yours. I hope these grades, which showed the wines' staying power in an everyday setting, will give you the confidence to enjoy wine more often with your everyday meals:

Avg = a "one-day wine," which tastes noticeably less fresh the next day. This doesn't mean the wine is less worthy, just less sturdy— so plan accordingly by inviting someone to share it with you.

B = holds its freshness for 2–3 days after opening

B+ = holds *and gets better* over 2–3 days after opening

A = has a 3- to 4-day "freshness window"

A+ = holds *and gets better* over 3–4 days

To learn how to lengthen the survival rate of your wine leftovers, see "Handling Wine Leftovers" in "The *Great Wine Made Simple* Mini-Course" later in this book.

Your Notes

Would you join my tasting panel? Of course, I would love for you to record your wine impressions and share them with me for the next edition of the *Andrea Robinson's Guide* (you may do so at www.andreawine. com). But even if you are not the survey type, do it for yourself. Whether you're at home or in a restaurant, the guide is a handy place to keep notes on what you drank, what you paid, what food you had with it, and what you thought. Don't you hate it when you've enjoyed a wine, then can't remember the name when you want to buy it again?

A Few Questions about the Wine Entries

How Were Wines Chosen for Inclusion in the Book?

The wines represented are top sellers in stores and restaurants nationally, in each style category. I featured mostly the top-selling premium, cork-finished wines because they outsell generics overall. However, I did include the dominant jug and bag-in-box wines, and my tasters did not ignore them. Don't see one of your favorite wines? Keep in mind that both popularity and availability of specific wines can vary a lot regionally, so a big brand in your area may not have the same sales and presence in other markets. This is especially true with local wines—for example, the Texas Chenin Blanc or New York Riesling that's on every table in your neck of the woods may not even be distributed in the next state. I also included worthy write-ins—those with decent availability that got the highest number of positive mentions from my tasters, although in some cases that availability may be skewed heavily to restaurants. Why, you ask? Many buyers have told me of their frustration at seeing the wines they'd like to purchase available only in restaurants. It's a phenomenon that became increasingly common in the wine boom of the 1990s. Simply put, wineries with a limited supply often concentrate on restaurant lists because of the image enhancement they can offer—good food, nice setting, and (usually) fewer competing selections than in a shop.

Why No Vintage Years?

This guide deals with the top-selling wines in the market, and so, for the most part, the year available in stores and restaurants is the winery's current release. But I am also making a philosophical statement about vintages for the wines in the guide, and it is this: I believe that the leading wines in the market *should* be fairly consistent from one year to the next so that consumers, and the retail and restaurant wine buyers who serve them, need not sweat the vintage, as long as it's current and fresh. There are certain wine categories for which vintage is a bigger consideration—among them expensive California reds, French Bordeaux and Burgundy, and upscale Italian reds. But even with these, if you do not intend to cellar the wines (very few buyers do), vintage isn't so critical. A few of the tasters mentioned the vintage issue, but most were comfortable with my approach.

> **ANDREA INSIGHT:** About 95% of the quality wines on the market are meant to be consumed within 1–3 years of the harvest (the vintage date on the label), while they are young, fresh, and in good condition. Most wines do not get better with age, so why wait?

Can You Really Define "Outstanding" Wine?

Indeed I can. We all can. Broadly, it is a wine that captures your attention. It could be the scent, the taste, the texture, or all three that make you say first, "Mmm. . . ," and then, "Wow" as your impressions register in the moment, in the context of all your prior experience and the price you paid. If it all sounds very personal and subjective, you're exactly right—it is. That is why I felt a guide like this, showcasing the impressions of real-world buyers, was so important. The fact that the wines herein are big sellers is already an endorsement. The details put each wine in context—of price, similar-style wines, occasion, and whatever else buyers feel is important. No other wine buying guide does that.

Who Are the Tasters? You

Over a 6-month period in 2005 I collected tasting data on my Web site from thousands of American wine buyers—trade colleagues (retail and restaurant buyers, sommeliers, hoteliers, chefs, waiters, importers, and distributors). The trade buyers included most major chain restaurants and stores, chefs, and my master sommelier colleagues, among others. I also recruit tasters through my restaurant guests; my students at the French Culinary Institute; and of course, the friends and family network, including family members I didn't even know I had until I found them on the e-mail trail. I originally thought consumers would be less keen than trade to share their wine opinions, but I was wrong. As noted previously, consumers account for more than 70% of the responses. Although I don't purposely exclude anyone, I do review every survey returned for signs of ballot stuffing from winery companies and eliminate all suspicious responses (there were literally just a couple).

Why Do These Tasters' Opinions Matter?

Clearly, this guide for everyone takes an utterly populist perspective that's different from every other wine publication on the market—and that is exactly what I intend. I think the honest assessments and perspective of consumers who have to pay their own money for wine (while wine journalists rarely do), and the restaurateurs and retailers who serve them, are extremely important and helpful—because they're the real world. (With so little of that perspective in the marketplace, can it be any wonder that wine is barely a blip on Americans' cultural radar screen?) I am not dismissing the value of and expertise behind the leading critics' scoring reports. But I do think they often further the notion that there are haves and have-nots in the wine world: the 90+–rated "good stuff" that none of us can afford; and the rest—the wines we see every day whose lower scores seem bad by comparison. That perspective is perhaps valuable to a tiny, elite group of luxury wine buyers. But for what I call the OTC (other than collectors) market, which makes up the bulk of the nation's buyers (including just about everyone I know), this dichotomy leaves us feeling utterly insecure about our own taste and budget, skeptical about the quality of the selection at the stores and restaurants we frequent, and self-conscious about our (legitimate) desire for value for the money—in the vernacular: good, cheap wine. If I've achieved my goal, this *Guide*'s real-world information will give you a renewed sense of confidence in your own taste and some great word-of-mouth guidance on new wines to try that are actually available where you shop and dine. Enjoy!

MOST POPULAR WINES—REFLECTING BOTH TASTE AND VALUE FOR THE MONEY

25 Most Popular Whites*
Based on Taste and Value

Name	Wtd. Avg. T/V Score**	Price Cate- gory
Nobilo Sauvignon Blanc	28	$
Casa Lapostolle Sauvignon Blanc	28	$
Chateau Ste. Michelle Columbia Valley Chardonnay	27	$
Dr. Loosen Riesling Kabinett Estate	27	$$$
Dry Creek Chenin Blanc	27	$
J. Lohr Bay Mist Riesling	27	$
Kim Crawford Sauvignon Blanc	27	$$
Mer Soleil Chardonnay	27	$$$$
Reichsgraf von Kesselstatt Piesporter Goldtropfchen Riesling Kabinett	27	$$$
Spy Valley Sauvignon Blanc	27	$
Chalone Chardonnay	26	$$$
Columbia Winery Cellarmaster's Reserve Riesling	26	$
Kendall–Jackson Vintner's Reserve Riesling	26	$
J. Lohr Riverstone Chardonnay	26	$
Louis Jadot Pouilly-Fuisse	26	$$$
St. Supery Sauvignon Blanc	26	$$

*To find the complete tasting notes for each wine, refer to the Winery Index in the back of the book.

**Scores were rounded off. Wines are listed in order of actual score ranking. The number of wines in each "Most Popular" listing reflects the overall number of wines in the category. So our "Top Whites" list numbers 25, whereas the Top Rieslings ranking shows just 10 entries. It's also a fairly close reflection of each category's sales and prominence in the fine wine market overall.

Name		
Conundrum White Blend	26	$$$
Fetzer Valley Oaks Gewurztraminer	26	$
Geyser Peak Chardonnay	26	$
Kurt Darting Riesling Kabinett	26	$$
Babich Marlborough Sauvignon Blanc	25	$
Frog's Leap Sauvignon Blanc	25	$$
Kenwood Sauvignon Blanc	25	$
Ferrari-Carano Fume Blanc	25	$$
Sonoma-Cutrer Russian River Ranches Chardonnay	25	$$$

25 Most Popular Reds
Based on Taste and Value

Name	Wtd. Avg. T/V Score*	Price Cate-gory
Alice White Shiraz	27	$
Bogle Petite Sirah	27	$
Estancia Alexander Valley Red Meritage	27	$$$
Navarro Correas Malbec	27	$
Ferrari-Carano Siena Sonoma County	27	$$$
Montecillo Rioja Crianza	27	$
Santa Rita 120 Cabernet Sauvignon	27	$
Sokol Blosser Willamette Pinot Noir	27	$$$
Franciscan Magnificat	26	$$$$
Joseph Phelps Pastiche Rouge	26	$$
Lindemans Bin 50 Shiraz	26	$
Chateau St. Jean Cinq Cepages Cabernet Blend	26	$$$$
D'Arenberg The Footbolt Shiraz	26	$$
Solaris Pinot Noir	26	$
Concannon Petite Sirah	26	$
Franciscan Oakville Estate Merlot	26	$$$
Penfolds Grange	26	$$$$
Casa Lapostolle Cuvee Alexandre Cabernet Sauvignon	26	$$
Chateau Les Ormes de Pez Bordeaux	26	$$$
Domaine Drouhin Oregon Willamette Valley Pinot Noir	26	$$$$
Osborne Solaz Tempranillo	26	$
Rafanelli Zinfandel	26	$$$$
Ramsay Pinot Noir	26	$$

*Scores were rounded off. Wines are listed in order of actual ranking.

Name	Wtd. Avg. T/V Score*	Price Category
Gallo Family Vineyards Merlot	25	$
Hill of Content Grenache/Shiraz	25	$$

Best of the Big Six Grapes

Name	Wtd. Avg. T/V Score*	Price Category
10 Most Popular Rieslings		
J.J. Prum Wehlener Sonnenuhr	28	$$
Dr. Loosen Kabinett Estate	27	$$$
Reichsgraf von Kesselstatt Piesporter Goldtropfchen Kabinett	27	$$
Trimbach Cuvee Frederic Emile	27	$$$
Columbia Winery Cellarmaster's Reserve	26	$
Kendall-Jackson Vintner's Reserve	26	$
Kurt Darting Kabinett	26	$$
Fetzer Valley Oaks Johannisberg	25	$
Eroica	25	$$$
J. Lohr Bay Mist	24	$
10 Most Popular Sauvignon/Fume Blancs		
Beaulieu Vineyard (BV) Coastal Estates	28	$
Nobilo	28	$
Casa Lapostolle	28	$
Kim Crawford	27	$$
St. Supery	26	$$
Spy Valley	27	$
Babich	25	$
Frog's Leap	25	$$
Kenwood	25	$
Ferrari-Carano Fume Blanc	25	$$
20 Most Popular Chardonnays		
Chateau Ste. Michelle Columbia Valley	27	$
Mer Soleil	27	$$$$
Chalone	26	$$$
J. Lohr Riverstone	26	$
Geyser Peak	26	$
Sonoma-Cutrer Russian River Ranches	25	$$$

*Scores were rounded off. Wines are listed in order of actual ranking.

Talbott (Robert) Sleepy Hollow Vineyard	25	$$$$
Gallo Family Vineyards Sonoma Reserve	24	$
Ferrari-Carano Carneros	24	$$$
Acacia Carneros	24	$$$
Chateau St. Jean Robert Young	24	$$$
R.H. Phillips Toasted Head	24	$$
La Crema	23	$$
Blackstone Monterey	23	$$
R.H. Phillips Dunnigan Hills	23	$
Casa Lapostolle Cuvee Alexandre	23	$$
Chateau Montelena	23	$$$
Kistler Durell	23	$$$$
Landmark Overlook	23	$$$
Rombauer	23	$$$

15 Most Popular Pinot Noirs

Sokol Blosser Willamette	27	$$$
Solaris	26	$
Domaine Drouhin Willamette Valley	26	$$$$
Ramsay	26	$$
Etude Carneros	25	$$$$
Merry Edwards Russian River Valley	25	$$$$
Cristom Jefferson Cuvee	25	$$$
Sanford	26	$$$
Elk Cove	24	$$
Robert Sinskey Los Carneros	24	$$$
Au Bon Climat Santa Barbara	24	$$
Au Bon Climat Rincon and Rosemary's	24	$$$$
Benton Lane	24	$$
Deloach	24	$$
Flowers	24	$$$$

10 Most Popular Merlots

Franciscan Oakville Estate	26	$$$
Gallo Family Vineyards Sonoma Reserve	25	$
Columbia Crest Two Vines	25	$
Stag's Leap Wine Cellars, Napa	25	$$$$
Chateau Souverain Alexander Valley	25	$$
Rodney Strong Sonoma	24	$$
St. Francis Sonoma	24	$$
Shafer	24	$$$$
Fetzer Valley Oaks	24	$
Bogle	23	$

Name	Wtd. Avg. T/V Score*	Price Category
20 Most Popular Cabernet Sauvignons and Blends		
Estancia Alexander Valley Red Meritage	27	$$$
Santa Rita 120	27	$
Franciscan Magnificat Meritage	26	$$$$
Chateau St. Jean Cinq Cepages	26	$$$$
Casa Lapostolle Cuvee Alexandre	26	$$
Chateau Les Ormes de Pez	26	$$$
Baron Philippe de Rothschild Escudo Rojo Cabernet Blend	25	$$
Francis Coppola Diamond Series Claret	25	$$
Penfolds Bin 389 Cabernet Sauvignon/ Shiraz	25	$$$
Pine Ridge Stag's Leap District	25	$$$$
Arrowood	25	$$$$
Los Vascos	25	$
Simi	24	$$$
Gallo Family Vineyards Sonoma Reserve	24	$$
Columbia Crest Grand Estates	24	$
Black Opal	24	$
Caymus Napa	24	$$$$
Clos du Bois Marlstone	24	$$$$
J. Lohr Seven Oaks	24	$$
Justin Isosceles	24	$$$$

Best of the Rest

Name	Wtd. Avg. T/V Score*	Price Category
10 Most Popular Champagnes and Sparkling Wines		
Bollinger RD	27	$$$$
Domaine Chandon Riche	27	$$
Iron Horse Wedding Cuvee Brut NV	27	$$
Krug Grande Cuvee Multivintage	25	$$$$
Domaine Carneros Le Reve	24	$$$$
Perrier-Jouët Grand Brut	24	$$$$
Taittinger Brut La Française	24	$$$$
Domaine Chandon Blanc de Noirs	23	$$
Moët & Chandon Brut Imperial	23	$$$$
Domaine Chandon Brut Classic Sparkling	23	$$

*Scores were rounded off. Wines are listed in order of actual ranking.

5 Most Popular Pinot Gris/Grigios

Willamette Valley Vineyards	25	$$
Alois Lageder	24	$$
Folonari	23	$
Santa Margherita	23	$$$
Cavit	22	$

10 Most Popular Italian and Spanish Reds

Montecillo Rioja Crianza	27	$
Banfi Chianti Classico Riserva	26	$$
Osborne Solaz Tempranillo-Cabernet	26	$
Ruffino Tan Label Chianti Classico Riserva Ducale	25	$$$
Pesquera Ribera del Duero	24	$$$
Taurino Salice Salentino	24	$$
Ruffino Gold Label Chianti Classico Riserva Ducale	24	$$$$
Marques de Caceres Rioja	23	$$
Felsina Chianti Classico	23	$$$
Antinori (Marchese) Chianti Classico Riserva	23	$$$$

10 Most Popular Shiraz/Syrahs and Rhone-Style Reds

Alice White Shiraz	27	$
Jacob's Creek	27	$
Lindemans Bin 50 Shiraz	26	$
D'Arenberg The Footbolt Shiraz	26	$$
Penfolds Grange	26	$$$$
Jaboulet Parallele 45 Cotes-du-Rhone	25	$
Hill of Content Grenache/Shiraz	25	$$
Jacob's Creek Shiraz/Cabernet	25	$
Penfolds Kalimna Shiraz Bin 28	24	$$$
Rosemount Diamond Label Shiraz	24	$

10 Most Popular Red Zinfandels

Rafanelli	26	$$$$
Ridge Geyserville	25	$$$
Bogle Old Vines	25	$
Dancing Bull	25	$
Seghesio	24	$$
Montevina Amador	24	$
Rancho Zabaco Dry Creek Valley	24	$$
Robert Mondavi Napa	24	$$
Woodbridge	24	$
Ravenswood Sonoma Old Vines	23	$$

THE REVIEWS

WHITE WINES

Sparkling/Champagne

Style Profile: Although all the world's bubblies are modeled on Champagne, only the genuine article from the Champagne *region* of France is properly called *Champagne*. *Sparkling wine* is the proper term for the other bubblies, some of which can be just as good as the real thing. Limited supply and high demand—plus a labor-intensive production process—make Champagne expensive compared to other sparklers but still an affordable luxury in comparison to other world-class wine categories, like top French Burgundy or California Cabernet estates. The other sparklers, especially Cava from Spain and Italian Prosecco, are affordable for everyday drinking. *Brut* (rhymes with *root*) on the label means the wine is utterly dry, with no perceptible sweetness. But that *doesn't* mean they all taste the same. In fact, each French Champagne house is known for a signature style, which can range from delicate and elegant to rich, full, and toasty—meaning there's something for every taste and food partner.

Serve: Well chilled; young and fresh (only the rare luxury French Champagnes improve with age). Open with utmost care: flying corks can be dangerous.

When: Anytime! It's not just for special occasions, and it's great with meals.

With: Anything and anyone, but especially sushi and shellfish.

In: A narrow tulip- or flute-type glass; the narrow opening preserves the bubbles.

Kitchen Fridge Survivor™ Tip for Bubbly Wine: Kitchenware shops and wine stores often sell "clamshell" stoppers specially designed to close Champagnes and sparkling wines if you don't finish the bottle. I've found that if you open the bottle carefully in the first place (avoid "popping" the cork, which is also the safest technique), a stoppered sparkling wine will keep its fizz for at least three days in the fridge, often longer. Having a hard time thinking of something else to toast? How about, "Here's to [insert day of week]." That's usually good enough for me!

Argyle Brut Sparkling,	PC	T	V
Oregon	$$	21	24

The Asian pear scent and flavor are delicious for just sipping and with subtle foods like shellfish.
Kitchen Fridge Survivor™ Grade: A
Your notes: _____

Ballatore Gran Spumante,	PC	T	V
California	$	24	24

It's "a little sweet"; "crisp and fun."
Kitchen Fridge Survivor™ Grade: A
Your notes: _____

Bollinger (*BOLL-en-jur*) RD	PC	T	V
Champagne, France	$$$$	29	24

✓ "Expensive, but *sooo* good," with baked apple and croissant flavors and scents; endless finish.
Kitchen Fridge Survivor™ Grade: A
Your notes: _____

Bollinger Special	PC	T	V
Cuvee (coo-VAY) Brut Champagne,	$$$$	29	18
France			

"Big, toasty, full bodied," with a complexity that "really captures your attention."
Kitchen Fridge Survivor™ Grade: A
Your notes: _____

Price Ranges: **$** = $12 or less; **$$** = $12.01–20; **$$$** = $20.01–35; **$$$$** = > $35
Kitchen Fridge Survivor™ Grades: *Avg.* = a "one-day wine," tastes noticeably less fresh the next day; *B* = holds its freshness for 2–3 days after opening; *B+* = holds *and gets better* over 2–3 days after opening; *A* = a 3- to 4-day "freshness window"; *A+* = holds *and gets better* over 3–4 days

Bouvet (*boo-VAY*) Brut Sparkling,   PC   T   V
Loire Valley, France $$ 22   25

Classy and affordable, with a complex scent of wilted blossoms and sweet hay, a crisp apple-quince flavor, and creamy texture.

Kitchen Fridge Survivor™ Grade: B+
Your notes: _____

Charles Heidsieck (*HIDE-sick*) Brut   PC   T   V
Champagne, France $$$$ 24   24

This "well rounded and luxurious" bubbly is known for its creamy texture, full body, and toasted hazelnut scent.

Kitchen Fridge Survivor™ Grade: A
Your notes: _____

Codorniu Cava Rose,   PC   T   V
Spain $$ X   X

☺ As good as French Rose for a fraction of the price. Creamy bubble, dried cherry fruit, soft spicy finish.

Kitchen Fridge Survivor™ Grade: A
Your notes: _____

Domaine Carneros Brut Sparkling,   PC   T   V
California $$$ 22   20

This wine's definitely on my short list of favorite California sparklers. It has very ripe fruit, expertly balanced between generous juiciness and elegant restraint. Fabulous with food, too.

Kitchen Fridge Survivor™ Grade: B
Your notes: _____

Domaine Carneros Le Reve   PC   T   V
Sparkling, California $$$$ 26   23

This top bottling for Domaine Carneros is one of California's best bubblies, with a firm core of fresh pear fruit, floral and fresh-bread scent, and endless finish.

Kitchen Fridge Survivor™ Grade: A+
Your notes: _____

Domaine Chandon (*shahn-DOHN*)   PC   T   V
Blanc de Noirs Sparkling, California $$ 22   24

It's pronounced *blahnk-duh-NWAHR*, and it means this golden bubbly is made from black (Noir) grapes, which give it extra body and concentration.

Kitchen Fridge Survivor™ Grade: B
Your notes: _____

Domaine Chandon Brut Classic Sparkling, California	PC	T	V
	$$	23	23

This American sparkler sibling of France's famous Moët & Chandon is a huge hit with my tasters for its yeasty, creamy style that's "classy but affordable."

Kitchen Fridge Survivor™ Grade: B+

Your notes: _____

Domaine Chandon Riche Sparkling, California	PC	T	V
	$$	24	29

What makes it "riche" is a hint of sweetness—not at all cloying. A great accompaniment to foods with a kick.

Kitchen Fridge Survivor™ Grade: A

Your notes: _____

Domaine Ste. Michelle Blanc de Noir Sparkling, Washington	PC	T	V
	$	24	29

My tasters note, "you can't beat the price" of this nicely balanced, crisp, and appley sparkler.

Kitchen Fridge Survivor™ Grade: B

Your notes: _____

Dom Perignon Champagne Brut, France	PC	T	V
	$$$$	24	18

Though some say "you can do better for the price," you can't beat the pedigree "when you want to impress," and the "good fruit flavor" and "yeasty" scent are "always reliable."

Kitchen Fridge Survivor™ Grade: B

Your notes: _____

Freixenet (*fresh-uh-NETT*) Brut de Noirs, Cava Rose, Spain	PC	T	V
	$	22	24

☺ "Yum's the word" for this wine. The mouthwatering taste of tangy strawberries is great with fried foods, spicy foods . . . any foods. And it held up for weeks in the fridge.

Kitchen Fridge Survivor™ Grade: A+

Your notes: _____

Price Ranges: **$** = $12 or less; **$$** = $12.01–20; **$$$** = $20.01–35; **$$$$** = > $35

Kitchen Fridge Survivor™ Grades: *Avg.* = a "one-day wine," tastes noticeably less fresh the next day; *B* = holds its freshness for 2–3 days after opening; *B+* = holds *and gets better* over 2–3 days after opening; *A* = a 3- to 4-day "freshness window"; *A+* = holds *and gets better* over 3–4 days

Gosset (go-SAY) Brut Rose   PC   T   V
Champagne, France $$$$ 27   24

☺ This is one of my favorite Champagnes, period.
The scent and flavors of dried cherries, exotic spices,
and toasted nuts would please any serious wine
drinker. Forget toasting and serve it with salmon, tuna,
duck, or pork.

Kitchen Fridge Survivor™ Grade: A

Your notes: _____

Gruet (groo-AY) Brut St. Vincent   PC   T   V
Sparkling, New Mexico $$ 27   27

New Mexico? Gruet's "great bubblies, which are tasty
and of good value," prove "all that prickles in the
desert isn't cactus!"

Kitchen Fridge Survivor™ Grade: B+

Your notes: _____

Iron Horse Wedding Cuvee Brut   PC   T   V
Sparkling, California $$$ 27   24

Brides, of course, love the romantic name; and it is
my choice for receptions, having inspired more
"What was the name of that wine?" reactions than
any other in the history of my wine career. It's got
great acidity and crisp tangerine and green apple
flavors.

Kitchen Fridge Survivor™ Grade: B

Your notes: _____

J Vintage Brut Sparkling,   PC   T   V
California $$$ 24   21

It seems to get better every year, and the package is
gorgeous. Rich and yeasty.

Kitchen Fridge Survivor™ Grade: A

Your notes: _____

Korbel Brut Sparkling,   PC   T   V
California $ 20   19

Although this is the top-selling bubbly in America,
Korbel's use of the name *Champagne* on the label
furthers consumer confusion over the term: True
Champagne must come from that *region* in France.

Kitchen Fridge Survivor™ Grade: Avg.

Your notes: _____

Krug Grande Cuvee Multivintage	PC	T	V
Champagne, France	$$$$	27	22

☺ This is one of my favorite wines in the world, and one of the few I really feel are worth the splurge. Krug's full, nutty, baked-brioche style is truly unique among Champagnes.

Kitchen Fridge Survivor™ Grade: A

Your notes: _____

Laurent-Perrier Brut LP,	PC	T	V
Champagne, France	$$$$	27	20

This wine's known for its elegance and racy acidity, which makes it a great food partner *and* a great Fridge Survivor.

Kitchen Fridge Survivor™ Grade: A+

Your notes: _____

Mionetto (*me-oh-NETT-oh*) DOC	PC	T	V
Prosecco (*pro-SECK-oh*) Brut,	$$	20	18
Veneto, Italy			

This Prosecco is dry, refreshing, and sophisticated but also affordable. Prosecco is the grape name. If you want, add peach puree to make the Bellini, Venice's signature cocktail.

Kitchen Fridge Survivor™ Grade: B

Your notes: _____

Moët & Chandon (*MWETT eh*	PC	T	V
shahn-DOHN) Brut Imperial	$$$$	25	20
Champagne, France			

This is one of the best Brut NVs on the market at the moment, with "medium body and more fruit flavor and acidity" than its sister bottling, Moët & Chandon White Star.

Kitchen Fridge Survivor™ Grade: B

Your notes: _____

Price Ranges: **$** = $12 or less; **$$** = $12.01–20; **$$$** = $20.01–35; **$$$$** = > $35

Kitchen Fridge Survivor™ Grades: *Avg.* = a "one-day wine," tastes noticeably less fresh the next day; *B* = holds its freshness for 2–3 days after opening; *B+* = holds *and gets better* over 2–3 days after opening; *A* = a 3- to 4-day "freshness window"; *A+* = holds *and gets better* over 3–4 days

Moët & Chandon Nectar Imperial	PC	T	V
Rose Champagne, France	$$$$	24	16

"Wow" bubbly dripping with sweet cherry and soft spice.

Kitchen Fridge Survivor™ Grade: B

Your notes: _____

Moët & Chandon White Star	PC	T	V
Champagne, France	$$$	24	20

Because of its famous pedigree, flower and biscuit scents, and peachy finish, my trade and consumer tasters alike tout this as "fantastic Champagne," and I agree. Its "reliable, crowd-pleasing style" is great with spicy foods and sushi.

Kitchen Fridge Survivor™ Grade: A

Your notes: _____

Mumm Napa Brut Cuvee	PC	T	V
Sparkling, California	$$	19	19

It's more popular than ever with my tasters, who rave about the "French style, for a great price."

Kitchen Fridge Survivor™ Grade: B

Your notes: _____

Mumm Napa Cuvee M,	PC	T	V
California	$$	X	X

✗ Juicy with honey and pear flavors and a creamy bubble.

Kitchen Fridge Survivor™ Grade: A

Your notes: _____

Perrier-Jouët (*PEAR-ee-ay JHWETT*)	PC	T	V
Flower Bottle, Champagne, France	$$$$	24	28

The wine is as beautiful as the bottle, with elegant scents of biscuits, flower, and baked apples.

Kitchen Fridge Survivor™ Grade: A

Your notes: _____

Perrier-Jouët Grand Brut	PC	T	V
Champagne, France	$$$$	28	20

"PJ" was historically one of my favorites in the lighter-bodied Champagne style. My tastings of late have revealed a decline—less flavor depth and a touch of bitterness. The tasting panel still gives it high marks, however.

Kitchen Fridge Survivor™ Grade: NA

Your notes: _____

Piper-Heidsieck (*HIDE-sick*) Brut | **PC** | **T** | **V**
Cuvee Champagne, France | **$$$** | **26** | **20**

This "really dry brut style" has a tangy, snappy acidity that makes it great with salty and fatty flavors and "an absolute joy to drink."

Kitchen Fridge Survivor™ Grade: A

Your notes: _____

Piper-Sonoma Brut Sparkling, | **PC** | **T** | **V**
California | **$$** | **22** | **20**

This California outpost of the French Champagne Piper-Heidsieck yields one of California's best bubblies. It's got a toasty quality that's wonderful on its own and with food.

Kitchen Fridge Survivor™ Grade: A+

Your notes: _____

Pol Roger Brut Reserve | **PC** | **T** | **V**
Champagne, France | **$$$** | **27** | **18**

"Wonderful producer. Great product at this price point," noted my tasters. It is one of the top brut Champagnes in the delicate, elegant style.

Kitchen Fridge Survivor™ Grade: A+

Your notes: _____

Pommery (*POMM-er-ee*) Brut | **PC** | **T** | **V**
Royal Champagne, France | **$$$$** | **23** | **20**

Pommery became well known in the United States thanks to the trendy "Pops" mini-bottles. It's an elegant style with a creamy scent and subtle pear flavor.

Kitchen Fridge Survivor™ Grade: A

Your notes: _____

Roederer Estate Brut Sparkling, | **PC** | **T** | **V**
California | **$$$** | **24** | **24**

☺ About as close to Champagne as you can get without buying French. The full, toasty style is the best of both worlds: "reasonably priced," with the taste of "a special occasion wine."

Kitchen Fridge Survivor™ Grade: A

Your notes: _____

Price Ranges: **$** = $12 or less; **$$** = $12.01–20; **$$$** = $20.01–35; **$$$$** = > $35

Kitchen Fridge Survivor™ Grades: ***Avg.*** = a "one-day wine," tastes noticeably less fresh the next day; ***B*** = holds its freshness for 2–3 days after opening; ***B+*** = holds *and gets better* over 2–3 days after opening; ***A*** = a 3- to 4-day "freshness window"; ***A+*** = holds *and gets better* over 3–4 days

Segura Viudas (*seh-GUHR-uh vee-YOU-duss*) **Aria Estate Cava Brut, Spain**

PC	T	V
$	24	29

☺ For the money, one of the most delicious sparklers on the market, with ripe, vibrant pear fruit and a creamy texture.

Kitchen Fridge Survivor™ Grade: A

Your notes: _____

Sofia Blanc de Blancs, California

PC	T	V
$$	24	24

Fun to drink from the cans (available in bottles, too), with fresh pear flavors and a touch of sweetness.

Kitchen Fridge Survivor™ Grade: Avg.

Your notes: _____

Taittinger (*TAIT-in-jur*) **Brut La Française Champagne, France**

PC	T	V
$$$$	26	22

One of my favorites among the subtle, elegant house-style Champagnes, with finesse and delicacy that "simply dance across the tongue."

Kitchen Fridge Survivor™ Grade: A

Your notes: _____

Veuve Clicquot (*voov klee-COH*) **La Grande Dame Champagne, France**

PC	T	V
$$$$	24	20

"Pricey but worth it" is the consensus for this powerful yet elegant, biscuity, nutty/pear/cream–scented wine.

Kitchen Fridge Survivor™ Grade: A

Your notes: _____

Veuve Clicquot Yellow Label Champagne, France

PC	T	V
$$$$	23	20

Again this year, pro and consumer tasters were wishy-washy, some saying "great, as always," and others saying "not what it used to be." I still like the full-bodied house style, but judge for yourself.

Kitchen Fridge Survivor™ Grade: B+

Your notes: _____

Pinot Gris/Pinot Grigio

Grape Profile: Pinot Gris (*pee-no GREE*) is the French and Grigio (*GREE-jee-oh*) the Italian spelling for this crisp, delicate white wine grape whose sales under the "Grigio" label continue to see scorching growth. The French and American versions tend toward the luscious style; the Italians are more tangy and crisp. To many of my trade tasters it's "the quintessential quaffing wine" and "a real winner by the glass" in restaurants. Happily, many of the cheapest Pinot Grigios remain among the best. I couldn't put it better than the taster who wrote, "If it doesn't *taste* a lot better, why should I *pay* a lot more?" As the Italians would say, *Ecco!*

Serve: Well chilled; young and fresh (as one of my wine buying buddies says to the waiters *she* teaches: "The best vintage for Pinot Grigio? As close to yesterday as possible!").

When: Anytime, but ideal with cocktails, outdoor occasions, lunch, big gatherings (a crowd pleaser).

With: Very versatile, but perfect with hors d'oeuvres, salads, salty foods, and fried foods.

In: An all-purpose wine stem is fine.

	PC	T	V
Alois Lageder (*la-GAY-der;* no one says the first part) Pinot Grigio, Italy	**$$**	**24**	**24**

☺ The pear fruit, floral scent, and smoky finish add up to complexity that few expect from Pinot Grigio.
Kitchen Fridge Survivor™ Grade: B
Your notes: _____

	PC	T	V
Banfi Le Rime Pinot Grigio/ Chardonnay, Italy	**$**	**X**	**X**

✗ A citrusy, mouthwatering, made-for-food value wine.
Kitchen Fridge Survivor™ Grade: B
Your notes: _____

Price Ranges: **$** = $12 or less; **$$** = $12.01–20; **$$$** = $20.01–35; **$$$$** = > $35
Kitchen Fridge Survivor™ Grades: *Avg.* = a "one-day wine," tastes noticeably less fresh the next day; *B* = holds its freshness for 2–3 days after opening; *B+* = holds *and gets better* over 2–3 days after opening; *A* = a 3- to 4-day "freshness window"; *A+* = holds *and gets better* over 3–4 days

The Reviews   31

Bolla (BOWL-uh) Pinot Grigio,   PC   T   V
Italy $ 21   21

I keep looking for a quality leap from the Bolla name, but it still offers less flavor for the money than other PGs at the same price.

Kitchen Fridge Survivor™ Grade: Avg.

Your notes: _____

Cavit (*CAV-it;* rhymes with   PC   T   V
"have it") Pinot Grigio, Italy $ 22   22

Fans say this wine's "a nice summertime sipper" or for cocktail parties. It's light, crisp, and bargain priced.

Kitchen Fridge Survivor™ Grade: B

Your notes: _____

Chehalem Pinot Gris,   PC   T   V
Oregon $$ 24   26

✗ "Ruby red grapefruit" flavor with a hint of earthiness.

Kitchen Fridge Survivor™ Grade: B

Your notes: _____

Clos du Bois Pinot Grigio,   PC   T   V
California $ X   X

✗ A top California Pinot Grigio; ripe pear fruit, a hint of mineral.

Kitchen Fridge Survivor™ Grade: A

Your notes: _____

Columbia Winery Pinot Gris,   PC   T   V
Washington $$ X   X

✗ Mmm. Spicy grapefruit and crisp pear; a delightful white from a red-wine specialist.

Kitchen Fridge Survivor™ Grade: B

Your notes: _____

Ecco Domani (*ECK-oh dough-*   PC   T   V
***MAH-nee*) Pinot Grigio, Italy** $ 18   20

"Tastes clean and refreshing," say fans of Gallo's Italian offspring that tastes crisp and lemony. Pros point out that it's "a great value for the money."

Kitchen Countertop Survivor™ Grade: B

Your notes: _____

Erath Pinot Gris,   PC   T   V
Oregon $$ X   X

✗ Ripe pear-pineapple flavors and a touch of mineral.

Kitchen Fridge Survivor™ Grade: A

Your notes: _____

Flora Springs Pinot Grigio, PC   T   V
California **$$** 26 24

"Delicious" pineapple fruit, long finish, "good value."

Kitchen Fridge Survivor™ Grade: B

Your notes: _____

Folonari (*foe-luh-NAH-ree*) PC   T   V
Pinot Grigio, Italy **$** 22 24

Trade buyers say this "underrated overachiever" is ideal when you're seeking a crisp, sippable, value-priced white.

Kitchen Fridge Survivor™ Grade: Avg.

Your notes: _____

Gallo Family Vineyards Reserve PC   T   V
Pinot Gris, California **$** 24 24

As winemaker Gina Gallo says, this wine is "all about the fruit: white peach, fig, and apricot." Yum!

Kitchen Fridge Survivor™ Grade: Avg.

Your notes: _____

King Estate Pinot Gris, PC   T   V
Oregon **$$** 22 22

After a few years of inflation, this wine's price has returned to good (in most markets) for the quality. Enjoy the "cornucopia of tropical fruit flavors" with sushi, spicy fare, or just for sipping.

Kitchen Fridge Survivor™ Grade: A

Your notes: _____

Kris Pinot Grigio, PC   T   V
Italy **$** 24 26

Apple, honey, "cheap and better than Santa Margherita."

Kitchen Fridge Survivor™ Grade: B

Your notes: _____

Price Ranges: **$** = $12 or less; **$$** = $12.01–20; **$$$** = $20.01–35; **$$$$** = > $35

Kitchen Fridge Survivor™ Grades: *Avg.* = a "one-day wine," tastes noticeably less fresh the next day; *B* = holds its freshness for 2–3 days after opening; *B+* = holds *and gets better* over 2–3 days after opening; *A* = a 3- to 4-day "freshness window"; *A+* = holds *and gets better* over 3–4 days

Livio Felluga (*LIV-ee-oh fuh-LOO-guh*) Pinot Grigio, Italy

PC	T	V
$$$	24	24

Lean, stylish, and *exciting* are words pros use to describe this standout Pinot Grigio. I like the pretty floral nose and ripe apricot flavor.

Kitchen Fridge Survivor™ Grade: B

Your notes: _____

MacMurray Ranch Pinot Gris, California

PC	T	V
$$	X	X

✗ Subtle honeyed pear and peach; one of California's best Pinot Grises/Grigios.

Kitchen Fridge Survivor™ Grade: B

Your notes: _____

Ponzi Pinot Gris, Oregon

PC	T	V
$$	21	18

The mineral and ripe pear scent and flavor are like Alsace Pinot Grises, but without the weight.

Kitchen Fridge Survivor™ Grade: A

Your notes: _____

Robert Mondavi Private Selection Pinot Grigio, California

PC	T	V
$	19	22

One of the best budget Pinot Grigios from California! Easy-drinking, with lots of lively apricot and peach flavors.

Kitchen Fridge Survivor™ Grade: B

Your notes: _____

Ruffino Lumina Pinot Grigio, Italy

PC	T	V
$	X	X

✗ More to it than the usual Italian Pinot Grigio; pear flavor and mineral with scents of flowers and hay.

Kitchen Fridge Survivor™ Grade: B

Your notes: _____

Santa Margherita Pinot Grigio, Italy

PC	T	V
$$$	24	21

Although some consumers and most trade tasters appraise Santa Margherita as "way overpriced," many still say it's a "favorite" that will "impress your friends." In my book, the exploding PG category offers so many better and cheaper alternatives.

Kitchen Fridge Survivor™ Grade: Avg.

Your notes: _____

Trimbach Pinot Gris Reserve,   PC   T   V
Alsace, France $$ X   X

☺ ✗ Subtle pear, with a "wow!" finish of almond croissant.

Kitchen Fridge Survivor™ Grade: B

Your notes: _____

Twin Fin Pinot Grigio,   PC   T   V
California $ X   X

✗ Juicy-crisp pear; the best price/value California Grigio, period.

Kitchen Fridge Survivor™ Grade: Avg.

Your notes: _____

WillaKenzie Pinot Gris,   PC   T   V
Oregon $$ X   X

✗ Juicily sippable canned pears and vanilla. Yum!

Kitchen Fridge Survivor™ Grade: Avg.

Your notes: _____

Willamette Valley Vineyard Pinot   PC   T   V
Gris, Oregon $$ 26   24

✓ "Great with food," thanks to the "crisp tartness" and "loads of flavor"—pears and dried pineapple.

Kitchen Fridge Survivor™ Grade: Avg.

Your notes: _____

Woodbridge (Robert Mondavi)   PC   T   V
Pinot Grigio, California $ 24   18

My favorite Woodbridge wine, with "lively peach fruit," that's "lipsmacking as a sipping wine."

Kitchen Fridge Survivor™ Grade: B

Your notes: _____

Zemmer Pinot Grigio,   PC   T   V
Italy $$ 20   18

This Pinot Grigio has "more concentration than most" in its price range, and has "a great nose, great food

---

Price Ranges: **$** = $12 or less; **$$** = $12.01–20; **$$$** = $20.01–35; **$$$$** = > $35

Kitchen Fridge Survivor™ Grades: *Avg.* = a "one-day wine," tastes noticeably less fresh the next day; *B* = holds its freshness for 2–3 days after opening; *B+* = holds *and gets better* over 2–3 days after opening; *A* = a 3- to 4-day "freshness window"; *A+* = holds *and gets better* over 3–4 days

compatibility, thanks to the lively acidity and crisp apple fruit.

Kitchen Fridge Survivor™ Grade: B

Your notes: _____

Riesling

Grape Profile: I'm thrilled to see that nationwide sales of Riesling (REES-ling—my favorite white grape) are growing! Clearly consumers are appreciating its virtues. Among them are great prices. Also, check out all the high survivor grades. Thanks to their tangy, crisp acidity, Riesling wines really hold up in the fridge. That makes them ideal for lots of everyday dining situations—you want a glass of white with your takeout sushi, but your dinner mate wants red with the beef teriyaki. At home I sometimes want to start with a glass of white while I'm cooking and then switch to red with the meal. It's nice to know that I can go back to the wine over several days, and every glass will taste as good as the first one.

Germany, the traditional source of great Rieslings, continues to grow its presence in the *Guide*. And that's great, because no other region offers so many *world class* wines for under $25. Look for German Rieslings from the Mosel, Rheingau, Pfalz, and Nahe regions. Other go-to Riesling regions are Washington State, Australia, New Zealand, and Alsace, France.

Prepare to be impressed. Rieslings are light bodied but loaded with stunning fruit flavor, balanced with tangy acidity.

Serve: Lightly chilled is fine (the aromas really shine when it's not ice cold); it's good young and fresh, but the French and German versions can evolve nicely for up to 5 years.

When: Every day (okay, my personal taste there); classy enough for "important" meals and occasions.

With: Outstanding with shellfish and ethnic foods with a "kick" (think Asian, Thai, Indian, Mexican). There's also an awesome rule-breaker match: braised meats!

In: An all-purpose wineglass.

Banrock Station Riesling,	PC	T	V
Australia	$	X	X

✗ Zesty citrus peel, floral scents, juicy peach finish. Yum!

Kitchen Fridge Survivor™ Grade: Avg.

Your notes: _____

Beringer Johannisberg Riesling,	PC	T	V
California	$	22	24

The fruit-salad-in-a-glass flavor of this wine rocks. I think it's one of the best values in the Beringer lineup.

Kitchen Fridge Survivor™ Grade: B+

Your notes: _____

Bonny Doon Pacific Rim Riesling,	PC	T	V
USA/Germany	$	23	25

☺ This endures as one of the most written-about wines in the survey—with raves about the "yummy, juicy-fruity yet dry" flavor. *Pacific Rim* is the winery's shorthand for "drink this with Asian foods."

Kitchen Fridge Survivor™ Grade: A

Your notes: _____

Chateau Ste. Michelle Johannisberg	PC	T	V
Riesling, Washington	$	23	24

Peach and apricot flavor and crisp, lively acidity give this wine the balance that is the hallmark of well-made Riesling. Bravo!

Kitchen Fridge Survivor™ Grade: A

Your notes: _____

Columbia Crest Johannisberg	PC	T	V
Riesling, Washington	$	22	22

This honeysuckle-peachy wine is "lip-smacking with spicy foods," and "a super value."

Kitchen Fridge Survivor™ Grade: A

Your notes: _____

Price Ranges: $ = $12 or less; **$$** = $12.01–20; **$$$** = $20.01–35; **$$$$** = > $35
Kitchen Fridge Survivor™ Grades: *Avg.* = a "one-day wine," tastes noticeably less fresh the next day; *B* = holds its freshness for 2–3 days after opening; *B+* = holds *and gets better* over 2–3 days after opening; *A* = a 3- to 4-day "freshness window"; *A+* = holds *and gets better* over 3–4 days

Columbia Winery Cellarmaster's	PC	T	V
Reserve Riesling, Washington	$	26	27

☺ Lush with ripe peach, apricot, and honey flavors, spiked with crisp acidity, at a bargain price.

Kitchen Fridge Survivor™ Grade: A+

Your notes: _____

Dr. Konstantin Frank Dry Riesling,	PC	T	V
New York	$$	25	24

☺ What an impressive fan base for this wine; the "best dry Riesling in the United States" (I concur), which "comes close to German quality," with incredible peachy fruit density and zingy acidity.

Kitchen Fridge Survivor™ Grade: A

Your notes: _____

Dr. Loosen Riesling Kabinett	PC	T	V
Estate, Germany	$$$	26	24

"Perfect with Asian meals," say my tasters, because the mineral/petrol scents and steely acidity set off spicy and pungent flavors beautifully.

Kitchen Fridge Survivor™ Grade: A

Your notes: _____

Eroica (ee-ROY-cuh) Riesling,	PC	T	V
Washington	$$$	26	23

☺ "The best Riesling made in America . . ."? It's a contender. The dense core of apple and peach fruit and mineral complexity make it "as good as German Riesling."

Kitchen Fridge Survivor™ Grade: A+

Your notes: _____

Felton Road Riesling,	PC	T	V
New Zealand	$$$	X	X

✗ Wow sophistication: mineral, kumquat, creamy finish.

Kitchen Fridge Survivor™ Grade: A

Your notes: _____

Fetzer Valley Oaks Johannisberg	PC	T	V
Riesling, California	$	24	26

My tasters "love" this "bold" Riesling, with "huge pear fruit" and a hint of sweetness "with spicy foods."

Kitchen Fridge Survivor™ Grade: B+

Your notes: _____

Gunderloch Riesling Estate, | PC | T | V
Germany | $$ | 18 | 18

This wine exemplifies great German Riesling—so approachable, yet with amazing complexity: flowers, chamomile tea, fresh cream, white peach.

Kitchen Fridge Survivor™ Grade: A

Your notes: _____

Hogue Johannisberg Riesling, | PC | T | V
Washington | $ | 22 | 22

Attention all white Zin fans: Here's a great alternative that's a little on the sweet side, with ripe, peachy fruit flavor and a candied orange finish.

Kitchen Fridge Survivor™ Grade: B

Your notes: _____

Jekel Riesling, | PC | T | V
California | $ | 24 | 18

I love this wine's floral nose and juicy peach flavor. The touch of sweetness makes it a perfect partner for spicy foods.

Kitchen Fridge Survivor™ Grade: B+

Your notes: _____

J.J. Prum Riesling Kabinett | PC | T | V
Wehlener Sonnenuhr, Germany | $$ | 29 | 27

✓ This is textbook Mosel Riesling—peaches-and-cream and petrol character, packed with concentration.

Kitchen Fridge Survivor™ Grade: A+

Your notes: _____

J. Lohr Bay Mist Riesling, | PC | T | V
California | $ | 24 | 24

This wine's enticing floral scent and apple fruit, balanced by crisp acidity, make it a perfect aperitif.

Kitchen Fridge Survivor™ Grade: B+

Your notes: _____

Price Ranges: **$** = $12 or less; **$$** = $12.01–20; **$$$** = $20.01–35; **$$$$** = > $35

Kitchen Fridge Survivor™ Grades: *Avg.* = a "one-day wine," tastes noticeably less fresh the next day; *B* = holds its freshness for 2–3 days after opening; *B+* = holds *and gets better* over 2–3 days after opening; *A* = a 3- to 4-day "freshness window"; *A+* = holds *and gets better* over 3–4 days

Kendall-Jackson Vintner's Reserve Riesling, California

PC	T	V
$	26	26

For tasters new to Riesling, I often recommend this one: a blue chip winery pedigree, lush peach and tangerine fruit, great price.

Kitchen Fridge Survivor™ Grade: A+

Your notes: _____

Kurt Darting Riesling Kabinett, Germany

PC	T	V
$$	27	24

I'm always thrilled when I find this on wine lists. Its bewitching floral aromas and spicy-tangy core are just glorious—with food or without.

Kitchen Fridge Survivor™ Grade: A+

Your notes: _____

Leasingham Bin 7 Riesling, Australia

PC	T	V
$$	X	X

✗ Like a lemon meringue pie, but not sweet. Yum!

Kitchen Fridge Survivor™ Grade: A

Your notes: _____

Leitz Dragonstone Riesling, Germany

PC	T	V
$$	26	28

"Excellent" lively, citrus zest and tangerine flavors.

Kitchen Fridge Survivor™ Grade: A+

Your notes: _____

Lingenfelder Bird Label Riesling, Germany

PC	T	V
$$	21	24

This "awsome value from a top producer" has amazing acidity and snappy apple flavor that make it "perfect to sip on," great with food.

Kitchen Fridge Survivor™ Grade: A+

Your notes: _____

McWilliams Hanwood Estate Riesling, Australia

PC	T	V
$	X	X

✗ Lively peach, green apple, and mineral at a great price.

Kitchen Fridge Survivor™ Grade: Avg.

Your notes: _____

Mirassou Riesling,	PC	T	V
California	$	X	X

✗ Classic style with a touch of petrol and ripe peach fruit.

Kitchen Fridge Survivor™ Grade: B+

Your notes: _____

Pierre Sparr Carte D'Or Riesling,	PC	T	V
Alsace, France	$	24	21

"When you're sick of oak, take this for the cure," say my tasters of this sleek, tangy, mouthwatering Riesling with the scent of honey and Asian pears. Yum!

Kitchen Fridge Survivor™ Grade: A+

Your notes: _____

Reichsgraf von Kesselstatt	PC	T	V
Piesporter Goldtropfchen	$$$	27	27
Riesling Kabinett, Germany			

The light body, honeysuckle and petrol scent, delicate peach-apple flavors, and creamy finish are textbook Mosel Riesling.

Kitchen Fridge Survivor™ Grade: A

Your notes: _____

Robert Mondavi Private Selection	PC	T	V
Riesling, California	$	19	20

How do they do it? The petrol and peach are classic Riesling, but the yum factor and great price are "house wine" material. Bravo!

Kitchen Fridge Survivor™ Grade: B+

Your notes: _____

Selbach-Oster (*ZELL-bock OH-stir*)	PC	T	V
"Fish Label" Riesling, Germany	$	24	24

This wine has neither a tongue-twister name nor a flabby-sweet taste. It *does* have a delicate peaches-and-cream scent, tangerine and apricot fruit, and long finish.

Kitchen Fridge Survivor™ Grade: A

Your notes: _____

Price Ranges: **$** = $12 or less; **$$** = $12.01–20; **$$$** = $20.01–35; **$$$$** = > $35

Kitchen Fridge Survivor™ Grades: *Avg.* = a "one-day wine," tastes noticeably less fresh the next day; *B* = holds its freshness for 2–3 days after opening; *B+* = holds *and gets better* over 2–3 days after opening; *A* = a 3- to 4-day "freshness window"; *A+* = holds *and gets better* over 3–4 days

Strub Niersteiner Paterberg   PC   T   V
Riesling Spatlese, Germany $$ 24   18

☺ "One of the best" Rieslings under $20. The creaminess and lively acidity remind me of lemon custard.

Kitchen Fridge Survivor™ Grade: A+

Your notes: _____

Trimbach Riesling,   PC   T   V
Alsace, France $$ 24   21

The fan club grows and grows for this Alsace classic. It's bone dry, with an amazing acidity and deep lemon-–-green apple flavor. World class.

Kitchen Fridge Survivor™ Grade: A+

Your notes: _____

Trimbach Riesling Cuvee   PC   T   V
Frederic Emile, France $$$$ 27   24

☺ I agree, it's "one of the world's great Rieslings" and "a great value considering the quality." The rich buttermilk scent, steely acidity, and lemon-pear fruit are subtle and layered. Ages great.

Kitchen Fridge Survivor™ Grade: A

Your notes: _____

Sauvignon Blanc/Fume Blanc

Grape Profile: Sauvignon Blanc (*soh-veen-yoan BLAHNK*), one of my favorite white wine grapes, is on the rise, and for good reason: Truly great ones are still available for under $15—something you can't say about many wine categories these days. Depending on where it's grown (cool, moderate, or warm zones), the exotically pungent scent and taste range from zesty and herbal to tangy lime-grapefruit to juicy peach and melon, with vibrant acidity. The grape's home base is France's Loire Valley and Bordeaux regions. California and Washington State make excellent versions, sometimes labeled Fume Blanc (*FOO-may BLAHNK*). In the Southern Hemisphere, New Zealand Sauvignon Blancs continue to earn pro and consumer raves. Another of Sauvignon Blanc's major virtues is its food versatility: It goes so well with the foods many people eat regularly (especially those following a less-red-meat regimen), like chicken and turkey, salads, sushi, Mexican, and vegetarian.

> **THANKS, KIWIS!** Many New Zealand Sauvignon Blancs are now bottled with a screw cap for your convenience and to ensure you get fresh wine without "corkiness" (see "Buying Lingo" for a definition). Hooray!

Serve: Chilled but not ice cold.

When: An amazing food partner, but the tasting notes also spotlight styles that are good on their own, as an aperitif.

With: As noted, great with most everyday eats as well as popular ethnic tastes like Mexican food.

In: An all-purpose wineglass.

	PC	T	V
Andretti Sauvignon Blanc, California	$$	22	27

Fast-lane flavors of "juicy peach"; "fantastic value."
Kitchen Fridge Survivor™ Grade: B
Your notes: _____

	PC	T	V
Babcock 11 Oaks Sauvignon Blanc, California	$$$	20	24

Super-Sauv-me! This is the no-oak, zingy, lemongrass, and tropical fruit style at its mouthwatering best.
Kitchen Fridge Survivor™ Grade: A
Your notes: _____

	PC	T	V
Babich Marlborough Sauvignon Blanc, New Zealand	$	24	26

This "zingy, appley" bottling "gets better every year." It's "a great value and a great food wine."
Kitchen Fridge Survivor™ Grade: B+
Your notes: _____

Price Ranges: **$** = $12 or less; **$$** = $12.01–20; **$$$** = $20.01–35; **$$$$** = > $35
Kitchen Fridge Survivor™ Grades: *Avg.* = a "one-day wine," tastes noticeably less fresh the next day; *B* = holds its freshness for 2–3 days after opening; *B+* = holds *and gets better* over 2–3 days after opening; *A* = a 3- to 4-day "freshness window"; *A+* = holds *and gets better* over 3–4 days

Beaulieu (BV) Coastal Estates   PC   T   V
Sauvignon Blanc, California $ 27   29

Lively and zesty kiwi and lime flavors, great price.

Kitchen Fridge Survivor™ Grade: B

Your notes: _____

Benziger Sauvignon Blanc,   PC   T   V
California $$ 23   21

A "great wine list buy," say fans, citing the bright citrus, apple, and melon aromas and crisp acidity that make it great with a wide range of foods.

Kitchen Fridge Survivor™ Grade: B+

Your notes: _____

Brancott Reserve Sauvignon Blanc,   PC   T   V
New Zealand $$ 26   24

"One of New Zealand's best" Sauvignon Blancs, with "lavish" herb and passion fruit flavors. Holds up great in the fridge or by the glass.

Kitchen Fridge Survivor™ Grade: A+

Your notes: _____

Brancott Sauvignon Blanc,   PC   T   V
New Zealand $ 22   21

One of my panel's perennial favorites: "Like summertime on the front porch," said one taster—and I couldn't agree more. "Forget the lemonade and pass the Brancott!"

Kitchen Fridge Survivor™ Grade: B+

Your notes: _____

Cakebread Sauvignon Blanc,   PC   T   V
California $$$ 26   21

Fans of Cakebread's Chardonnay should try this. The vibrant grapefruit aromas with a hint of fig and vanilla give a much better bang for the buck.

Kitchen Fridge Survivor™ Grade: A

Your notes: _____

Casa Lapostolle (*lah-poh-STOLE*)   PC   T   V
Sauvignon Blanc, Chile $ 26   28

This bottling has so much more than I expect at this price: vivid honeydew, kiwi flavors, and a long finish.

Kitchen Fridge Survivor™ Grade: A

Your notes: _____

Chateau Ste. Michelle Columbia	**PC**	**T**	**V**
Valley Sauvignon Blanc,	**$**	**23**	**24**
Washington			

Three cheers: tasty, affordable, consistent. Okay, four—exotic: grapefruit and lemongrass scent, ginger flavor, creamy texture.

Kitchen Fridge Survivor™ Grade: B

Your notes: _____

Chateau St. Jean Fume Blanc,	**PC**	**T**	**V**
California	**$**	**24**	**20**

A touch of barrel aging gives this wine a creamy scent, balanced by fruit flavors of grapefruit, melon, and fig, plus tangy acidity. Yum!

Kitchen Fridge Survivor™ Grade: B+

Your notes: _____

Cloudy Bay Sauvignon Blanc,	**PC**	**T**	**V**
New Zealand	**$$$**	**25**	**22**

This wine put the now-famous kiwi-lime, "grassy" character of New Zealand Sauvignon Blancs on the map in the 1980s. The consensus now is that it's "hard to find" and "expensive" but "still yummy."

Kitchen Fridge Survivor™ Grade: A

Your notes: _____

Dancing Bull Sauvignon Blanc,	**PC**	**T**	**V**
California	**$**	**X**	**X**

✗ Peachy fruit with a lively twist of lime. Tasty!

Kitchen Fridge Survivor™ Grade: B

Your notes: _____

Domaine Vincent Delaporte	**PC**	**T**	**V**
Sancerre, France	**$$$**	**24**	**18**

"Classic" Sancerre with lime, mineral, and grapefruit.

Kitchen Fridge Survivor™ Grade: A+

Your notes: _____

Price Ranges: **$** = $12 or less; **$$** = $12.01–20; **$$$** = $20.01–35; **$$$$** = > $35

Kitchen Fridge Survivor™ Grades: ***Avg.*** = a "one-day wine," tastes noticeably less fresh the next day; ***B*** = holds its freshness for 2–3 days after opening; ***B+*** = holds *and gets better* over 2–3 days after opening; ***A*** = a 3- to 4-day "freshness window"; ***A+*** = holds *and gets better* over 3–4 days

Dry Creek Fume Blanc,	PC	T	V
California	$$	24	24

☺ Although the price has nudged up a bit, there's still flavor bang for the buck. You get "jam-packed, tangy" tangerine and peach flavors that get better and better over several days in the fridge.

Kitchen Fridge Survivor™ Grade: A+

Your notes: _____

Drylands Sauvignon Blanc,	PC	T	V
New Zealand	$$	X	X

✗ Passion fruit, pineapple, grapefruit, and crushed mint.

Kitchen Fridge Survivor™ Grade: A

Your notes: _____

Duckhorn Sauvignon Blanc,	PC	T	V
California	$$$	23	21

The "high price" reflects a premium for the famous Duckhorn name. I think the tangerine fruit, nice balance, and good length are worth it when you want to impress.

Kitchen Fridge Survivor™ Grade: A

Your notes: _____

Dyed in the Wool Sauvignon Blanc,	PC	T	V
New Zealand	$	18	24

The cheeky sense of humor and the grassy-lime-melon wine style are both classically kiwi, and the price is great.

Kitchen Fridge Survivor™ Grade: A

Your notes: _____

Ferrari-Carano Fume Blanc,	PC	T	V
California	$$	26	25

This is one of California's benchmark Fumes, balancing crisp tanginess with melony fig fruit and richness due to the oak-barrel aging. Delish!

Kitchen Fridge Survivor™ Grade: B+

Your notes: _____

Frei Brothers Redwood Creek	PC	T	V
Sauvignon Blanc, California	$	18	18

Lively, "tropical" fruit flavor for a "good price."

Kitchen Fridge Survivor™ Grade: Avg.

Your notes: _____

| Frog's Leap Sauvignon Blanc, | PC | T | V |
| California | $$ | 25 | 25 |

This is a fine-dining wine list regular worth looking for. The 100% Sauvignon Blanc character of gooseberries and flinty, penetrating citrus is delicious.

Kitchen Fridge Survivor™ Grade: A

Your notes: _____

| Geyser Peak Sauvignon Blanc, | PC | T | V |
| California | $ | 22 | 24 |

This is a lovely, classic California Sauvignon Blanc, combining the crisp tang of citrus with the juicier taste of kiwi.

Kitchen Fridge Survivor™ Grade: B+

Your notes: _____

Grgich (*GER-gich;* both are hard	PC	T	V
g as in *girl*) Hills Fume Blanc,	$$$	27	21
California			

I'm happy that Grgich keeps true to its high-quality distinct style: crisp, with scents of fresh herbs and citrus and flavors of grapefruit and melon.

Kitchen Fridge Survivor™ Grade: B

Your notes: _____

| Henri Bourgeois (ahn-REE buh- | PC | T | V |
| *JHWAH*) Pouilly Fume, France | $$ | 27 | 18 |

This wine offers classic French subtlety and complexity: floral and smoky scents, zingy acidity, and elegance.

Kitchen Fridge Survivor™ Grade: B+

Your notes: _____

| Hogue Fume Blanc, Washington | PC | T | V |
| | $ | 23 | 25 |

"A very good wine at a very good price," with fresh apple, herbs, and citrus peel plus a juicy mouthfeel.

Kitchen Fridge Survivor™ Grade: A+

Your notes: _____

Price Ranges: **$** = $12 or less; **$$** = $12.01–20; **$$$** = $20.01–35; **$$$$** = > $35

Kitchen Fridge Survivor™ Grades: ***Avg.*** = a "one-day wine," tastes noticeably less fresh the next day; ***B*** = holds its freshness for 2–3 days after opening; ***B+*** = holds *and gets better* over 2–3 days after opening; ***A*** = a 3- to 4-day "freshness window"; ***A+*** = holds *and gets better* over 3–4 days

Honig Sauvignon Blanc, | PC | T | V
California | $$ | 24 | 23

"Excellent!" and one of the few California Sauvignon Blancs in the flinty, grassy, Loire Valley style.

Kitchen Fridge Survivor™ Grade: B+

Your notes: _____

Joel Gott Sauvignon Blanc, | PC | T | V
California | $ | 23 | 24

For the price, a scrumptious Sauvignon Blanc dripping with honeydew, kiwi, and lime flavors.

Kitchen Fridge Survivor™ Grade: A

Your notes: _____

Jolivet (Pascal) Sancerre | PC | T | V
(*jhoe-lee-VAY sahn-SAIR*), France | $$ | 23 | 21

☺ A perennial favorite with my tasters, this wine's well balanced and utterly "alive" taste and scent (lemongrass, lime cream, and honey) are great for the price.

Kitchen Fridge Survivor™ Grade: A+

Your notes: _____

Joseph Phelps Sauvignon Blanc, | PC | T | V
California | $$$ | 24 | 24

"Lots of *zing* and *zang*" for the money, including "grapefruit and citrus flavors" and "softer fruit flavors" like peach and melon.

Kitchen Fridge Survivor™ Grade: B+

Your notes: _____

Kenwood Sauvignon Blanc, | PC | T | V
California | $ | 23 | 28

The taste of this gorgeous Sauvignon Blanc reminds me of a summer melon salad with lime, honey, and mint.

Kitchen Fridge Survivor™ Grade: A+

Your notes: _____

Kim Crawford Sauvignon Blanc, | PC | T | V
New Zealand | $$ | 28 | 26

A "major favorite" with my panel; with the purest Sauvignon Blanc fruit—key lime, kiwi, and honeydew.

Kitchen Fridge Survivor™ Grade: A

Your notes: _____

Lucien Crochet (*loo-SYEN crow-SHAY*) **Sancerre, France**

PC	T	V
$$$	27	18

"Definitive Sauvignon Blanc" is the consensus on this top-scoring wine. The floral-herbaceous nose, creamy-but-not-heavy texture, crisp citrus flavor, and finesse are "a huge relief for the oak-weary."

Kitchen Fridge Survivor™ *Grade: B+*

Your notes: _____

Mason Sauvignon Blanc, California

PC	T	V
$$	24	23

You'll love this kiwi and passion fruit–scented wine that's "like New Zealand Sauvignon Blanc without the grassiness." Great for spicy food.

Kitchen Fridge Survivor™ *Grade: B*

Your notes: _____

Merryvale Sauvignon Blanc, California

PC	T	V
$$	22	20

One of the best in Merryvale's lineup, with lush and lively kiwi, honeydew, and lime flavors.

Kitchen Fridge Survivor™ *Grade: B*

Your notes: _____

Monkey Bay Sauvignon Blanc, New Zealand

PC	T	V
$	24	27

Amazing—this wine bested benchmark Cloudy Bay *twice* in blind tastings with pro palates. Cut grass, lime, grapefruit, long finish—cool label, too!

Kitchen Fridge Survivor™ *Grade: A*

Your notes: _____

Murphy-Goode Fume Blanc, California

PC	T	V
$	21	22

While some call it "too Chardonnay like," many tasters were thumbs-up on the less herbaceous, passion fruit, and tropical flavor profile.

Kitchen Fridge Survivor™ *Grade: Avg.*

Your notes: _____

Price Ranges: **$** = $12 or less; **$$** = $12.01–20; **$$$** = $20.01–35; **$$$$** = > $35

Kitchen Fridge Survivor™ Grades: *Avg.* = a "one-day wine," tastes noticeably less fresh the next day; *B* = holds its freshness for 2–3 days after opening; *B+* = holds *and gets better* over 2–3 days after opening; *A* = a 3- to 4-day "freshness window"; *A+* = holds *and gets better* over 3–4 days

Nobilo Sauvignon Blanc,   PC   T   V
New Zealand $ 28   28

✓ This kiwi Sauvignon Blanc has taken the market by storm, offering the signature grapefruit/herbal style the region is known for, at a "great price."

Kitchen Fridge Survivor™ Grade: A+

Your notes: _____

Orrin Swift Sauvignon Blanc,   PC   T   V
California $$ X   X

✗ A lot of juicy kiwi and grapefruit flavor for the price.

Kitchen Fridge Survivor™ Grade: B+

Your notes: _____

Pavillon Blanc du Chateau Margaux   PC   T   V
Bordeaux, France $$$$ 24   18

An atypical white Bordeaux (because it's 100% Sauvignon Blanc), with intense lime and Granny Smith apple flavors and a racy mineral scent.

Kitchen Fridge Survivor™ Grade: B+

Your notes: _____

Robert Mondavi Napa Fume Blanc,   PC   T   V
California $$ 25   23

☺ Perennially one of Robert Mondavi's best offerings, as the scores show. It's got fruit, spice, and lemongrass; vivid citrus; and a rich texture.

Kitchen Fridge Survivor™ Grade: B

Your notes: _____

St. Supery Sauvignon Blanc,   PC   T   V
California $$ 26   25

"One of the best" California Sauvignon Blancs, with a "bright, crisp and amazingly complex" flavor—"peach and lime."

Kitchen Fridge Survivor™ Grade: A+

Your notes: _____

Silverado Sauvignon Blanc,   PC   T   V
California $$ 24   22

Free of oak, full of fruit: melon, apple, and grapefruit.

Kitchen Fridge Survivor™ Grade: B

Your notes: _____

Simi Sauvignon Blanc,   PC   T   V
California $$ 24   21

This is Sauvignon Blanc in the rich style, with creamy roundness from integrated oak and a proportion of Semillon grapes in the blend.

Kitchen Fridge Survivor™ Grade: B+

Your notes: _____

Smoking Loon Sauvignon Blanc,   PC   T   V
California $ X   X

✗ So much juicy honeydew-lime flavor for the price.

Kitchen Fridge Survivor™ Grade: Avg.

Your notes: _____

Spy Valley Sauvignon Blanc,   PC   T   V
New Zealand $$ 24   28

"Tart apples with a nice grassy finish" make this "wonderful" wine a New Zealand classic, and one of the best on the market for the money.

Kitchen Fridge Survivor™ Grade: A

Your notes: _____

Sterling Vineyards Napa   PC   T   V
Sauvignon Blanc, California $$ 18   18

This "go-to brand" has grapefruit, nectarines, and key lime flavors and scents.

Kitchen Fridge Survivor™ Grade: B

Your notes: _____

Sterling Vintner's Collection   PC   T   V
Sauvignon Blanc, California $ X   X

☺ ✗ Gorgeous peach and passion fruit flavor; better and cheaper than their Napa bottling.

Kitchen Fridge Survivor™ Grade: A+

Your notes: _____

Price Ranges: **$** = $12 or less; **$$** = $12.01–20; **$$$** = $20.01–35; **$$$$** = > $35

Kitchen Fridge Survivor™ Grades: *Avg.* = a "one-day wine," tastes noticeably less fresh the next day; *B* = holds its freshness for 2–3 days after opening; *B+* = holds *and gets better* over 2–3 days after opening; *A* = a 3- to 4-day "freshness window"; *A+* = holds *and gets better* over 3–4 days

Veramonte Sauvignon Blanc,   PC   T   V
Chile $ 24   24

☺ Here's a great-value Sauvignon Blanc, with exotic kiwi, honeydew, and passion fruit flavors.

Kitchen Fridge Survivor™ Grade: B+

Your notes: _____

Villa Maria Private Bin Sauvignon   PC   T   V
Blanc, New Zealand $ 25   24

This New Zealand Sauvignon Blanc offers a nice balance between the grassy/herbal scent and the tangy passion fruit-melon taste.

Kitchen Fridge Survivor™ Grade: B+

Your notes: _____

Voss Sauvignon Blanc,   PC   T   V
California $$ 24   24

A super-lively Sauvignon Blanc—juicy with kiwi, white peach, and grapefruit flavors.

Kitchen Fridge Survivor™ Grade: B+

Your notes: _____

Whitehaven Sauvignon Blanc,   PC   T   V
New Zealand $$ X   X

✗ Like New Zealand's Cloudy Bay, but cheaper! Explosive passion fruit, herbs, and kiwi.

Kitchen Fridge Survivor™ Grade: A

Your notes: _____

Chardonnay

Grape Profile: Chardonnay is the top-selling white varietal wine in this country and the fullest-bodied of the major white grapes. That rich body, along with Chardonnay's signature fruit intensity, could explain its extraordinary popularity with Americans, although in truth this grape's style is pretty chameleonlike. It can yield wines of legendary quality, ranging from crisp and austere to soft and juicy to utterly lush and exotic (and very often oaky), depending on whether it's grown in a cool, moderate, or warm climate. I am pleased to say that, as these notes indicate, buyers find all of these styles worthy, perhaps offering some hope to pros who bemoan a noticeable "sameness" to many of the brand names. All Chardonnays are modeled on white Burgundy wines from France. The world-class versions are known for complexity, and often oakiness; the very best are age worthy. The rest, in the $ and $$ price categories, are pleasant styles meant for current drinking. California Chardonnays by far dominate store and restaurant sales, but the quality and value of both Washington State's and Australia's are just as good. Although no New Zealand or Oregon offerings made the survey due to limited production, they're worth sampling.

Serve: Chilled; however, extreme cold mutes the complexity of the top bottlings. Pull them off the ice if they get too cold.

When: There's no occasion where Chardonnay *isn't* welcomed by the majority of wine lovers; the grape's abundant fruit makes it great on its own, as an aperitif or a cocktail alternative.

With: Some sommeliers carp that Chardonnay "doesn't go well with food," but I don't think most consumers agree. Maybe they have a point that it "overpowers" some delicate culinary creations in luxury restaurants, but for those of us doing most of our eating and drinking in less-rarefied circumstances, it's a great partner for all kinds of food. The decadent, oaky/buttery styles that are California's calling card can even handle steak.

In: An all-purpose wineglass.

Acacia Chardonnay Carneros,	PC	T	V
California	$$$	24	24

An elegant Chardonnay with apple-vanilla subtlety that lets the food star.
Kitchen Fridge Survivor™ Grade: B
Your notes: _____

Price Ranges: **$** = $12 or less; **$$** = $12.01–20; **$$$** = $20.01–35; **$$$$** = > $35
Kitchen Fridge Survivor™ Grades: *Avg.* = a "one-day wine," tastes noticeably less fresh the next day; *B* = holds its freshness for 2–3 days after opening; *B+* = holds *and gets better* over 2–3 days after opening; *A* = a 3- to 4-day "freshness window"; *A+* = holds *and gets better* over 3–4 days

Alice White Chardonnay,   PC   T   V
Australia $ 21   24

A lot of lip-smacking Golden Delicious apple fruit for not a lot of money. Holds up well over several days, too.

Kitchen Fridge Survivor™ Grade: B+

Your notes: _____

Au Bon Climat Santa Barbara   PC   T   V
Chardonnay, California $$$ 20   18

The "elegant tropical fruit" makes this "twice the wine at half the price" compared to many big-name California Chardonnays.

Kitchen Fridge Survivor™ Grade: A

Your notes: _____

Beaulieu Vineyard (BV) Coastal   PC   T   V
Estates Chardonnay, California $ 20   22

This Chardonnay is a solid performer with my tasters, with textbook apple-pear flavors and a not-too-heavy style.

Kitchen Fridge Survivor™ Grade: Avg.

Your notes: _____

Beringer Napa Chardonnay,   PC   T   V
California $ 22   22

A benchmark Napa Valley Chardonnay with ripe fruit and toasty oak.

Kitchen Fridge Survivor™ Grade: Avg.

Your notes: _____

Black Box Napa Chardonnay,   PC   T   V
California $ 24   28

Lush tropical fruit that tasters "can't believe comes in a box.

Kitchen Fridge Survivor™ Grade: A

Your notes: _____

Blackstone Monterey Chardonnay,   PC   T   V
California $$ 24   22

"Fruity" and buttery, with great roundness in the mouth.

Kitchen Fridge Survivor™ Grade: B

Your notes: _____

Buena Vista Carneros Chardonnay,   PC   T   V
California $$ X   X

✗ A gem, with buttery grilled pineapple flavors, long finish.

Kitchen Fridge Survivor™ Grade: B+

Your notes: _____

| **Cakebread Napa Chardonnay,** | PC | T | V |
| **California** | $$$$ | 24 | 19 |

This is a Napa classic, though I've noticed increasing oak overtaking the pear and green apple fruit. The blue-chip name is a top seller in fine restaurants.

Kitchen Fridge Survivor™ Grade: B

Your notes: _____

| **Cambria Katherine's Vineyard** | PC | T | V |
| **Chardonnay, California** | $$ | 24 | 22 |

A "big seller" in the big oaky style, with rich tropical fruit—for a decent price.

Kitchen Fridge Survivor™ Grade: Avg.

Your notes: _____

| **Casa Lapostolle Cuvee Alexandre** | PC | T | V |
| **Chardonnay, Chile** | $$ | 22 | 24 |

☺ A benchmark "oaky" Chardonnay with toasty, cinnamon-spice, vanilla, and rich tropical fruit.

Kitchen Fridge Survivor™ Grade: B

Your notes: _____

| **Catena Chardonnay,** | PC | T | V |
| **Argentina** | $$ | 22 | 22 |

A "rarity" among New World Chardonnays that "strikes the ideal balance" between ripe fruit and oak.

Kitchen Fridge Survivor™ Grade: B

Your notes: _____

| **Chalk Hill Chardonnay,** | PC | T | V |
| **California** | $$$ | 22 | 16 |

☺ The rich oak and luscious tropical fruit flavor are big enough to pair even with steak. And the price is reasonable compared to other luxury California Chards.

Kitchen Fridge Survivor™ Grade: B

Your notes: _____

Price Ranges: **$** = $12 or less; **$$** = $12.01–20; **$$$** = $20.01–35; **$$$$** = > $35

Kitchen Fridge Survivor™ Grades: *Avg.* = a "one-day wine," tastes noticeably less fresh the next day; *B* = holds its freshness for 2–3 days after opening; *B+* = holds *and gets better* over 2–3 days after opening; *A* = a 3- to 4-day "freshness window"; *A+* = holds *and gets better* over 3–4 days

Chalone Chardonnay,   PC   T   V
California $$$ 29   24

☺ For decades, a favorite of wine lovers—a bit "pricey," but "worth it," with "unique mineral quality," elegance, and "beautiful stone fruit" flavor. Ages nicely.

Kitchen Fridge Survivor™ Grade: B+

Your notes: _____

Chateau Montelena Chardonnay,   PC   T   V
California $$$ 24   22

"Worth every penny," say tasters of Montelena's understated elegance, featuring flinty-spicy aromas; crisp apple fruit; and a subtle, long finish. An ager.

Kitchen Fridge Survivor™ Grade: A

Your notes: _____

Chateau Ste. Michelle Columbia   PC   T   V
Valley Chardonnay, Washington $ 24   28

✔ "A lot of yum for the money": tasty pear-citrus fruit and a buttery scent.

Kitchen Fridge Survivor™ Grade: B

Your notes: _____

Chateau St. Jean Robert Young   PC   T   V
Vineyard Chardonnay, California $$$ 27   21

A "California classic" with "amazing balance" of "subtle" oak framing the Asian pear fruit.

Kitchen Fridge Survivor™ Grade: Avg.

Your notes: _____

Chateau St. Jean Sonoma   PC   T   V
Chardonnay, California $ 21   23

A classic, offering great "quality for the price," rich tropical and pear fruit, and restrained oak.

Kitchen Fridge Survivor™ Grade: B

Your notes: _____

Clos du Bois Sonoma Chardonnay,   PC   T   V
California $ 24   21

A huge seller, for good reason: lots of citrus and melon fruit and subtle oak—at a good price.

Kitchen Fridge Survivor™ Grade: A+

Your notes: _____

Columbia Crest Grand Estates   PC   T   V
Chardonnay, Washington $ 22   23

"Great value" thanks to the sweet spices, baked-apple fruit, and a hint of butter, at an easy price.

Kitchen Fridge Survivor™ Grade: B+

Your notes: _____

Cousino Macul Antiguas Reservas   PC   T   V
Chardonnay, Chile $$ 24   24

Raves for its "great value" and "buttery, honey" flavors.

Kitchen Fridge Survivor™ Grade: B

Your notes: _____

Cuvaison (*KOO-veh-sahn*) Napa   PC   T   V
Valley Chardonnay, California $$ 24   24

This is a "wow" for the price, with a luscious tropical richness and lavish-but-balanced oak.

Fridge Survivor Grade: B

Your notes: _____

Estancia Pinnacles Chardonnay,   PC   T   V
California $ 22   23

This Chard remains balanced with vibrant acidity and soft tropical fruit.

Kitchen Fridge Survivor™ Grade: A

Your notes: _____

Faiveley Mercurey Clos Rochette,   PC   T   V
France $$$ X   X

✗ Classic Burgundy: nice toasty hazelnut and baked apple.

Kitchen Fridge Survivor™ Grade: A+

Your notes: _____

Far Niente Chardonnay,   PC   T   V
California $$$$ 26   17

California ripeness along with French-style subtlety. With concentrated pineapple fruit and a toasty mineral scent, it is delicious young but ages well for 7+ years.

Price Ranges: **$** = $12 or less; **$$** = $12.01–20; **$$$** = $20.01–35; **$$$$** = > $35
Kitchen Fridge Survivor™ Grades: *Avg.* = a "one-day wine," tastes noticeably less fresh the next day; *B* = holds its freshness for 2–3 days after opening; *B+* = holds *and gets better* over 2–3 days after opening; *A* = a 3- to 4-day "freshness window"; *A+* = holds *and gets better* over 3–4 days

Fat Bastard Chardonnay,   PC   T   V
France $ 24   24
Lively apple fruit that's "pleasant for the price."
Kitchen Fridge Survivor™ *Grade: Avg.*
Your notes: _____

Ferrari-Carano Carneros   PC   T   V
Chardonnay, California $$$ 27   22
"A value if you can afford it" sums up the fact that of
the luxury Chards, this is among the most accessible,
with its spicy fruit, oak, and luscious tropical flavors.
Kitchen Fridge Survivor™ *Grade: B*
Your notes: _____

Fetzer Valley Oaks Chardonnay,   PC   T   V
California $ 24   21
The style remains consistent—fruity, and oaky—for a
good price.
Kitchen Fridge Survivor™ *Grade: B*
Your notes: _____

Flora Springs Barrel Fermented   PC   T   V
Chardonnay, California $$$ X   X
✗ Tropical fruit, crème brûlée and butter, all in
balance.
Kitchen Fridge Survivor™ *Grade: B+*
Your notes: _____

Franciscan Oakville Chardonnay,   PC   T   V
California $$ 22   20
"The same characteristics" of the monster Chards—
toasty oak and ripe pineapple/mango fruit but "not
overblown;" "lets you (affordably) impress."
Kitchen Fridge Survivor™ *Grade: Avg.*
Your notes: _____

Frank Family Vineyards   PC   T   V
Chardonnay, California $$$ 26   26
"Pops" with "fruit salad in a glass" and buttery
flavors.
Kitchen Fridge Survivor™ *Grade: B+*
Your notes: _____

Frei Brothers Reserve Russian   **PC**   **T**   **V**
River Chardonnay, California   **$$**   X   X

✗ Subtle tropical and vanilla with a silky texture; very classy.

Kitchen Fridge Survivor™ *Grade: B*

Your notes: _____

Gallo Family Vineyards Reserve   **PC**   **T**   **V**
Chardonnay, California   **$**   24   25

☺ I keep waiting for this "outstanding for the price" Chard to slip, but it still offers ripe, intense flavors of pineapples, pears, and apples and nice balance.

Kitchen Fridge Survivor™ *Grade: A*

Your notes: _____

Geyser Peak Chardonnay,   **PC**   **T**   **V**
California   **$**   22   24

Pleasant apple, pear, and melon fruit and nuances of buttery oak.

Kitchen Fridge Survivor™ *Grade: B*

Your notes: _____

Grgich (*GER-gich;* both are hard *g*,   **PC**   **T**   **V**
as in *girl*) Hills Chardonnay,   **$$$$**   26   18
California

The name has for decades promised blue-chip Napa Chard that's packed with rich fruit, yet elegant.

Kitchen Fridge Survivor™ *Grade: A*

Your notes: _____

Hess Select Chardonnay,   **PC**   **T**   **V**
California   **$**   22   23

A "great value for the money" favorite with my panel thanks to the incredible fruit: pineapple, mango, pear, and lemon.

Kitchen Fridge Survivor™ *Grade: B*

Your notes: _____

Price Ranges: **$** = $12 or less; **$$** = $12.01–20; **$$$** = $20.01–35; **$$$$** = > $35

Kitchen Fridge Survivor™ Grades: *Avg.* = a "one-day wine," tastes noticeably less fresh the next day; *B* = holds its freshness for 2–3 days after opening; *B+* = holds *and gets better* over 2–3 days after opening; *A* = a 3- to 4-day "freshness window"; *A+* = holds *and gets better* over 3–4 days

Jacob's Creek Chardonnay, PC T V
Australia $ 21 22

Both trade and consumers rate this a value star. I give it extra credit for consistency and for the bright citrus and peach flavor.

Kitchen Fridge Survivor™ Grade: Avg.

Your notes: _____

J. Lohr Riverstone Chardonnay, PC T V
California $ 26 26

This Chard in the big buttery style is a great value for the price, with flavors and scents of lime, peaches, minerals, and toasty oak.

Kitchen Fridge Survivor™ Grade: B

Your notes: _____

Joseph Drouhin Pouilly-Fuisse PC T V
(*poo-YEE fwee-SAY*), France $$ 22 22

Classic Pouilly-Fuisse, with creamy apple and fresh almond scents, steely dryness, and a long finish.

Kitchen Fridge Survivor™ Grade: A

Your notes: _____

Kendall-Jackson Vintner's Reserve PC T V
Chardonnay, California $ 21 21

Competition has brought this top-selling Chard's price down a bit. It still shines for its juicy fruit and soft oak—and the quality remains high, so I think the fan club will endure.

Kitchen Fridge Survivor™ Grade: A

Your notes: _____

Kim Crawford Unoaked PC T V
Chardonnay, New Zealand $$ 24 21

My tasters love the "pure fruit"—apple, pineapple, and peach—uncluttered by oak, and so will you.

Kitchen Fridge Survivor™ Grade: A+

Your notes: _____

Kistler Durell Chardonnay, PC T V
California $$$$ 28 18

A "beautiful," "very powerful" Chardonnay with incredible apples and mangoes fruit density, a bewitching hazelnut scent, and good ageability.

Kitchen Fridge Survivor™ Grade: B+

Your notes: _____

Laboure-Roi Macon Villages,   PC   T   V
France $$ 18   24

"Crisp" "pear and peach," with a mineral-"slate" finish.
Kitchen Fridge Survivor™ Grade: A
Your notes: _____

La Crema Chardonnay,   PC   T   V
California $$ 24   23

"Balanced and yummy" and classically California: ripe
peach/tropical fruit; toasty-sweet oak.
Kitchen Fridge Survivor™ Grade: Avg.
Your notes: _____

Landmark Vineyards Overlook   PC   T   V
Chardonnay, California $$$ 24   22

This "California tropical" Chard has "huge body,
heavy-duty oak, and smooooth" texture.
Kitchen Fridge Survivor™ Grade: Avg.
Your notes: _____

Leflaive (luh-FLEV) (Domaine)   PC   T   V
Puligny-Montrachet, France $$$$ 21   18

Domaine Leflaive's "delicious," "finessed" white
Burgundies sing with style, complexity, and layers of
baked apple and peach fruit.
Kitchen Fridge Survivor™ Grade: B+
Your notes: _____

Leflaive (Olivier) (oh-LIV-ee-ay)   PC   T   V
St. Aubin, France $$$ 24   22

A good "starter Burgundy," with refined citrus and
pear fruit, minerals, and toasted nuts.
Kitchen Fridge Survivor™ Grade: B
Your notes: _____

Lindemans Bin 65 Chardonnay,   PC   T   V
Australia $ 21   23

☺ This wine encores as one of the top
Chardonnay values with my tasters. The fragrant

Price Ranges: **$** = $12 or less; **$$** = $12.01–20; **$$$** = $20.01–35;
$$$$ = > $35
Kitchen Fridge Survivor™ Grades: **Avg.** = a "one-day wine," tastes
noticeably less fresh the next day; **B** = holds its freshness for 2–3
days after opening; **B+** = holds *and gets better* over 2–3 days after
opening; **A** = a 3- to 4-day "freshness window"; **A+** = holds *and gets
better* over 3–4 days

tropical fruit is balanced with bright acidity, "for a great price."

Kitchen Fridge Survivor™ *Grade: B+*

Your notes: _____

Louis Jadot Macon-Villages	PC	T	V
(*LOO-ee jhah-DOUGH mah-COHN vill-AHJH*) Chardonnay, France	$	21	21

The clean, refreshing green apple and citrus fruit, sparked with vivid acidity is free of oak heaviness.

Kitchen Fridge Survivor™ *Grade: B+*

Your notes: _____

Louis Jadot Pouilly-Fuisse,	PC	T	V
France	$$	27	25

Fresh, unoaked Chardonnay fruit with a touch of mineral and a long finish.

Kitchen Fridge Survivor™ *Grade: A*

Your notes: _____

Matanzas Creek Chardonnay,	PC	T	V
California	$$$	24	21

◉ A "wine list stalwart" that's dropped in price (yay!) and always delivers on intense fruit and toasty oak.

Kitchen Fridge Survivor™ *Grade: B*

Your notes: _____

McWilliams Hanwood Estate	PC	T	V
Chardonnay, Australia	$	24	27

"Great Value!" with a "fruity, melons and vanilla taste."

Kitchen Fridge Survivor™ *Grade: Avg.*

Your notes: _____

Mer Soleil (mare sew-*LAY*)	PC	T	V
Chardonnay, California	$$$$	27	27

The oak is subtle on this dripping-with-banana/mango fruit Chard.

Kitchen Fridge Survivor™ *Grade: B*

Your notes: _____

Michel Laroche Chablis St. Martin	PC	T	V
Burgundy, France	$$$	22	19

True French Chablis that's relatively available and affordable, with piercingly pure apple and citrus and a bit of mineral (like the smell of wet rocks).

Kitchen Fridge Survivor™ *Grade: A+*

Your notes: _____

Mirassou Chardonnay,	PC	T	V
California	$	23	24

The pineapple and lemon flavors make this lush; nice quality for the price.

Kitchen Fridge Survivor™ Grade: B+

Your notes: _____

Penfolds Koonunga Hill	PC	T	V
Chardonnay, Australia	$	22	22

Tropical fruit, butterscotch, and character offer great bang for the buck.

Kitchen Countertop Survivor™ Grade: B

Your notes: _____

R.H. Phillips Chardonnay,	PC	T	V
California	$	23	24

This wine's always a solid value, with vivid citrus and nectarine fruit and a nice kiss of not-too-heavy oak.

Kitchen Fridge Survivor™ Grade: A

Your notes: _____

R.H. Phillips Toasted Head	PC	T	V
Chardonnay, California	$$	24	23

"Toasted Head" means more oakiness—they toast not only the sides of the barrels but the "head" (end piece) too, yielding a very toasty, rich, butterscotch scent.

Kitchen Fridge Survivor™ Grade: Avg.

Your notes: _____

Robert Mondavi Napa Chardonnay,	PC	T	V
California	$$	22	21

This blue-chip brand delivers the baked-apple and toasty-spice flavor of benchmark Napa Chardonnay.

Kitchen Fridge Survivor™ Grade: Avg.

Your notes: _____

Rodney Strong Sonoma	PC	T	V
Chardonnay, California	$	23	22

This huge seller is classic Sonoma: a coconut-sweet scent from oak and ripe apple fruit.

Price Ranges: **$** = $12 or less; **$$** = $12.01–20; **$$$** = $20.01–35; **$$$$** = > $35

Kitchen Fridge Survivor™ Grades: ***Avg.*** = a "one-day wine," tastes noticeably less fresh the next day; ***B*** = holds its freshness for 2–3 days after opening; ***B+*** = holds *and gets better* over 2–3 days after opening; ***A*** = a 3- to 4-day "freshness window"; ***A+*** = holds *and gets better* over 3–4 days

Kitchen Fridge Survivor™ Grade: Avg.
Your notes: _____

Rombauer Chardonnay,   **PC**   **T**   **V**
California   **$$$**   **28**   **18**
"Buttery and lightly toasty" with baked-apple fruit.
Kitchen Fridge Survivor™ Grade: B
Your notes: _____

Rosemount Diamond Label   **PC**   **T**   **V**
Chardonnay, Australia   **$**   **20**   **22**
This Aussie's "still solid," with peach and citrus fruit, a
little oak, and a clean finish.
Kitchen Fridge Survivor™ Grade: B+
Your notes: _____

St. Francis Sonoma Chardonnay,   **PC**   **T**   **V**
California   **$**   **22**   **22**
Lots of real Sonoma Chardonnay character for the
price: ripe pear and tropical fruit, soft vanilla oak, buttery scent, and nice balance.
Kitchen Fridge Survivor™ Grade: A+
Your notes: _____

Silverado Chardonnay,   **PC**   **T**   **V**
California   **$$$**   **X**   **X**
✗ Lots of crisp apple flavor; excellent structure and
length for the money.
Kitchen Fridge Survivor™ Grade: A
Your notes: _____

Simi Russian River Reserve   **PC**   **T**   **V**
Chardonnay, California   **$$$**   **X**   **X**
✗ Thanks to new winemaker Steve Reeder, it's better
than ever—with gorgeous tropical fruit and toasted
nut flavors.
Kitchen Fridge Survivor™ Grade: Avg.
Your notes: _____

Smoking Loon Chardonnay,   **PC**   **T**   **V**
California   **$**   **21**   **23**
This Chard packs a lot of fruit flavor—pineapple and
juicy citrus—for the price.
Kitchen Fridge Survivor™ Grade: Avg.
Your notes: _____

Sonoma-Cutrer Russian River	PC	T	V
Ranches Chardonnay, California	$$$	27	24

In contrast to the "monster Chardonnay genre," this classic holds out for elegance and complexity.

Kitchen Fridge Survivor™ Grade: B+

Your notes: _____

Sterling Vineyards Napa	PC	T	V
Chardonnay, California	$$	23	22

A California classic with a vanilla scent and light apple fruit.

Kitchen Fridge Survivor™ Grade: A

Your notes: _____

Sterling Vintner's Collection	PC	T	V
Chardonnay, California	$	X	X

✗ Crisp, appley, and not too heavy for sipping or pairing.

Kitchen Fridge Survivor™ Grade: Avg.

Your notes: _____

Talbott (Robert) Sleepy Hollow	PC	T	V
Vineyard Chardonnay, California	$$$$	26	23

Every guest I've ever served adored the exotic marzipan, toasted nut, and tart pear flavors of this "restaurant wine" (rarely found in stores).

Kitchen Fridge Survivor™ Grade: B

Your notes: _____

Talus Chardonnay,	PC	T	V
California	$	X	X

✗ An old brand reborn and better than ever with a nice balance between juicy-tropical and clean citrus.

Kitchen Fridge Survivor™ Grade: B

Your notes: _____

Price Ranges: **$** = $12 or less; **$$** = $12.01–20; **$$$** = $20.01–35; **$$$$** = > $35

Kitchen Fridge Survivor™ Grades: *Avg.* = a "one-day wine," tastes noticeably less fresh the next day; *B* = holds its freshness for 2–3 days after opening; *B+* = holds *and gets better* over 2–3 days after opening; *A* = a 3- to 4-day "freshness window"; *A+* = holds *and gets better* over 3–4 days

Three Blind Moose Chardonnay,	PC	T	V
California	$	X	X

✗ Juicy apple-pineapple fruit; great value for the money.

Kitchen Fridge Survivor™ Grade: B

Your notes: _____

Trefethen Estate Chardonnay,	PC	T	V
California	$$$	24	16

Trefethen's signature wine, with classy and subtle oak, pear, and pineapple fruit.

Kitchen Fridge Survivor™ Grade: B

Your notes: _____

Twin Fin Chardonnay,	PC	T	V
California	$	X	X

✗ A "hip-label" wine that also tastes great—tangerine and apple fruit, soft oak, lively take-another-sip finish.

Kitchen Fridge Survivor™ Grade: B

Your notes: _____

Veramonte Chardonnay,	PC	T	V
Chile	$	21	21

This Chard gives you lovely tropical fruit flavor that "tastes more expensive than it is."

Kitchen Fridge Survivor™ Grade: Avg.

Your notes: _____

Wolf Blass Yellow Label	PC	T	V
Chardonnay, Australia	$	X	X

✗ Lively apple-peach-melon fruit and just a touch of oak.

Kitchen Fridge Survivor™ Grade: B

Your notes: _____

Yellow Tail Chardonnay,	PC	T	V
Australia	$	20	24

This wine's "delicious, easy-drinking" Chardonnay fruit makes this "hugely popular" wine "a value."

Kitchen Fridge Survivor™ Grade: Avg

Your notes: _____

Other Whites

Category Profile: A label of "other" for wines that don't fit neatly into a major category means some do not get the respect they deserve. The group includes a wildly diverse collection of wine types, from uncommon grapes and regions to unique blends and proprietary branded wines. Here is some background on each:

Uncommon Grapes and Regions—This category includes the grapes Albarino (from Spain), Pinot Blanc, Gewurztraminer, Gruner-Veltliner (from Austria), and Viognier, all meriting high marks from tasters and definitely worth your attention. The other-than-Pinot-Grigio Italian whites are also here, along with Spanish regional whites. (See the "Wine List Decoder" for more on these.)

Unique Blends—Blends of the white grapes Semillon and Chardonnay, mainly from Australia and Washington State, are increasingly popular. This category also includes a growing crop of specialty multi-grape blends well worth trying—a sign consumers are continuing to branch out—yay!

Proprietary Brands—These used to dominate the wine market in the seventies, and a few like Blue Nun have retained significant market presence.

Serve: Well chilled.

When: The uncommon grapes (like Gewurztraminer) and unique blends are wonderful when you want to surprise guests with a different flavor experience.

With: In my opinion, Gewurztraminer, Albarino, and the unusual grape blends are some of the most exciting food partners out there.

In: An all-purpose wineglass.

	PC	T	V
Alice White Lexia,			
Australia	**$**	**24**	**25**

"Nice Tasting," "nice price," with honey-pear flavor.
Kitchen Fridge Survivor™ *Grade: B*
Your notes: _____

Price Ranges: **$** = $12 or less; **$$** = $12.01–20; **$$$** = $20.01–35; **$$$$** = > $35
Kitchen Fridge Survivor™ Grades: *Avg.* = a "one-day wine," tastes noticeably less fresh the next day; *B* = holds its freshness for 2–3 days after opening; *B+* = holds *and gets better* over 2–3 days after opening; *A* = a 3- to 4-day "freshness window"; *A+* = holds *and gets better* over 3–4 days

Alice White Semillon   PC   T   V
(sem-ee-*YOHN*)/Chardonnay, $ 19   20
Australia

"What a great value" for such juicy peach flavor streaked with a zingy lime tanginess.

Kitchen Fridge Survivor™ Grade: Avg.

Your notes: _____

Antinori Orvieto Campogrande,   PC   T   V
Italy $ 18   18

"Refreshing" with crisp apple fruit for a "good price."

Kitchen Fridge Survivor™ Grade: B

Your notes: _____

Arrowood Saralee's Vineyard   PC   T   V
Viognier, California $$$ 29   24

Classic Viognier: "peaches, melon, and a floral aroma."

Kitchen Fridge Survivor™ Grade: Avg.

Your notes: _____

Becker Viognier,   PC   T   V
Texas $$ 23   22

One of the best Viogniers made in America, so it's worth the search. Gorgeous white peach and floral scents and tangerine-mango flavors.

Kitchen Fridge Survivor™ Grade: B

Your notes: _____

Beringer Chenin Blanc,   PC   T   V
California $ 26   28

My tasters "love" this "huge bargain" with huge fruit—juicy tangerine and peach—and some sweetness.

Kitchen Fridge Survivor™ Grade: Avg.

Your notes: _____

Beringer Gewurztraminer,   PC   T   V
California $ 22   22

My tasters "adore the price" and the apricot fruit flavor that makes this wine a "great aperitif."

Kitchen Fridge Survivor™ Grade: Avg.

Your notes: _____

Burgans Albarino (*boor-GAHNS*   PC   T   V
***all-buh-REEN-yoh*), Bodegas** $$ 24   23
Vilarino-Cambados, Spain

"A wonderful alternative to Chardonnay; great with shellfish," say my tasters, who love the peachy, aromatic style.

Kitchen Fridge Survivor™ Grade: B+
Your notes: _____

Ca' del Solo Big House White,	PC	T	V
California	$	24	24

This "great blend of ABCs" (anything but Chardonnay white grapes) offers "totally refreshing" flavors of peach and kiwi.

Kitchen Fridge Survivor™ Grade: B
Your notes: _____

Chateau Ste. Michelle	PC	T	V
Gewurztraminer, Washington	$	24	24

Fragrant! Candied ginger and apricots, and delicious "with Chinese food."

Kitchen Fridge Survivor™ Grade: B
Your notes: _____

Columbia Crest Columbia Valley	PC	T	V
Gewurztraminer, Washington	$	20	21

This wine's honey and sweet spice flavor makes it "great with spicy and ethnic foods."

Kitchen Fridge Survivor™ Grade: B+
Your notes: _____

Columbia Crest Semillon/	PC	T	V
Chardonnay, Washington	$	18	24

Blending the Semillon grape with Chard adds acidity, earthiness, honey, and lime flavors.

Kitchen Fridge Survivor™ Grade: B
Your notes: _____

Conundrum White Blend,	PC	T	V
California	$$$	27	24

This "interesting combination" of grapes (Chard, Sauvignon Blanc, Chenin Blanc, and more) has an exotic tropical style and a wine's devoted following.

Kitchen Fridge Survivor™ Grade: B
Your notes: _____

Price Ranges: **$** = $12 or less; **$$** = $12.01–20; **$$$** = $20.01–35; **$$$$** = > $35
Kitchen Fridge Survivor™ Grades: *Avg.* = a "one-day wine," tastes noticeably less fresh the next day; *B* = holds its freshness for 2–3 days after opening; *B+* = holds *and gets better* over 2–3 days after opening; *A* = a 3- to 4-day "freshness window"; *A+* = holds *and gets better* over 3–4 days

Domaine Weinbach   **PC**   **T**   **V**
Gewurztraminer Cuvee Theo,   **$$$$**   27   24
France

"Immense" tropical, lychee, and apricot fruit,
unctuous texture, yet not heavy. An Alsace classic.

Kitchen Fridge Survivor™ Grade: A

Your notes: _____

Dry Creek Vineyard Chenin Blanc,   **PC**   **T**   **V**
California   **$**   27   27

"Like biting a Golden Delicious apple"—juicy, with a
pretty snap of acidity and a creamy finish. De-lish.

Kitchen Fridge Survivor™ Grade: B

Your notes: _____

Fall Creek Chenin Blanc,   **PC**   **T**   **V**
Texas   **$**   X   X

✗ Crisp, appley, and slightly sweet; a picnic in a
bottle.

Kitchen Fridge Survivor™ Grade: Avg.

Your notes: _____

Fetzer Valley Oaks Gewurztraminer,   **PC**   **T**   **V**
California   **$**   25   26

Here's a "favorite" of my tasters for its luscious floral
and apricot aromas and flavors.

Kitchen Fridge Survivor™ Grade: B

Your notes: _____

Francis Coppola Presents Bianco,   **PC**   **T**   **V**
California   **$**   X   X

✗ Floral scent, zesty citrus flavor; a great "house" wine.

Kitchen Fridge Survivor™ Grade: Avg.

Your notes: _____

Herbauges Muscadet,   **PC**   **T**   **V**
France   **$**   20   21

This carafe quaff of Parisian bistros offers crisp
apple flavors, mineral scents, and maximum
refreshment.

Kitchen Fridge Survivor™ Grade: B

Your notes: _____

Hildago La Gitana (*ee-DAHL-go*   **PC**   **T**   **V**
***la hee-TAH-nuh*) Manzanilla**   **$**   24   24
Sherry, Spain

This sherry's "nutty," "clean" flavor is super with salty
fare and fried foods, too.

Kitchen Fridge Survivor™ Grade: A

Your notes: _____

Hirsch Gruner Veltliner #1,   PC   T   V
Austria $$ X   X

✗ "Delicious" grapefruit and pineapple; a great food wine.

Kitchen Fridge Survivor™ Grade: B+

Your notes: _____

Hogue Gewurztraminer,   PC   T   V
Washington $ 22   24

This apricot-gingery Gewurz is "del-ish for sipping" and with "Chinese food."

Kitchen Fridge Survivor™ Grade: B+

Your notes: _____

Hugel (*hew-GELL*) Gewurztraminer,   PC   T   V
France $$ 25   22

☺ A fave of my tasters for the floral and sweet spice scent and lychee-nut/apricot flavor.

Kitchen Fridge Survivor™ Grade: A

Your notes: _____

Hugel Pinot Blanc,   PC   T   V
France $ 21   21

The apple-pear flavor, mineral complexity, and liveliness of this Pinot Blanc are great for the price.

Kitchen Fridge Survivor™ Grade: B

Your notes: _____

Indaba Chenin Blanc,   PC   T   V
South Africa $ 24   24

Yum's the word from tasters for this wine's lively Golden Delicious apple flavor at a "great price."

Kitchen Fridge Survivor™ Grade: B+

Your notes: _____

Price Ranges: **$** = $12 or less; **$$** = $12.01–20; **$$$** = $20.01–35; **$$$$** = > $35

Kitchen Fridge Survivor™ Grades: ***Avg.*** = a "one-day wine," tastes noticeably less fresh the next day; ***B*** = holds its freshness for 2–3 days after opening; ***B+*** = holds *and gets better* over 2–3 days after opening; ***A*** = a 3- to 4-day "freshness window"; ***A+*** = holds *and gets better* over 3–4 days

Knoll Gruner-Veltliner (*kuh-NOLL GROO-ner Velt-LEEN-er*) Smaragd Trocken Wachau, Austria

	PC	T	V
	$	22	23

Sommeliers (including me) "love" the "zippy, grapefruit-spice character" that's "magic with food."

Kitchen Fridge Survivor™ Grade: A

Your notes: _____

Marques de Riscal Rueda (*mar-KESS deh ree-SCAHL roo-AY-duh*), Spain

	PC	T	V
	$	22	18

This wine is fresh, sleek, and vibrant, tasting of key lime and kiwi, without oak flavor, great with food. In my book, a value star.

Kitchen Fridge Survivor™ Grade: B+

Your notes: _____

Martin Codax Albarino (*all-buh-REEN-yo*), Spain

	PC	T	V
	$	24	21

This "magic-with-food" wine's got floral, citrus, passion fruit, and pear, all oak free.

Kitchen Fridge Survivor™ Grade: B+

Your notes: _____

Martinsancho Verdejo, Spain

	PC	T	V
	$	24	26

"Citrus" and crisp apple with lively acidity.

Kitchen Fridge Survivor™ Grade: A

Your notes: _____

Menage a Trois White Blend, California

	PC	T	V
	$	20	20

The trios (three) grapes are Chard, Sauvignon Blanc, and Chenin Blanc; and the tutti-fruiti flavor is juicy.

Kitchen Fridge Survivor™ Grade: Avg.

Your notes: _____

Muros Antiguos Albarino Vinho Verde, Portugal

	PC	T	V
	$$	18	18

Enjoy the appley flavor and crispness "with fish."

Kitchen Fridge Survivor™ Grade: A

Your notes: _____

Navarro Gewurztraminer, California

	PC	T	V
	$$$	24	21

Apricot fruit and wilted rose-petal scents make this one of my panel's "favorite Gewurztraminers."

Kitchen Fridge Survivor™ Grade: B+

Your notes: _____

Paul Blanck Gewurztraminer | PC | T | V
Classique, France | $$ | 24 | 24

I think this is one of Alsace's best Gewurztraminers for the money: lychee, rose petal, peach, minerals, *balance*.
Kitchen Fridge Survivor™ Grade: B+
Your notes: _____

Penfolds Koonunga Hill | PC | T | V
Semillon/Chardonnay, Australia | $ | 22 | 22

My tasters call this a "delicious sleeper of a wine," with provocative pear aromas and citrus flavors.
Kitchen Fridge Survivor™ Grade: B+
Your notes: _____

Pepperwood Grove Viognier, | PC | T | V
California | $ | 20 | 21

A rarity! Real Viognier character—honeysuckle, lavender, ripe pineapple—at a great price.
Kitchen Fridge Survivor™ Grade: Avg.
Your notes: _____

Pierre Sparr Alsace-One, | PC | T | V
France | $ | 24 | 24

☺ This Riesling, Pinot Blanc, Muscat, Gewurztraminer, and Pinot Gris mix, with lots of peach and pear fruit, is "great with food; great price."
Kitchen Fridge Survivor™ Grade: B
Your notes: _____

Pierre Sparr Pinot Blanc, | PC | T | V
France | $ | 21 | 20

No oak or high alcohol to distract from the lip-smacking pear and quince fruit. Yum.
Kitchen Fridge Survivor™ Grade: B
Your notes: _____

Rosemount Traminer Riesling, | PC | T | V
Australia | $ | 26 | 28

"Refreshing" fruit-salad flavor that's "heaven" for Riesling lovers.

Price Ranges: **$** = $12 or less; **$$** = $12.01–20; **$$$** = $20.01–35; **$$$$** = > $35
Kitchen Fridge Survivor™ Grades: *Avg.* = a "one-day wine," tastes noticeably less fresh the next day; *B* = holds its freshness for 2–3 days after opening; *B+* = holds *and gets better* over 2–3 days after opening; *A* = a 3- to 4-day "freshness window"; *A+* = holds *and gets better* over 3–4 days

Kitchen Fridge Survivor™ Grade: B
Your notes: _____

Ruffino Orvieto,   PC   T   V
Italy $ 19   21
This wine's crisp acidity, clean melon fruit, and nutty
qualities are what everyday Italian white wine should be.
Kitchen Fridge Survivor™ Grade: B
Your notes: _____

Sella & Mosca Vermentino,   PC   T   V
Italy $$ X   X
✗ Yum! Juicy pear fruit, lively acidity, nice price.
Kitchen Fridge Survivor™ Grade: A
Your notes: _____

Smoking Loon Viognier,   PC   T   V
California $ 19   21
Lots of character for the price—floral/apricot scents
and flavors, and juicy acidity.
Kitchen Fridge Survivor™ Grade: B
Your notes: _____

Sokol Blosser Evolution,   PC   T   V
Oregon $$ 23   20
Like an aromatherapy treatment—honeysuckle,
peach, apricot, pear, and more—but a lot cheaper!
Kitchen Fridge Survivor™ Grade: B
Your notes: _____

Sutter Home Gewurztraminer,   PC   T   V
California $ 19   20
From one of the top-selling wine brands, a fruit salad
in a glass, with a gingery scent.
Kitchen Fridge Survivor™ Grade: B
Your notes: _____

Walter Glatzer Gruner-Veltliner   PC   T   V
Kabinett, Austria $ 23   21
This sommelier favorite's "tangy, mouthwatering
lemongrass and spice" are an exotic, affordable treat.
Kitchen Fridge Survivor™ Grade: A
Your notes: _____

Weingartner (*WINE-gart-ner*)   PC   T   V
Gruner-Veltliner Federspiel, Austria $ 22   22
☺ Austrians call this grape Gru-V (as in *groovy*)
for short. And that it is—ginger, grapefruit, and

spice scents; apple, peach, and lemon zest flavors.
Try it!

Kitchen Fridge Survivor™ Grade: A

Your notes: _____

Wollersheim Prairie Fume,	PC	T	V
Wisconsin	$	24	24

Juicy pineapple and peach; lively, refreshing.

Kitchen Fridge Survivor™ Grade: A

Your notes: _____

Zind-Humbrecht Wintzenheim	PC	T	V
Gewurztraminer, France	$$	27	21

My tasters "love" the "apricot," "lychee," and tangerine
fruit from this famous estate.

Kitchen Fridge Survivor™ Grade: Avg.

Your notes: _____

BLUSH/PINK/ROSE WINES

Category Profile: Although many buyers are snobby
about the blush category, the truth is that for most of
us white Zinfandel was probably the first wine we
drank that had a cork. It's a juicy, uncomplicated style
that makes a lot of buyers, and their wallets, very
happy. Now for the gear switch—rose. The only thing
true roses have in common with the blush category is
appearance. Rose wines are classic to many world-
class European wine regions. They are absolutely dry,
tangy, crisp, and amazingly interesting wines for the
money. I often say that with their spice and complexity they have red wine flavor, but the lightness of body
and chillability gives them white wine style. They are
great food wines. Don't miss the chance to try my recommendations or those of your favorite shop or
restaurant. You will love them.

Price Ranges: **$** = $12 or less; **$$** = $12.01–20; **$$$** = $20.01–35;
$$$$ = > $35

Kitchen Fridge Survivor™ Grades: ***Avg.*** = a "one-day wine," tastes
noticeably less fresh the next day; ***B*** = holds its freshness for 2–3
days after opening; ***B+*** = holds *and gets better* over 2–3 days after
opening; ***A*** = a 3- to 4-day "freshness window"; ***A+*** = holds *and gets
better* over 3–4 days

Serve: The colder the better.

When: The refreshing touch of sweetness in blush styles makes them great as an aperitif. Roses are great for both sipping and meals.

With: A touch of sweetness in wine can tone down heat, so spicy foods are an especially good partner for blush wine. Dry roses go with everything.

In: An all-purpose wineglass.

	PC	T	V
Beringer White Zinfandel, California	$	17	20

The standard-bearer in the White Zinfandel category, with fresh strawberry and raspberry flavors, and a juicy texture.
Kitchen Fridge Survivor™ Grade: B
Your notes: _____

	PC	T	V
Bodegas Ochoa (oh-CHOH-uh) Garnacha Rosado, Spain	$	22	26

This "wonderful summer rosé," completely dry with scents of "strawberry" and a "beautiful color," is "further proof that Spain is coming on strong."
Kitchen Fridge Survivor™ Grade: B+
Your notes: _____

	PC	T	V
Bonny Doon Big House Pink, California	$	X	X

✗ A fun sipper with juicy strawberry-watermelon flavor.
Kitchen Fridge Survivor™ Grade: B
Your notes: _____

	PC	T	V
Bonny Doon Vin Gris de Cigare Pink Wine, California	$$	19	20

A bone-dry, tangy, spicy refresher that's great with food.
Kitchen Fridge Survivor™ Grade: B
Your notes: _____

	PC	T	V
Domaine Ott Bandol Rose, France	$$	27	24

"One of the best from southern France" and a classically styled rose: spicy, strawberry-fruity, thirst quenching.
Kitchen Fridge Survivor™ Grade: B
Your notes: _____

Goats Do Roam Rose,   PC   T   V
South Africa $ 24   24

A "delicious" blend of Pinotage and Syrah, totally dry, with white pepper spice and tangy red currant fruit.

Kitchen Fridge Survivor™ *Grade: B*

Your notes: _____

La Vieille Ferme Rose,   PC   T   V
France $ 22   24

"Delicious" and "not sweet." Great with herbal dishes.

Kitchen Fridge Survivor™ *Grade: B*

Your notes: _____

Marques de Caceres Rioja Rosado,   PC   T   V
Spain $ 18   21

This wine's tangy strawberry-watermelon-spice flavor is de-lish! You can invite *any* food to this party.

Kitchen Fridge Survivor™ *Grade: Avg.*

Your notes: _____

Menage a Trois Rose,   PC   T   V
California $ X   X

✗ Juicy watermelon flavor; the perfect pair for spicy food.

Kitchen Fridge Survivor™ *Grade: A*

Your notes: _____

Solorosa Rose,   PC   T   V
California $$ 23   22

☺ This not-at-all-sweet rose has lots of spice, savor, and richness from barrel fermentation. Fabulous with grill fare.

Kitchen Fridge Survivor™ *Grade: B+*

Your notes: _____

Sutter Home White Zinfandel,   PC   T   V
California $ 14   16

This trailblazing White Zinfandel is still juicy and pleasing and one of the best.

Kitchen Fridge Survivor™ *Grade: B*

Your notes: _____

Price Ranges: **$** = $12 or less; **$$** = $12.01–20; **$$$** = $20.01–35; **$$$$** = > $35

Kitchen Fridge Survivor™ Grades: **Avg.** = a "one-day wine," tastes noticeably less fresh the next day; **B** = holds its freshness for 2–3 days after opening; **B+** = holds *and gets better* over 2–3 days after opening; **A** = a 3- to 4-day "freshness window"; **A+** = holds *and gets better* over 3–4 days

Toad Hollow Eye of the Toad Pinot	PC	T	V
Noir Dry Rose, California	$	23	23

"Wow" dry rose dripping with "juicy strawberry taste."
Kitchen Fridge Survivor™ Grade: Avg.
Your notes: _____

RED WINES

Beaujolais/Gamay

Category Profile: Beaujolais (*bow-jhoe-LAY*) Nouveau, the new wine of the vintage that each year is shipped from France on the third Thursday in November (just in time for Thanksgiving), dominates sales in this category. (It also inspires scores of nouveau imitators riding its cash-cow coattails.) You can have fun with nouveau, but don't skip the real stuff—particularly Beaujolais-Villages (*vill-AHJH*) and Beaujolais Cru (named for the town where they're grown, for example, Morgon, Brouilly, and Moulin-à-Vent). These Beaujolais categories are a wine world rarity, in that they offer real character at a low price. The signature style of Beaujolais is a juicy, grapey fruit flavor and succulent texture with, in the crus, an added layer of earthy spiciness. All red Beaujolais is made from the Gamay grape.

Serve: Lightly chilled, to enhance the vibrant fruit.

When: Great as an aperitif and for alfresco occasions such as picnics and barbecues.

With: Many tasters said they swear by it for Thanksgiving. It's so soft, smooth, and juicy I think it goes with everything, from the simplest of sandwich meals to brunch, lunch, and beyond. It's often a great buy on restaurant wine lists and versatile for those really tough matching situations where you've ordered everything from oysters to osso bucco but you want one wine.

In: An all-purpose wineglass.

Chateau de la Chaize Brouilly,	PC	T	V
France	$$	18	17

This is classic Beaujolais, with lots of soft berry fruit and a smoky, earthy scent like autumn leaves.
Kitchen Countertop Survivor™ Grade: B
Your notes: _____

Duboeuf (*Duh-BUFF*) (Georges)	PC	T	V
Beaujolais Nouveau, France	$	19	22

A fun, juicy crowd pleaser that consumers find "drink-able with or without food" and bargain priced.

Kitchen Countertop Survivor™ Grade: Avg.

Your notes: _____

Duboeuf (Georges) Beaujolais-	PC	T	V
Villages, France	$	19	21

It's "hard not to love" the plump berry flavor; good for those who don't normally drink red.

Kitchen Countertop Survivor™ Grade: B

Your notes: _____

Duboeuf (Georges) Moulin-A-Vent,	PC	T	V
France	$$	24	21

This is "great for the money" with lots of "spice, smooth berry fruit," and complexity.

Kitchen Countertop Survivor™ Grade: B

Your notes: _____

Louis Jadot Beaujolais-Villages,	PC	T	V
France	$	22	24

☺ The light body and berry fruit make this "the perfect sipping wine."

Kitchen Countertop Survivor™ Grade: B

Your notes: _____

Pinot Noir

Category Profile: Pinot Noir is my favorite of the major classic red grape varieties, because I love its smoky-ripe scent; pure fruit flavor; and, most of all, silken texture. It also offers red wine intensity and complexity, without being heavy. Although Pinot Noir's home turf is the Burgundy region of France, few of those wines make the list of top sellers in the United States, because production is tiny. The coolest parts of coastal California

Price Ranges: **$** = $12 or less; **$$** = $12.01–20; **$$$** = $20.01–35; **$$$$** = > $35

Kitchen Countertop Survivor™ Grades: *Avg.* = a "one-day wine," tastes noticeably less fresh the next day; *B* = holds its freshness for 2–3 days after opening; *B+* = holds *and gets better* over 2–3 days after opening; *A* = a 3- to 4-day "freshness window"; *A+* = holds *and gets better* over 3–4 days

(especially the Russian River Valley, Carneros, Monterey, Sonoma Coast, and Santa Barbara County) specialize in Pinot Noir, as does Oregon's Willamette (*will-AM-ett*) Valley. New Zealand is also becoming an important Pinot source. Pinot Noir from all the major regions is typically oak aged, but as with other grapes the amount of oakiness is matched to the intensity of the fruit. Generally the budget bottlings are the least oaky.

Serve: *Cool* room temperature; don't hesitate to chill the bottle briefly if needed.

When: Although the silky texture makes Pinot Noir quite bewitching on its own, it is also the ultimate "food wine." It is my choice to take to dinner parties and to order in restaurants, because I know it will probably delight both white and red wine drinkers and will go with most any food.

With: Pinot's versatility is legendary, but it is *the* wine for mushroom dishes, salmon, rare tuna, and any bird (especially duck).

In: An all-purpose wineglass. Or try a larger balloon stem; the extra air space enhances the wine's aroma.

	PC	T	V
Acacia Carneros Pinot Noir, California	**$$$**	**20**	**20**

This "smooth as silk Pinot" has a "lovely berry flavor," "spice and earth" scent, and "ages nicely for a few years."
Kitchen Countertop Survivor™ Grade: B+
Your notes: _____

	PC	T	V
Adelsheim Pinot Noir, Oregon	**$$$**	**24**	**21**

This Oregon classic's subtle dried-cranberry fruit and dusty-herbal scent are quite distinctive.
Kitchen Countertop Survivor™ Grade: B
Your notes: _____

	PC	T	V
Archery Summit Arcus Estate Pinot Noir, Oregon	**$$$$**	**26**	**19**

The "intense and opulent" black cherry fruit has lots of fans, but some pros find it "over-oaked for the amount of fruit." It needs aeration to soften up.

Kitchen Countertop Survivor™ Grade: B

Your notes: _____

Argyle Pinot Noir,   PC   T   V
Oregon $$ 21   19

One of Oregon's tastiest Pinots is also one of its most affordable, with a flavor like cherry Life Savers.

Kitchen Fridge Survivor™ Grade: B

Your notes: _____

Au Bon Climat Rincon and   PC   T   V
Rosemary's Pinot Noir, California $$$$ 24   24

Downright sexy, with a layer of bacony-smoky complexity enveloping the strawberry-rhubarb fruit.

Kitchen Fridge Survivor™ Grade: A

Your notes: _____

Au Bon Climat Santa Barbara   PC   T   V
Pinot Noir, California $$ 26   23

☺ *Oh-bohn-clee-MAHT* has a cult following and a nickname—"ABC" (for short) is among the truly great American Pinots, with vivid black cherry fruit, and perfect balance.

Kitchen Countertop Survivor™ Grade: B+

Your notes: _____

Au Bon Climat Talley Vineyard   PC   T   V
Pinot Noir, California $$$$ 24   21

Rich but elegant with pure cherry Jolly Rancher fruit and a cinnamon spice scent.

Kitchen Countertop Survivor™ Grade: B

Your notes: _____

Beaulieu Vineyard (BV) Carneros   PC   T   V
Pinot Noir, California $$ 18   18

The "classic Carneros Pinot" style delivers silky cherry fruit, spice, and soft texture.

Kitchen Countertop Survivor™ Grade: Avg.

Your notes: _____

Price Ranges: **$** = $12 or less; **$$** = $12.01–20; **$$$** = $20.01–35; **$$$$** = > $35

Kitchen Countertop Survivor™ Grades: ***Avg.*** = a "one-day wine," tastes noticeably less fresh the next day; ***B*** = holds its freshness for 2–3 days after opening; ***B+*** = holds *and gets better* over 2–3 days after opening; ***A*** = a 3- to 4-day "freshness window"; ***A+*** = holds *and gets better* over 3–4 days

Beaulieu Vineyard (BV) Coastal Estates Pinot Noir, California

PC	T	V
$	X	X

☺ ✗ Lively juicy cherry Jolly Rancher flavor; a major bargain.

Kitchen Countertop Survivor™ Grade: B

Your notes: _____

Beaulieu Vineyard (BV) Reserve Pinot Noir, California

PC	T	V
$$	X	X

✗ Bing cherry pie with vanilla, cinnamon, and great length.

Kitchen Countertop Survivor™ Grade: B+

Your notes: _____

Benton Lane Pinot Noir, Oregon

PC	T	V
$$	26	22

"Lovely" red berry and earthy tea-leaf flavors at a nice price.

Kitchen Countertop Survivor™ Grade: Avg.

Your notes: _____

Brancott Vineyards Marlborough Reserve Pinot Noir, New Zealand

PC	T	V
$$	22	19

This wine's cherry cola scent and cinnamon–black cherry flavors are lush but structured. Good stuff.

Kitchen Countertop Survivor™ Grade: B

Your notes: _____

Buena Vista Carneros Pinot Noir, California

PC	T	V
$$	20	20

Classic Carneros, with aromas of potpourri and tea leaves and flavors of dried cherry and spice.

Kitchen Countertop Survivor™ Grade: B

Your notes: _____

Calera Santa Barbara Pinot Noir, California

PC	T	V
$$$	24	20

Sweet sun-dried tomato and "dried cherry fruit" flavor.

Kitchen Countertop Survivor™ Grade: B+

Your notes: _____

Cambria (*CAME-bree-uh*) Julia's Vineyard Pinot Noir, California

PC	T	V
$$	24	22

This wine's savory earth and spice, lush plum flavor, and tug of tannin make it "memorable."

Kitchen Countertop Survivor™ Grade: B

Your notes: _____

Castle Rock Pinot Noir, PC T V
California $ 24 24

Tasters "love, love, love" the "soft," "lush" cherry fruit and concentrated flavor, especially for the price.

Kitchen Countertop Survivor™ Grade: Avg.

Your notes: _____

Chateau St. Jean Pinot Noir, PC T V
California $$ 24 23

"A great beginner's Pinot Noir," with "yummy" "cherry jam" fruit and silky texture.

Kitchen Countertop Survivor™ Grade: Avg.

Your notes: _____

Clos du Bois Sonoma County PC T V
Pinot Noir, California $$$ 20 21

The strawberry-rhubarb, smokiness, and "great Bing cherry flavors" are just delicious.

Kitchen Countertop Survivor™ Grade: A

Your notes: _____

Cloudline Pinot Noir, PC T V
Oregon $$ X X

Smoky! With dried cranberry fruit and an easy price.

Kitchen Countertop Survivor™ Grade: Avg.

Your notes: _____

Coldstream Hills Pinot Noir, PC T V
Australia $$ 19 19

This Aussie offering has a smokiness, and sun-dried tomato flavor.

Kitchen Countertop Survivor™ Grade: Avg.

Your notes: _____

Cristom Jefferson Cuvee Pinot PC T V
Noir, Oregon $$$ 27 23

This wine's signature smoky/cocoa scent, deep cherry fruit, and satiny texture are amazing.

Price Ranges: **$** = $12 or less; **$$** = $12.01–20; **$$$** = $20.01–35; **$$$$** = > $35

Kitchen Countertop Survivor™ Grades: *Avg.* = a "one-day wine," tastes noticeably less fresh the next day; *B* = holds its freshness for 2–3 days after opening; *B+* = holds *and gets better* over 2–3 days after opening; *A* = a 3- to 4-day "freshness window"; *A+* = holds *and gets better* over 3–4 days

Kitchen Countertop Survivor™ *Grade: B*

Your notes: _____

David Bruce Santa Cruz Pinot   PC   T   V
Noir, California $$$ 24   21

This Pinot's gamy, savory spice, earth, and raspberry fruit are truly distinctive.

Kitchen Countertop Survivor™ *Grade: B*

Your notes: _____

Dehlinger Pinot Noir,   PC   T   V
California $$$$ 24   21

This wine drips with cherry cola and rhubarb scent and flavor, and the satiny texture is downright sexy.

Kitchen Countertop Survivor™ *Grade: B*

Your notes: _____

Deloach Russian River Pinot Noir,   PC   T   V
California $$ 24   24

A consistent bet for rich, cinnamon-spiced cherry flavor and silky texture.

Kitchen Countertop Survivor™ *Grade: B*

Your notes: _____

Domaine Carneros Pinot Noir,   PC   T   V
California $$$ 26   21

A "sophisticated" scent, subtle oakiness, and long finish "like *great* red Burgundy," yet with the "bold fruit" of its California home base.

Kitchen Countertop Survivor™ *Grade: A*

Your notes: _____

Domaine Drouhin (*droo-AHN***)**   PC   T   V
Willamette Valley Pinot Noir, $$$$ 27   24
Oregon

This wine has "exuberant raspberry and cherry fruit" and intense oak, which dominates when the wine is young, but it ages well.

Kitchen Countertop Survivor™ *Grade: B*

Your notes: _____

Duck Pond Pinot Noir,   PC   T   V
Oregon $$ 23   24

A "light-on-the-wallet" Pinot with strawberry aromas, ripe raspberry flavors, and great food compatibility.

Kitchen Countertop Survivor™ *Grade: B*

Your notes: _____

Echelon Central Coast Pinot Noir, | PC | T | V
California | **$** | 23 | 25

The smoky, wild raspberry scent and flavor and silky texture are a triumph at this price.

Kitchen Countertop Survivor™ Grade: B+

Your notes: _____

Edna Valley Vineyard Pinot Noir, | PC | T | V
California | **$$** | 24 | 24

"Light bodied" but pure cherry that's true to the grape.

Kitchen Countertop Survivor™ Grade: Avg.

Your notes: _____

Elk Cove Pinot Noir, | PC | T | V
Oregon | **$$** | 26 | 23

Pinot in the lighter style, with savory spice and dried cherry character that make it versatile with food.

Kitchen Countertop Survivor™ Grade: Avg.

Your notes: _____

Estancia Pinnacles Pinot Noir, | PC | T | V
California | **$$** | 22 | 22

With its distinct herbal, strawberry compote, and smoky character, this is nice for the money.

Kitchen Countertop Survivor™ Grade: B+

Your notes: _____

Etude Carneros Pinot Noir, | PC | T | V
California | **$$$$** | 27 | 22

☺ This wine's elegance, cherry-spice scent, juicy cherry-cranberry fruit, and long finish have been style signatures since the first vintage. Gorgeous.

Kitchen Countertop Survivor™ Grade: A

Your notes: _____

Felton Road Pinot Noir, | PC | T | V
New Zealand | **$$$$** | X | X

✗ Amazing lush black cherry, toast, vanilla, smoke.

Kitchen Countertop Survivor™ Grade: B+

Your notes: _____

Price Ranges: **$** = $12 or less; **$$** = $12.01–20; **$$$** = $20.01–35; **$$$$** = > $35

Kitchen Countertop Survivor™ Grades: *Avg.* = a "one-day wine," tastes noticeably less fresh the next day; *B* = holds its freshness for 2–3 days after opening; *B+* = holds *and gets better* over 2–3 days after opening; *A* = a 3- to 4-day "freshness window"; *A+* = holds *and gets better* over 3–4 days

Fess Parker Santa Barbara Pinot   **PC**   **T**   **V**
Noir, California   **$$**   **24**   **26**

☺ "A find" with "chocolate, tobacco," and cherry-cola flavors.

Kitchen Countertop Survivor™ Grade: B+
Your notes: _____

Firesteed Pinot Noir,   **PC**   **T**   **V**
Oregon   **$**   **20**   **21**

☺ Delicious cranberry and dried cherry fruit, a nice kick of acid, and a "great price" make it "easy to love."

Kitchen Countertop Survivor™ Grade: Avg.
Your notes: _____

Five Rivers Ranch Pinot Noir,   **PC**   **T**   **V**
California   **$**   **21**   **22**

True Pinot Noir character at a super price: a touch of wet-clay earthiness and soft raspberry-strawberry fruit.

Kitchen Countertop Survivor™ Grade: B
Your notes: _____

Flowers Pinot Noir,   **PC**   **T**   **V**
California   **$$$$**   **28**   **20**

My Pinot-loving tasters are "obsessed" with the elegant cherry and intoxicating spice-tea notes.

Kitchen Countertop Survivor™ Grade: B
Your notes: _____

Frei Brothers Reserve Pinot Noir,   **PC**   **T**   **V**
California   **$$**   **23**   **20**

Cherry cola and cinnamon on the nose, and silky richness on the palate.

Kitchen Countertop Survivor™ Grade: B+
Your notes: _____

Gallo Family Vineyards Reserve   **PC**   **T**   **V**
Pinot Noir, California   **$**   **21**   **24**

Pure "raspberry and cherry" fruit, a cola scent, and supple-but-lively texture, at a nice price.

Kitchen Countertop Survivor™ Grade: B+
Your notes: _____

Iron Horse Estate Pinot Noir,   **PC**   **T**   **V**
California   **$$$**   **25**   **21**

☺ The "wow" black cherry compote and cola flavors and vanilla-scented oak are luscious yet balanced.

Kitchen Countertop Survivor™ Grade: B
Your notes: _____

| **J Wine Company Russian River** | PC | T | V |
| **Pinot Noir, California** | $$$ | 26 | 22 |

"So incredibly jammy and rich," yet it maintains the balance and silkiness Pinot lovers look for with sweet oak and ripe, black cherry flavor.
Kitchen Countertop Survivor™ Grade: B
Your notes: _____

| **Ken Wright Pinot Noir,** | PC | T | V |
| **Oregon** | $$$$ | 26 | 22 |

The sleek texture, subtle earth and tea-leaf scent, and subtle cherry-jam fruit are elegance in a bottle.
Kitchen Countertop Survivor™ Grade: Avg.
Your notes: _____

| **Kendall-Jackson Vintner's Reserve** | PC | T | V |
| **Pinot Noir, California** | $$ | 22 | 21 |

This is a good intro Pinot, with classic silky cherry and spice character at an affordable price.
Kitchen Countertop Survivor™ Grade: A
Your notes: _____

| **King Estate Pinot Noir,** | PC | T | V |
| **Oregon** | $$$ | 23 | 18 |

There's nice soft cherry fruit and rose-petal scent; the price to quality ratio has improved.
Kitchen Countertop Survivor™ Grade: B
Your notes: _____

| **La Crema Sonoma Pinot Noir,** | PC | T | V |
| **California** | $$ | 23 | 24 |

This fuller-bodied style is a "favorite Pinot" choice for many. It has deep cherry cola flavor and a toasty scent.
Kitchen Countertop Survivor™ Grade: Avg.
Your notes: _____

Price Ranges: **$** = $12 or less; **$$** = $12.01–20; **$$$** = $20.01–35; **$$$$** = > $35
Kitchen Countertop Survivor™ Grades: *Avg.* = a "one-day wine," tastes noticeably less fresh the next day; *B* = holds its freshness for 2–3 days after opening; *B+* = holds *and gets better* over 2–3 days after opening; *A* = a 3- to 4-day "freshness window"; *A+* = holds *and gets better* over 3–4 days

Lindemans Bin 99 Pinot Noir, Australia   PC $ T 20   V 25

You "can't beat the value" of this light, soft Pinot with supple cherry fruit and a silky texture.

Kitchen Countertop Survivor™ Grade: Avg.

Your notes: _____

MacMurray Ranch Russian River Valley Pinot Noir, California   PC $$$ T X   V X

✗ Cola, black cherry; a nice trade up from the Sonoma Coast.

Kitchen Countertop Survivor™ Grade: B

Your notes: _____

MacMurray Ranch Sonoma Coast Pinot Noir, California   PC $$ T 29   V 23

Fred's (as in *My Three Sons*) daughter Kate works with the Gallo family to make this silky Pinot with deep, black cherry–raspberry fruit and a vanilla scent. De-lish.

Kitchen Countertop Survivor™ Grade: B+

Your notes: _____

Mark West Central Coast Pinot Noir, California   PC $ T 24   V 28

"Very good value" with "cherry," oak, and kirsch flavors.

Kitchen Countertop Survivor™ Grade: Avg.

Your notes: _____

Meridian Pinot Noir, California   PC $ T 20   V 20

Perfect for every day, especially for the price. The mouthwatering flavor "tastes like biting into fresh cherries."

Kitchen Countertop Survivor™ Grade: B

Your notes: _____

Merry Edwards Russian River Valley Pinot Noir, California   PC $$$$ T 28   V 23

This elegant Pinot is silky but very rich and plump, with flavors of cola, dark cherry, and chocolate.

Kitchen Countertop Survivor™ Grade: B

Your notes: _____

Miner Pinot Noir, California   PC $$$$ T 27   V 18

"Bold fruit" and a "wonderful earthy" finish make it "one of the best U.S. Pinots" and "worth" the price.

Kitchen Countertop Survivor™ Grade: B

Your notes: _____

Mirassou Pinot Noir,	PC	T	V
California	$	21	24

A soft cherry-and-spice value Pinot. Perfect for every day.

Kitchen Countertop Survivor™ Grade: A

Your notes: _____

Morgan 12 Clones Pinot Noir,	PC	T	V
California	$$$	21	24

Ripe cherry fruit, exotic smoky character, and solid quality every year. Bravo!

Kitchen Countertop Survivor™ Grade: B+

Your notes: _____

Pepperwood Grove Pinot Noir,	PC	T	V
California	$	18	22

Tasters laud the smoothness, "lively cherry fruit," and "great price."

Kitchen Countertop Survivor™ Grade: Avg.

Your notes: _____

Ponzi Pinot Noir,	PC	T	V
Oregon	$$$	25	21

An Oregon classic with spicy cherry and wilted rose-petal scent, earthiness, complexity, and elegance.

Kitchen Countertop Survivor™ Grade: Avg.

Your notes: _____

Ramsay Pinot Noir,	PC	T	V
California	$$	24	27

So much character for the money! A smoky-meaty quality, strawberry-jam fruit, and silky texture.

Kitchen Countertop Survivor™ Grade: B

Your notes: _____

Price Ranges: **$** = $12 or less; **$$** = $12.01–20; **$$$** = $20.01–35; **$$$$** = > $35

Kitchen Countertop Survivor™ Grades: ***Avg.*** = a "one-day wine," tastes noticeably less fresh the next day; ***B*** = holds its freshness for 2–3 days after opening; ***B+*** = holds *and gets better* over 2–3 days after opening; ***A*** = a 3- to 4-day "freshness window"; ***A+*** = holds *and gets better* over 3–4 days

Rex Hill Willamette Valley   PC   T   V
Pinot Noir, Oregon $$ 26   23

Quality's improved for this wine, with spicy "cherry and earthy flavors" typical of the Willamette Pinot style.

Kitchen Countertop Survivor™ Grade: Avg.

Your notes: _____

Robert Mondavi Carneros Pinot   PC   T   V
Noir, California $$$ 26   20

Classic Carneros Pinot Noir character with herbal tea scents, dried cherry, earthiness, and elegance.

Kitchen Countertop Survivor™ Grade: B

Your notes: _____

Robert Mondavi Napa Reserve Pinot   PC   T   V
Noir, California $$$ 24   21

A bit of aeration is needed to unlock the "gorgeous cherry fruit," smoky spice, and complexity. Delicious.

Kitchen Countertop Survivor™ Grade: B

Your notes: _____

Robert Mondavi Private Selection   PC   T   V
Pinot Noir, California $ 24   21

One of the better Pinots at this price, with silky berry fruit.

Kitchen Countertop Survivor™ Grade: B+

Your notes: _____

Robert Sinskey Los Carneros   PC   T   V
Pinot Noir, California $$$ 26   23

The beloved-by-my-tasters Sinskey style emphasizes oak, along with spicy, supple, dark berry fruit.

Kitchen Countertop Survivor™ Grade: B

Your notes: _____

Rochioli Pinot Noir,   PC   T   V
California $$$$ 27   20

One of the greatest California Pinot Noirs made, with a scent of cola, pure cherry fruit, mineral finish, and *very* subtle oak.

Kitchen Countertop Survivor™ Grade: A

Your notes: _____

Saintsbury Carneros Pinot Noir,   PC   T   V
California $$$ 23   20

This "Carneros stalwart" is all about elegance: cranberry, rhubarb, spice scents and flavors, sleek texture, and an "endless finish."

Kitchen Countertop Survivor™ Grade: B+

Your notes: _____

Sanford Pinot Noir,   PC   T   V
California $$$ 27   22

A Santa Barbara classic, with exotic strawberry-rhubarb fruit touched with a meaty-smoky scent.

Kitchen Countertop Survivor™ Grade: B

Your notes: _____

Sea Smoke Botella Pinot Noir,   PC   T   V
California $$$ 24   28

The fruit intensity—spiced cherry, strawberry-rhubarb—and earthy complexity are exactly what Pinot Noir lovers are looking for.

Kitchen Countertop Survivor™ Grade: B

Your notes: _____

Sebastiani Sonoma County Pinot   PC   T   V
Noir, California $$ 24   23

A price/value star, with sleek mineral-pomegranate-strawberry compote flavors and spicy nose.

Kitchen Countertop Survivor™ Grade: B

Your notes: _____

Siduri Pinot Noir,   PC   T   V
California $$$ 23   20

A unique, high-impact Pinot Noir style with a heady meaty-gaminess and big plum fruit.

Kitchen Countertop Survivor™ Grade: B

Your notes: _____

Price Ranges: **$** = $12 or less; **$$** = $12.01–20; **$$$** = $20.01–35; **$$$$** = > $35

Kitchen Countertop Survivor™ Grades: *Avg.* = a "one-day wine," tastes noticeably less fresh the next day; *B* = holds its freshness for 2–3 days after opening; *B+* = holds *and gets better* over 2–3 days after opening; *A* = a 3- to 4-day "freshness window"; *A+* = holds *and gets better* over 3–4 days

Smoking Loon Pinot Noir, | PC | T | V
California | $ | 18 | 24

Budget Pinot Noir with character: a hint of herbal-spice in the scent, and lovely strawberry fruit flavor.

Kitchen Countertop Survivor™ Grade: Avg.

Your notes: _____

Sokol Blosser Willamette Pinot | PC | T | V
Noir, Oregon | $$$ | 28 | 26

✓ My panel and I love this distinctive Pinot Noir style: pomegranate and sun-dried tomato notes and a savory herbal smokiness.

Kitchen Countertop Survivor™ Grade: B

Your notes: _____

Solaris Pinot Noir, | PC | T | V
California | $ | 24 | 28

✓ With a "fruity" style that pairs "with almost anything," it's hard to go wrong at this price, and Pinot Noir lovers will be amazed at the varietal character.

Kitchen Countertop Survivor™ Grade: B

Your notes: _____

Talus Pinot Noir, | PC | T | V
California | $ | X | X

✗ Surprisingly silky, cherry-earthiness at a great price.

Kitchen Countertop Survivor™ Grade: Avg.

Your notes: _____

Traminer Roncier Pinot Noir, | PC | T | V
France | $ | 24 | 27

A "silk on the tongue" "steal" with "lovely earthiness."

Kitchen Countertop Survivor™ Grade: Avg.

Your notes: _____

Trinchero Family Estates Pinot | PC | T | V
Noir, California | $$$ | X | X

✗ Satiny, plump cherry fruit, a hint of earth, and a long finish.

Kitchen Countertop Survivor™ Grade: B+

Your notes: _____

Truchard Pinot Noir, | PC | T | V
California | $$$ | 22 | 19

I love the raspberry tea and mineral scents, and especially the satiny texture, of this Carneros classic.

Kitchen Countertop Survivor™ Grade: B

Your notes: _____

Twin Fin Pinot Noir,   PC   T   V
California $ 24   24

☺ Smooth strawberry-cranberry flavor; the best budget Pinot Noir out there.

Kitchen Countertop Survivor™ Grade: Avg.

Your notes: _____

Whitehaven Pinot Noir,   PC   T   V
New Zealand $$$ X   X

✗ One of New Zealand's nicer Pinot Noirs: pure cherry fruit, sleek and earthy.

Kitchen Countertop Survivor™ Grade: B+

Your notes: _____

WillaKenzie Willamette Valley   PC   T   V
Pinot Noir, Oregon $$$ 24   21

A value for this quality, with "luscious black cherry fruit" and licorice-mineral nuances.

Kitchen Countertop Survivor™ Grade: B

Your notes: _____

Willamette Valley Vineyards Whole   PC   T   V
Berry Pinot Noir, Oregon $$ 23   21

A soft cherry-grapey style and a nice price.

Kitchen Countertop Survivor™ Grade: Avg.

Your notes: _____

Williams-Selyem Hirsch Vineyard   PC   T   V
Pinot Noir, California $$$$ 29   24

"Expensive, but so worth it" is the view for this silky cherry-vanilla-spice Pinot Noir that's "one of the best made."

Kitchen Countertop Survivor™ Grade: B

Your notes: _____

Price Ranges: **$** = $12 or less; **$$** = $12.01–20; **$$$** = $20.01–35; **$$$$** = > $35

Kitchen Countertop Survivor™ Grades: *Avg.* = a "one-day wine," tastes noticeably less fresh the next day; *B* = holds its freshness for 2–3 days after opening; *B+* = holds *and gets better* over 2–3 days after opening; *A* = a 3- to 4-day "freshness window"; *A+* = holds *and gets better* over 3–4 days

Williams-Selyem Pinot Noir,	PC	T	V
Sonoma Coast, California	$$$$	26	20

"Pricey" but "great," though some tasters note it's "not legendary" as it once was. Still, I've found the wine's benchmark quality—with earthy tea leaf–dried spice scents and pure, ripe cherry fruit—continues to endure.
Kitchen Countertop Survivor™ Grade: B

Your notes: _____

Chianti and Sangiovese

Category Profile: Remember the days when "Chianti" meant those kitschy straw-covered bottles? Tuscany's signature red has come a long way in quality since then, pulling much of the Italian wine world with it. But let me clear up some understandable confusion about the labels and styles. As quality has improved, Chianti has "morphed" into three tiers of wine—varietal Sangiovese (*san-joe-VAY-zay*), labeled with the grape name; traditional Chianti in a range of styles; and the luxury tier, which includes top regional wines like Brunello, and the so-called Super Tuscan reds. Many of the major Tuscan wineries produce wines in all three categories. The basic Sangioveses largely populate the one-dollar-sign price tier, and some offer good value. (Most are, in my opinion, just "red wine" without a lot of character.) Chianti itself now spans the entire price and quality spectrum from budget quaff to boutique collectible, with the top-quality *classico* and *riserva* versions worthy of aging in the cellar. Finally, the Super Tuscans emerged because wineries wanted creative license to use international grapes outside the traditional Chianti "recipe" (and, I guess, with fantasy names like Summus, Sassicaia, and Luce, poetic license, too!). What they all have in common is that Italian "zest"—savory rustic spice in the scent, plus vibrant acidity—and international sophistication from the use of French oak barrels for aging and some French grapes (like Cab and Merlot) for blending. The wines are often cellar worthy and nearly always pricey.

Serve: Room temperature (the varietal Sangioveses are also nice with a light chill); the "bigger" wines—classicos, riservas, and Super Tuscans—benefit from aeration (pour into the glass and swirl or decant into a pitcher or carafe with plenty of air space).

When: Any food occasion, from snack to supper to celebration.

With: Especially great wherever tomato sauce, cheese, olive oil, or savory herbs (rosemary, basil, oregano) are present.

In: An all-purpose wineglass or larger-bowled red wine stem.

	PC	T	V
Antinori (Marchese) (*ahn-tee-NORE-ee mar-KAY-zee*) Chianti Classico Riserva, Italy	**$$$$**	**24**	**21**

This wine's intensity, strawberry fruit, tannin grip, and peppery spice will also reward aging.
Kitchen Countertop Survivor™ Grade: B+
Your notes: _____

	PC	T	V
Banfi Brunello di Montalcino, Italy	**$$$$**	**22**	**16**

This wine needs some bottle age to soften the palate-coating tannin and dense fig and mocha flavors. It is no longer the "value" Brunello it once was.
Kitchen Countertop Survivor™ Grade: A
Your notes: _____

	PC	T	V
Banfi Chianti Classico Riserva, Italy	**$$**	**X**	**X**

✗ Classic Chianti with savory spice and strawberry fruit.
Kitchen Countertop Survivor™ Grade: A
Your notes: _____

	PC	T	V
Castello di Brolio Chianti Classico, Italy	**$$$**	**22**	**22**

This wine's got the spice, zing, and fruit to go with most any food and please a lot of palates.

Price Ranges: **$** = $12 or less; **$$** = $12.01–20; **$$$** = $20.01–35; **$$$$** = > $35
Kitchen Countertop Survivor™ Grades: *Avg.* = a "one-day wine," tastes noticeably less fresh the next day; *B* = holds its freshness for 2–3 days after opening; *B+* = holds *and gets better* over 2–3 days after opening; *A* = a 3- to 4-day "freshness window"; *A+* = holds *and gets better* over 3–4 days

Kitchen Countertop Survivor™ *Grade: B*
Your notes: _____

Castello di Gabbiano Chianti PC T V
Classico, Italy $ 20 20
A soft, light Chianti, with red cherry flavors and spicy
nuances that "can't be beat for the price."
Kitchen Countertop Survivor™ *Grade: B*
Your notes: _____

Castello di Gabbiano Chianti PC T V
Classico Riserva, Italy $$ 24 19
☺ You get a lot for the money with this "textbook
Chianti Classico Riserva," with a cornucopia of red
fruit, lively acidity, and a nice tug of tannin.
Kitchen Countertop Survivor™ *Grade: B*
Your notes: _____

Cecchi (*CHECK-ee*) Chianti, PC T V
Italy $ 23 21
A "basic Chianti" with "nice flavors" (dried cherry and
savory spice) that are "great for pizza."
Kitchen Countertop Survivor™ *Grade: Avg.*
Your notes: _____

Felsina (*FELL-see-nuh*) Chianti PC T V
Classico, Italy $$$ 24 22
A "worth the price," "ageable" Tuscan with subtle
strawberry-raspberry fruit and savory-earthy notes.
Kitchen Countertop Survivor™ *Grade: B+*
Your notes: _____

Frescobaldi Nippozano Chianti PC T V
Rufina (*ROO-fin-uh*) Riserva, Italy $$ 24 29
Hard to find, but worth the search, with plenty of ripe
plum fruit, balsamic, and peppery nuances.
Kitchen Countertop Survivor™ *Grade: B+*
Your notes: _____

Luce Super Tuscan, PC T V
Italy $$$$ 28 18
"Complex and luxurious" with cherries, nuts, dried
spices, and oak in the scent and palate.
Kitchen Countertop Survivor™ *Grade: A*
Your notes: _____

Monte Antico (*MOHN-tay ann-TEE-coh*) Toscana, Italy

	PC	T	V
	$	24	27

Served "by the glass at in-the-know Italian restaurants," because the "plum fruit" and lively spice are "a tasty package" that's "robust but not overpowering" for food.
Kitchen Countertop Survivor™ Grade: B+
Your notes: _____

Nozzole (*NOTES-oh-lay*) Chianti Classico Riserva, Italy

	PC	T	V
	$$	24	24

The "rich red plum fruit," "great acidity," and "savory spice" make it "ready to drink" and "great with food."
Kitchen Countertop Survivor™ Grade: A
Your notes: _____

Rocca della Macie (*ROH-cuh dell-eh mah-CHEE-eh*) Chianti Classico, Italy

	PC	T	V
	$$	22	22

The "cherry and blackberry" flavor and "smooth" texture make this great for food, and "good value," too.
Kitchen Countertop Survivor™ Grade: B
Your notes: _____

Ruffino Chianti Classico Riserva Ducale (*doo-CALL-eh*) Gold Label, Italy

	PC	T	V
	$$$$	26	22

One of the most-tasted wines by my panel! "Pricey" but "worth it," with "wow-level complexity and leathery-ness," and "roasted fig" fruit.
Kitchen Countertop Survivor™ Grade: A+
Your notes: _____

Ruffino Chianti Classico Riserva Ducale Tan Label, Italy

	PC	T	V
	$$$	26	24

✓ "Worth the extra money" over a bargain Chianti because its softness and spicy cranberry fruit "pairs beautifully."
Kitchen Countertop Survivor™ Grade: B
Your notes: _____

Price Ranges: **$** = $12 or less; **$$** = $12.01–20; **$$$** = $20.01–35; **$$$$** = > $35
Kitchen Countertop Survivor™ Grades: **Avg.** = a "one-day wine," tastes noticeably less fresh the next day; **B** = holds its freshness for 2–3 days after opening; **B+** = holds *and gets better* over 2–3 days after opening; **A** = a 3- to 4-day "freshness window"; **A+** = holds *and gets better* over 3–4 days

Santa Cristina Sangiovese,   PC   T   V
Antinori, Italy $ 20   23

"What a deal" for this "easy to drink for everyday" wine with soft, earthy cranberry fruit and good balance.
Kitchen Countertop Survivor™ Grade: B

Your notes: _____

Straccali Chianti,   PC   T   V
Italy $ 21   24

"I'd buy it again," say my tasters of this soft, juicy Chianti that's "a bargain for everyday drinking."
Kitchen Countertop Survivor™ Grade: Avg.

Your notes: _____

Merlot

Grape Profile: When early 1990s news reports linked heart health and moderate red wine drinking, Merlot joined the ranks of go-to wine grapes that inspire instant customer recognition. As with other market-leading varietals like Chardonnay and Cabernet Sauvignon, Merlot can range both in price, from budget to boutique, and in complexity, from soft and simple to "serious." Across the spectrum, Merlot is modeled on the wines from its home region of Bordeaux, France. At the basic level, that means medium body and soft texture, with nice plum and berry fruit

---

MERLOT'S KISSING COUSINS: If you are looking for something different but similar to Merlot, check out two South American specialties. First, there's Argentina's Malbec (*MAHL-beck*), a red grape originally from Bordeaux. It's similar in body and smoothness to Merlot, with lots of smoky aromatic complexity. Some wineries to look for: Altos Las Hormigas, Navarro Correas, Catena, and Chandon Terrazas. Second, from Chile, try Carmenere (*carmuh-NAIR-eh*), also a Bordeaux import that was originally misidentified as Merlot in many Chilean vineyards. Its smooth texture and plum fruit are complemented by an exotically meaty-smoky scent. Look for Carmeneres from Concha y Toro, Carmen, and Veramonte Primus. Check out "Other Reds" for more on these.

---

flavor. The more ambitious versions have more body, tannin, and fruit concentration and usually a good bit of oakiness in the scent and taste. Washington State, California's Sonoma and Napa regions, and Chile are my favorite growing regions for varietal Merlot. Most Merlot producers follow the Bordeaux practice of blending in some Cabernet Sauvignon (or another of the classic Bordeaux red grapes) to complement and enhance the wines' taste and complexity.

Serve: *Cool* room temperature.

When: With meals, of course; and the basic bottlings are soft enough to enjoy on their own as a cocktail alternative.

With: Anything with which you enjoy red wine, especially cheeses, roasts, fuller-bodied fish, and grilled foods.

In: An all-purpose wineglass or larger-bowled red wine stem.

Beaulieu Vineyard (BV) Coastal Estates Merlot, California	PC	T	V
	$	X	X

✗ What a great deal—juicy plummy fruit, smoke, and spice.
Kitchen Countertop Survivor™ Grade: Avg.
Your notes: _____

Beringer Napa Merlot, California	PC	T	V
	$$	X	X

One of Beringer's best reds—velvety, dusty, cocoa, juicy-ripe dark cherries, vanilla, spice . . . Yum!
Kitchen Countertop Survivor™ Grade: B+
Your notes: _____

Black Box Napa Merlot, California	PC	T	V
	$	24	28

Juicy berry fruit that tasters say is "great for a box" and a good price.

Price Ranges: **$** = $12 or less; **$$** = $12.01–20; **$$$** = $20.01–35; **$$$$** = > $35
Kitchen Countertop Survivor™ Grades: *Avg.* = a "one-day wine," tastes noticeably less fresh the next day; *B* = holds its freshness for 2–3 days after opening; *B+* = holds *and gets better* over 2–3 days after opening; *A* = a 3- to 4-day "freshness window"; *A+* = holds *and gets better* over 3–4 days

Kitchen Countertop Survivor™ *Grade: A*

Your notes: _____

Blackstone Merlot, PC T V
California $ 21 23
☺ One of the most-tasted and "favorite value" wines
in the survey. Folks "love the smooth-'n'-juicy plum"
flavor.

Kitchen Countertop Survivor™ *Grade: Avg.*

Your notes: _____

Bogle Merlot, PC T V
California $ 22 24
A popular brand that's huge with my panel for the
"soft cherry flavor" and "awesome value."

Kitchen Countertop Survivor™ *Grade: Avg.*

Your notes: _____

Casa Lapostolle Cuvee Alexandre PC T V
Merlot, California $$ 24 25
New World ripe-cherry fruit, Bordeaux-like mocha,
earth, vanilla. Very classy.

Kitchen Countertop Survivor™ *Grade: B*

Your notes: _____

Chateau Souverain Alexander PC T V
Valley Merlot, California $$ 26 23
"Exceptional quality for the price," with a deep,
plummy scent and flavor plus a "wet leaves"
earthiness, and a "very long finish."

Kitchen Countertop Survivor™ *Grade: B*

Your notes: _____

Chateau Ste. Michelle Columbia PC T V
Valley Merlot, Washington $$ 20 21
This wine's "Bordeaux-style elegance" and smooth
plum flavor are reliable year in and year out.

Kitchen Countertop Survivor™ *Grade: B*

Your notes: _____

Christian Moueix (*Mwexx*) Merlot, PC T V
France $ 21 23
An Old-World Style, meaning elegant, soft, subtle,
earthy; best when paired with food.

Kitchen Countertop Survivor™ *Grade: Avg.*

Your notes: _____

Clos du Bois Alexander Valley Reserve Merlot, California	PC $$$	T X	V X

✗ Big velvety tannins, dark berry fruit, cocoa, and vanilla.

Kitchen Countertop Survivor™ Grade: B

Your notes: _____

Clos du Bois Sonoma Merlot, California	PC $$	T 22	V 23

Very popular, but I'm still underwhelmed by the thin fruit, although I'm outnumbered by the many fans who say it's "yummy."

Kitchen Countertop Survivor™ Grade: Avg.

Your notes: _____

Columbia Crest Grand Estates Merlot, Washington	PC $	T 23	V 23

A top choice for the money, with lots of plum fruit, and a vanilla-berry scent.

Kitchen Countertop Survivor™ Grade: B

Your notes: _____

Columbia Crest Two Vines Merlot, Washington	PC $	T 22	V 28

A major Merlot with subtle plum-berry fruit and earth, in balance. Yum!

Kitchen Countertop Survivor™ Grade: B

Your notes: _____

Columbia Winery Merlot, Washington	PC $$	T 21	V 22

"Amazing for the money," with succulent berry on the palate, "great structure," and a long finish.

Kitchen Countertop Survivor™ Grade: B+

Your notes: _____

Dallas Conte Merlot, Chile	PC $	T 26	V 26

The wood-smoke scent and chunky plum fruit give you a lot of yum for the money.

Price Ranges: **$** = $12 or less; **$$** = $12.01–20; **$$$** = $20.01–35; **$$$$** = > $35

Kitchen Countertop Survivor™ Grades: *Avg.* = a "one-day wine," tastes noticeably less fresh the next day; *B* = holds its freshness for 2–3 days after opening; *B+* = holds *and gets better* over 2–3 days after opening; *A* = a 3- to 4-day "freshness window"; *A+* = holds *and gets better* over 3–4 days

Kitchen Countertop Survivor™ *Grade: Avg.*

Your notes: _____

Duckhorn Napa Merlot,   PC   T   V
California $$$$ 25   20

The full-throttle blackberry fruit, toasty oak, and lush texture are "for lovers of *big* Merlot," who are prepared for the fact that this benchmark's "pricey."

Kitchen Countertop Survivor™ *Grade: B+*

Your notes: _____

Falesco Montiano,   PC   T   V
Italy $$$$ 26   18

"Merlot on steroids" with plush plum and cocoa flavors.

Kitchen Countertop Survivor™ *Grade: Avg.*

Your notes: _____

Fall Creek Merlot,   PC   T   V
Texas $$ X   X

✗ Smooth, plummy, and easy drinking.

Kitchen Countertop Survivor™ *Grade: B*

Your notes: _____

Fetzer Valley Oaks Merlot,   PC   T   V
California $ 23   25

Among the best basic California Merlots on the market, with "juicy" cherry-berry flavors and an impressive survivor grade.

Kitchen Countertop Survivor™ *Grade: B*

Your notes: _____

Franciscan Oakville Estate Merlot,   PC   T   V
California $$ 28   24

✓ The raves continue to rack up for this quintessential Napa Merlot with lush cherry fruit; plush tannins; and just enough light, toasty oak to give it "layers and layers."

Kitchen Countertop Survivor™ *Grade: B*

Your notes: _____

Francis Coppola Diamond Series   PC   T   V
Blue Label Merlot, California $$ 24   25

This is textbook California Merlot—plum flavors, soft earthiness, vanilla-scented oak, velvety tannins.

Kitchen Countertop Survivor™ *Grade: Avg.*

Your notes: _____

Frei Brothers Reserve Merlot,   PC   T   V
California $$ 21   20

Plum-berry fruit, subtle oak, and smooth tannins, but the price has gone up.

Kitchen Countertop Survivor™ Grade: B

Your notes: _____

Frog's Leap Merlot,   PC   T   V
California $$$$ 23   18

Though it's expensive, devotees (me among them) find the complex fig and cassis fruit worth the price.

Kitchen Countertop Survivor™ Grade: A

Your notes: _____

Gallo Family Vineyards Sonoma   PC   T   V
Reserve Merlot, California $ 24   27

Too oaky for me, but the "very luscious" plum jam flavor pleases fans of big reds.

Kitchen Countertop Survivor™ Grade: A

Your notes: _____

HRM Rex Goliath Merlot,   PC   T   V
California $ 18   24

Plums, cherries, and wild berries, soft and smooth.

Kitchen Countertop Survivor™ Grade: Avg.

Your notes: _____

Kendall-Jackson Vintner's Reserve   PC   T   V
Merlot, California $$ 20   20

This is Merlot in the luscious style—redolent with black cherry flavor and smooth texture.

Kitchen Countertop Survivor™ Grade: B+

Your notes: _____

L'Ecole No. 41 Walla Walla Valley   PC   T   V
Merlot, Washington $$$$ 24   22

"Not cheap," but there's "value" in the form of deep berry flavor and exotic coconutty oak.

Kitchen Countertop Survivor™ Grade: Avg.

Your notes: _____

Price Ranges: **$** = $12 or less; **$$** = $12.01–20; **$$$** = $20.01–35; **$$$$** = > $35

Kitchen Countertop Survivor™ Grades: *Avg.* = a "one-day wine," tastes noticeably less fresh the next day; *B* = holds its freshness for 2–3 days after opening; *B+* = holds *and gets better* over 2–3 days after opening; *A* = a 3- to 4-day "freshness window"; *A+* = holds *and gets better* over 3–4 days

Lindemans Bin 40 Merlot, PC T V
Australia $ 21 22

At this price, it's no wonder there's a huge fan club for this wine's "easy drinking" plump plum and berry fruit.

Kitchen Countertop Survivor™ Grade: Avg.

Your notes: _____

The Little Penguin Merlot, PC T V
Australia $ 25 24

Another soft, berry-flavored competitor to Yellow Tail. And this one tastes a lot better, with the soft berry flavor.

Kitchen Countertop Survivor™ Grade: Avg.

Your notes: _____

Markham Merlot, PC T V
California $$$ 24 21

Still a value compared to other high-end California Merlots, with smooth plum fruit and soft oak.

Kitchen Countertop Survivor™ Grade: B+

Your notes: _____

Montes Alpha "M," PC T V
Chile $$$$ 25 22

With its huge chocolately plum fruit, this mostly Merlot "super Chilean" can be mistaken for a big-time Napa Meritage wine.

Kitchen Countertop Survivor™ Grade: B

Your notes: _____

Montes Merlot, PC T V
Chile $ 24 20

Montes remains a standard-bearer among Chilean Merlots: concentrated dark-berry flavors and cedar and earth scents—all on an elegant frame.

Kitchen Countertop Survivor™ Grade: B

Your notes: _____

Ravenswood Vintners Blend PC T V
Merlot, California $ 21 21

It's got "jammy, smooth" plum and cherry fruit, but some say there are "better Merlots for the price."

Kitchen Countertop Survivor™ Grade: B+

Your notes: _____

Rodney Strong Sonoma Merlot,	PC	T	V
California	$$	25	24

Beats "other Merlots at this price" say my tasters, who love the "cedar, spice, plum, berry, and earth."
Kitchen Countertop Survivor™ Grade: Avg.
Your notes: _____

Rombauer Merlot,	PC	T	V
California	$$$	24	19

"Rich, deep, earthy" fruit and a "long finish."
Kitchen Countertop Survivor™ Grade: Avg.
Your notes: _____

St. Francis Sonoma Merlot,	PC	T	V
California	$$	25	22

"Excellent," "consistent," "very blackberry," and "rich."
Kitchen Countertop Survivor™ Grade: B
Your notes: _____

Sebastiani Sonoma County	PC	T	V
Merlot, California	$$	24	20

Where so many Merlots have become mundane, this one has the deep and layered plum fruit and plump texture of classic California Merlot. Excellent quality.
Kitchen Countertop Survivor™ Grade: Avg.
Your notes: _____

Shafer Merlot,	PC	T	V
California	$$$$	27	21

"Pricey but very tasty" sums it up for this rich, classy wine in the lush, powerful "cult" style (meaning huge dark-berry fruit and lavish vanilla-oak).
Kitchen Countertop Survivor™ Grade: B+
Your notes: _____

Simi Merlot,	PC	T	V
California	$$$	X	X

✗ Big black cherry fruit; vanilla, clove, and coconut scents.

Price Ranges: **$** = $12 or less; **$$** = $12.01–20; **$$$** = $20.01–35; **$$$$** = > $35
Kitchen Countertop Survivor™ Grades: *Avg.* = a "one-day wine," tastes noticeably less fresh the next day; *B* = holds its freshness for 2–3 days after opening; *B+* = holds *and gets better* over 2–3 days after opening; *A* = a 3- to 4-day "freshness window"; *A+* = holds *and gets better* over 3–4 days

Kitchen Countertop Survivor™ Grade: A
Your notes: _____

Stag's Leap Wine Cellars Napa   PC   T   V
Merlot, California $$$$ 26   24
"Dark and full of berry," earth, mocha, and mint.
Kitchen Countertop Survivor™ Grade: B
Your notes: _____

Sterling Vineyards Napa Merlot,   PC   T   V
California $$$ 25   17
Mixed reviews! Some say "pricey" and "too oaky";
others say the "smooth, berry" style is worth it for a
"special night."
Kitchen Countertop Survivor™ Grade: B+
Your notes: _____

Sutter Home Merlot,   PC   T   V
California $ 19   23
The "always consistent" soft plum flavor is a "great
surprise" at this price.
Kitchen Countertop Survivor™ Grade: Avg.
Your notes: _____

Swanson Vineyards Merlot,   PC   T   V
California $$$ 27   18
This "luscious" Merlot with lavish vanilla-
scented oak is "full of complexity" and "worth the
money."
Kitchen Countertop Survivor™ Grade: Avg.
Your notes: _____

Three Blind Moose Merlot,   PC   T   V
California $ X   X
✗ Smooth and juicy plum fruit; one of the best at this
price.
Kitchen Countertop Survivor™ Grade: Avg.
Your notes: _____

Twin Fin Merlot,   PC   T   V
California $ X   X
✗ Juicy cherry Jell-O flavors and a touch of spicy
oak.
Kitchen Countertop Survivor™ Grade: Avg.
Your notes: _____

Cabernet Sauvignon and Blends

Grape Profile: Although Merlot ranks above it, Cabernet Sauvignon remains a top-selling red varietal wine. It grows well virtually all over the wine world and gives good to excellent quality and flavor at every price level, from steal to splurge. Its style can vary, based on the wine's quality level, from uncomplicated everyday styles to the superintense boutique bottlings. The most famous and plentiful sources of Cabernet are Bordeaux in France, California (especially Sonoma and Napa), Washington State, and Italy on the high end with its Super Tuscan versions; and I think Chile shines in the mid-priced category. Classically, it has a scent and taste of dark berries (blueberry, blackberry), plus notes of spice, earth, cocoa, cedar, and even mint that can be very layered and complex in the best wines. It has medium to very full body and often more tannin—that bit of a tongue-gripping sensation that one of my waiters once described, perfectly I think, as "a slipcover for the tongue, ranging from terry cloth to suede to velvet," depending on the wine in question. Oakiness, either a little or a lot, depending on the growing region and price category, is also a common Cabernet feature. Combined, these can make for a primo mouthful of a wine, which surely explains why Cabernet is king of collectible wines.

A note about "blends": As described previously for Merlot, Cabernet Sauvignon wines follow the Bordeaux blending model, with one or more of the traditional Bordeaux red grapes—Merlot, Cabernet Franc, Petit Verdot, and Malbec—blended in for balance and complexity. Australia pioneered blending Cabernet Sauvignon with Shiraz—a delicious combination that the wine buying market has embraced. Those blends are listed either here or in the Shiraz section, according to which of the two grapes is dominant in the blend (it will be listed first on the label, too).

Price Ranges: **$** = $12 or less; **$$** = $12.01–20; **$$$** = $20.01–35; **$$$$** = > $35

Kitchen Countertop Survivor™ Grades: *Avg.* = a "one-day wine," tastes noticeably less fresh the next day; *B* = holds its freshness for 2–3 days after opening; *B+* = holds *and gets better* over 2–3 days after opening; *A* = a 3- to 4-day "freshness window"; *A+* = holds *and gets better* over 3–4 days

Serve: Cool room temperature; the fuller-bodied styles benefit from aeration—pour into the glass a bit ahead of time or decant into a carafe (but if you forget, don't sweat it; if you care to, swirling the glass does help).

When: With your favorite red wine meals, but the every-day bottlings are soft enough for cocktail-hour sipping.

With: Anything you'd serve alongside a red; especially complements beef, lamb, goat cheese and hard cheeses, pesto sauce, and dishes scented with basil, rosemary, sage, or oregano.

In: An all-purpose wineglass or larger-bowled red wine stem.

	PC	T	V
Alexander Valley Vineyards **Cabernet Sauvignon, California**	$	24	24

"Really nice" soft-'n'-drinkable blackberry fruit.
Kitchen Countertop Survivor™ Grade: B
Your notes: _____

	PC	T	V
Alice White Cabernet Sauvignon, **Australia**	$	X	X

✗ Another in this brand's value stable, with soft black-berry fruit and a hint of cedar and mint.
Kitchen Countertop Survivor™ Grade: Avg.
Your notes: _____

	PC	T	V
Alice White Cabernet Shiraz, **Australia**	$	20	23

This "yummy budget choice" has "nice plum fruit" and a touch of cedar in the scent.
Kitchen Countertop Survivor™ Grade: B
Your notes: _____

	PC	T	V
Arrowood Cabernet Sauvignon **Sonoma County, California**	$$$$	26	23

The classic Sonoma Cab style, with wild blackberry fruit and toasty-vanilla oak.
Kitchen Countertop Survivor™ Grade: B
Your notes: _____

	PC	T	V
Baron Philippe de Rothschild, **Escudo Rojo Cabernet Blend, Chile**	$$	24	26

☺ Lots of complexity—smokiness, dried spices, leather, coffee, figs, mint—and great balance.

Kitchen Countertop Survivor™ Grade: B+

Your notes: _____

Beaulieu Vineyard (BV) Coastal Estates Cabernet Sauvignon, California	PC	T	V
	$	21	22

"Especially for the price," most tasters found it "pretty good," in the lighter, soft, everyday style.

Kitchen Countertop Survivor™ Grade: Avg.

Your notes: _____

Beaulieu Vineyard (BV) George de Latour Private Reserve Cabernet Sauvignon, California	PC	T	V
	$$$$	25	20

"Amazing" say my tasters of this wine's licorice, cedar, black cherry, and mineral aromas, typical of the region's "Rutherford Dust" soil. An ager.

Kitchen Countertop Survivor™ Grade: B

Your notes: _____

Beaulieu Vineyard (BV) Napa Valley Cabernet Sauvignon, California	PC	T	V
	$$	X	X

☺ ✗ Nice! Dusty, minty, earthy with subtle dark berry fruit. Cheaper and better than their famous Rutherford bottling.

Kitchen Countertop Survivor™ Grade: B

Your notes: _____

Beaulieu Vineyard (BV) Rutherford Cabernet Sauvignon, California	PC	T	V
	$$$	24	22

The "typical Napa Cab" style of jammy Cabernet flavor and "big oak." "Used to be more affordable," but so did everything else. This is a really solid splurge choice.

Kitchen Countertop Survivor™ Grade: B

Your notes: _____

Price Ranges: **$** = $12 or less; **$$** = $12.01–20; **$$$** = $20.01–35; **$$$$** = > $35

Kitchen Countertop Survivor™ Grades: *Avg.* = a "one-day wine," tastes noticeably less fresh the next day; *B* = holds its freshness for 2–3 days after opening; *B+* = holds *and gets better* over 2–3 days after opening; *A* = a 3- to 4-day "freshness window"; *A+* = holds *and gets better* over 3–4 days

Beringer Knights Valley Cabernet Sauvignon, California

	PC	T	V
	$$$	24	23

The chewy cassis fruit with vanilla-scented oak are "as complex and balanced as a wine for twice the price." It "gets better" with age, too.

Kitchen Countertop Survivor™ Grade: A

Your notes: _____

Beringer Private Reserve Cabernet Sauvignon, California

	PC	T	V
	$$$$	24	18

Amazing aromas of cedar, olives, tobacco, and black currants, plus nice balance and ageability.

Kitchen Countertop Survivor™ Grade: B

Your notes: _____

Black Opal Cabernet Sauvignon, Australia

	PC	T	V
	$	22	26

It's "juicy, yummy," and offers "more for the money" than a lot of the competition.

Kitchen Countertop Survivor™ Grade: B

Your notes: _____

Black Opal Cabernet/Merlot, Australia

	PC	T	V
	$	21	21

This Cab/Merlot blend from Australia "goes with anything" and has "pretty berry" flavors.

Kitchen Countertop Survivor™ Grade: B

Your notes: _____

Blackstone Cabernet Sauvignon, California

	PC	T	V
	$	21	24

"Inexpensive for what you get"—namely, "delicious" blackberry and cocoa scents and flavors.

Kitchen Countertop Survivor™ Grade: B

Your notes: _____

Cain Cuvee Bordeaux Style Red, California

	PC	T	V
	$$$	26	21

A "wow" versus more expensive California Cab blends. The cassis fruit and cedary oak "command your attention."

Kitchen Countertop Survivor™ Grade: A

Your notes: _____

Cakebread Napa Cabernet Sauvignon, California

	PC	T	V
	$$$$	24	21

The "cedar, blackberry, and anise" complexity drew raves for this "great name from Napa."

Kitchen Countertop Survivor™ Grade: B+

Your notes: _____

Casa Lapostolle Cuvee Alexandre   **PC**   **T**   **V**
Cabernet Sauvignon, Chile   **$$**   **26**   **26**

The cedar, vanilla, cinnamon, dark dusky fruit, and earth give you "depth at an unbeatable price."

Kitchen Countertop Survivor™ Grade: Avg.

Your notes: _____

Caymus Napa Cabernet   **PC**   **T**   **V**
Sauvignon, California   **$$$$**   **27**   **21**

Pricey, but one of the most sought-after Napa Cabs: jam-packed with huge dark fruit and strapping tannins that make it cellar worthy.

Kitchen Countertop Survivor™ Grade: B

Your notes: _____

Chateau Clerc-Milon Bordeaux,   **PC**   **T**   **V**
France   **$$$$**   **27**   **18**

A classic Bordeaux that needs age, but the delicious vanilla, cedar, wild/sour berry, and baking spice scents are worth the wait.

Kitchen Countertop Survivor™ Grade: B

Your notes: _____

Chateau Cos d'Estournel (coss   **PC**   **T**   **V**
dess-tur-NELL) Bordeaux, France   **$$$$**   **26**   **24**

Dusty cedar, cassis, sweet tobacco, anise, and coffee bean just begin to describe this wine's complexity. Ages 25+ years in great vintages (2003, for example).

Kitchen Countertop Survivor™ Grade: B

Your notes: _____

Chateau Duhart-Milon Rothschild   **PC**   **T**   **V**
Bordeaux, France   **$$$$**   **26**   **21**

A favorite of my students, who love the wine's rhubarb, cedar, leather, and roasted coffee bean character.

Price Ranges: **$** = $12 or less; **$$** = $12.01–20; **$$$** = $20.01–35; **$$$$** = > $35

Kitchen Countertop Survivor™ Grades: *Avg.* = a "one-day wine," tastes noticeably less fresh the next day; *B* = holds its freshness for 2–3 days after opening; *B+* = holds *and gets better* over 2–3 days after opening; *A* = a 3- to 4-day "freshness window"; *A+* = holds *and gets better* over 3–4 days

Kitchen Countertop Survivor™ Grade: B
Your notes: _____

Chateau Greysac Bordeaux,   PC   T   V
France $$ 23   23
The cedar and earth scent and smooth plum fruit add up
to "excellent value Bordeaux" that's great "with cheese."
Kitchen Countertop Survivor™ Grade: B
Your notes: _____

Chateau Gruaud-Larose (*GROO-oh*   PC   T   V
***lah-ROSE*) Bordeaux, France** $$$$ 26   21
☺ "Pricey," but more affordable than many Bordeaux
of comparable quality, with palate-coating tannins,
dark fruit, cedar-coffee scents, and a long finish.
Kitchen Countertop Survivor™ Grade: A
Your notes: _____

Chateau Lagrange Bordeaux,   PC   T   V
France $$$$ 24   18
Affordable classic Bordeaux, with a textbook dusty,
blackcurrant, and roasted coffee character.
Kitchen Countertop Survivor™ Grade: B+
Your notes: _____

Chateau Les Ormes de Pez (lays   PC   T   V
ORM duh PEZZ) Bordeaux, France $$$ 27   24
The "cassis and earthy" (autumn leaves and wet
gravel) character is classic Bordeaux at a doable price.
Kitchen Countertop Survivor™ Grade: B
Your notes: _____

Chateau Lynch-Bages Bordeaux,   PC   T   V
France $$$$ 27   20
A "deal and ready to drink" in so-so years, and always
true to its style: cedar and lead-pencil scent, luscious
cassis fruit, velvety-powerful texture.
Kitchen Countertop Survivor™ Grade: B+
Your notes: _____

Chateau Meyney Bordeaux,   PC   T   V
France $$$ 20   22
Great bang for your Bordeaux buck, with smoky, dark
cherry cedar aromas that intensify with age.
Kitchen Countertop Survivor™ Grade: B
Your notes: _____

Chateau Montelena Cabernet Sauvignon, California	PC $$$$	T 25	V 22

One of the great Napa Cabs! Dense with blackberry fruit, licorice, and vanilla scents in youth, evolving amazingly to cigar box and dried fig with age.

Kitchen Countertop Survivor™ Grade: Avg.

Your notes: _____

Chateau Prieure-Lichine Bordeaux, France	PC $$$	T 24	V 21

Priced like "a poor man's Bordeaux" because quality suffered for a while, but now it's back on form, with "round and approachable" cassis and plum fruit.

Kitchen Countertop Survivor™ Grade: Avg.

Your notes: _____

Chateau Souverain Alexander Valley Cabernet Sauvignon, California	PC $$$	T 24	V 22

"Cellar-worthy Cab" at this price is a rarity. It's got powerful fig fruit and balanced tannins and oak.

Kitchen Countertop Survivor™ Grade: B

Your notes: _____

Chateau Ste. Michelle Columbia Valley Cabernet Sauvignon, Washington	PC $$	T 22	V 22

Great for the price, with intense black cherry scent, soft blackberry flavors, and a toasty-oak finish.

Kitchen Countertop Survivor™ Grade: A

Your notes: _____

Chateau St. Jean Cinq Cepages (*sank seh-PAHJH*) Cabernet Blend, California	PC $$$$	T 28	V 24

The full-throttle blackberry fruit, earthy-smoky-spice scent, and power-with-elegance make this one of my favorite California wines, period.

Kitchen Countertop Survivor™ Grade: B+

Your notes: _____

Price Ranges: **$** = $12 or less; **$$** = $12.01–20; **$$$** = $20.01–35; **$$$$** = > $35

Kitchen Countertop Survivor™ Grades: *Avg.* = a "one-day wine," tastes noticeably less fresh the next day; *B* = holds its freshness for 2–3 days after opening; *B+* = holds *and gets better* over 2–3 days after opening; *A* = a 3- to 4-day "freshness window"; *A+* = holds *and gets better* over 3–4 days

Clos du Bois Marlstone,   PC   T   V
California $$$$ 24   24

Lots of complexity, with a mineral, briary scent and layers of intensity—black olive, black cherry, tobacco.
Kitchen Countertop Survivor™ Grade: B
Your notes: _____

Clos du Bois Sonoma Cabernet   PC   T   V
Sauvignon, California $$ 23   21

A few tasters call it "light" and "pricey," but I think the wild berry and anise character is much better than the hugely popular Merlot.
Kitchen Countertop Survivor™ Grade: Avg.
Your notes: _____

Columbia Crest Grand Estates   PC   T   V
Cabernet Sauvignon, Washington $ 23   26

☺ "Delicious" and "a 'wow' at this price" sums up the raves for this plush blackberry-and-earth Cab.
Kitchen Countertop Survivor™ Grade: B+
Your notes: _____

Concha y Toro Casillero del Diablo   PC   T   V
Cabernet Sauvignon, Chile $ 22   23

A lot of Cab character for the money, with dusty-blackberry, cocoa, and cedar, plus a meaty gaminess.
Kitchen Countertop Survivor™ Grade: Avg
Your notes: _____

Concha y Toro Don Melchor   PC   T   V
Cabernet Sauvignon Reserva, Chile $$$$ 23   23

The velvety texture and blackberry fruit remain, but I think this wine, a former favorite, has lost its Bordeaux-like complexity.
Kitchen Countertop Survivor™ Grade: A
Your notes: _____

Concha y Toro Marques de Casa   PC   T   V
Concha Cabernet Sauvignon, Chile $$ 24   24

"Black cherry and plum"; "nice" for the price.
Kitchen Countertop Survivor™ Grade: Avg.
Your notes: _____

Cousino Macul Antiguas Reservas   PC   T   V
Cabernet Sauvignon, Chile $$ 26   26

"Terrific" for the price with lots of smoky layers.

Kitchen Countertop Survivor™ Grade: B

Your notes: _____

Dry Creek Vineyard Cabernet Sauvignon, California	PC	T	V
	$$	20	21

Tasters call this wild berry and spice Cab a "value" and "tasty," though some find the finish a little short.

Kitchen Countertop Survivor™ Grade: Avg.

Your notes: _____

Estancia Alexander Valley Red Meritage, California	PC	T	V
	$$$	27	27

☺ ✓ A "wow" for the price, with elegance, a cedar/mint/mocha scent, and deep blackberry fruit.

Kitchen Countertop Survivor™ Grade: B

Your notes: _____

Estancia Cabernet Sauvignon, California	PC	T	V
	$$	23	24

"Real-deal California Cabernet" flavor—mint and cassis—at a "good price" makes this a winner.

Kitchen Countertop Survivor™ Grade: B+

Your notes: _____

Far Niente Cabernet Sauvignon, California	PC	T	V
	$$$$	25	19

Classic, classy Napa Cab, with big fruit and layers of earth, leaves, smoke, and cedar that enrich with age.

Kitchen Countertop Survivor™ Grade: A

Your notes: _____

Ferrari-Carano Siena Sonoma County, California	PC	T	V
	$$$	28	26

This is Cabernet blended with Sangiovese like a Super Tuscan wine, so you get the leathery-spiciness of the Italian grape, with "huge berry ripeness" from the Sonoma sun.

Kitchen Countertop Survivor™ Grade: A

Your notes: _____

Price Ranges: **$** = $12 or less; **$$** = $12.01–20; **$$$** = $20.01–35; **$$$$** = > $35

Kitchen Countertop Survivor™ Grades: *Avg.* = a "one-day wine," tastes noticeably less fresh the next day; *B* = holds its freshness for 2–3 days after opening; *B+* = holds *and gets better* over 2–3 days after opening; *A* = a 3- to 4-day "freshness window"; *A+* = holds *and gets better* over 3–4 days

Fetzer Valley Oaks Cabernet   PC   T   V
Sauvignon, California $ 20   24

Just what a "bargain"-priced Cab should be: "generous fruit" (plum, berry) and "mild, food-friendly tannins."

Kitchen Countertop Survivor™ Grade: B

Your notes: _____

Fisher Coach Insignia,   PC   T   V
California $$$$ 26   18

This "always delicious" Cab-dominated wine's opulent vanilla, cassis, and chocolate character rivals Napa's best, at a doable price.

Kitchen Countertop Survivor™ Grade: B+

Your notes: _____

Flora Springs Trilogy,   PC   T   V
California $$$$ X   X

✗ A Napa original Bordeaux-style blend that's a fraction of the price of competitors; ages great.

Kitchen Countertop Survivor™ Grade: B+

Your notes: _____

Francis Coppola Diamond Series   PC   T   V
Claret (*CLARE-ett*), California $$ 26   25

Claret means it's a blend of Bordeaux's Cabernet and Merlot grapes, with cedary, mocha scents and firm blackberry fruit and tannins.

Kitchen Countertop Survivor™ Grade: B

Your notes: _____

Francis Coppola Rubicon,   PC   T   V
California $$$$ 24   18

This wine's kaleidoscope of flavors—roasted coffee, dense black cherries, cedar, mint, and earth—evolve beautifully with bottle age.

Kitchen Countertop Survivor™ Grade: B+

Your notes: _____

Franciscan Magnificat Meritage,   PC   T   V
California $$$$ 27   23

"A steal" in its category with "packed-in blackberry," cedar-vanilla, tobacco, and smokiness.

Kitchen Countertop Survivor™ Grade: A

Your notes: _____

Franciscan Oakville Estate Cabernet Sauvignon, California

	PC	T	V
	$$$	25	23

☺ The real Napa Cab character—a whiff of cedar-mint, dark cassis fruit, sweet vanilla from oak, and velvety tannins—make it one of the best for the money.

Kitchen Countertop Survivor™ Grade: B

Your notes: _____

Frei Brothers Reserve Cabernet Sauvignon, California

	PC	T	V
	$$	24	18

The dusty-cassis-mint-spice character of this wine is textbook Alexander Valley Cab.

Kitchen Countertop Survivor™ Grade: Avg.

Your notes: _____

Frog's Leap Cabernet Sauvignon, California

	PC	T	V
	$$$	23	19

One of Napa's most distinctive Cabs, jam-packed with blackberry flavor, kissed with vanilla, licorice, and briary scents; impeccably balanced.

Kitchen Countertop Survivor™ Grade: B

Your notes: _____

Gallo Family Vineyards Barelli Creek Cabernet Sauvignon, California

	PC	T	V
	$$$	X	X

✗ Back on form and delicious! Blackberry, earth, chocolate, and mint. It will age well, too.

Kitchen Countertop Survivor™ Grade: B+

Your notes: _____

Gallo Family Vineyards Reserve Cabernet Sauvignon, California

	PC	T	V
	$$	24	25

The price is edging up, and "it's gotten more oaky," but there's still lots of big, dark berry and fig fruit intensity.

Kitchen Countertop Survivor™ Grade: Avg.

Your notes: _____

Price Ranges: **$** = $12 or less; **$$** = $12.01–20; **$$$** = $20.01–35; **$$$$** = > $35

Kitchen Countertop Survivor™ Grades: *Avg.* = a "one-day wine," tastes noticeably less fresh the next day; *B* = holds its freshness for 2–3 days after opening; *B+* = holds *and gets better* over 2–3 days after opening; *A* = a 3- to 4-day "freshness window"; *A+* = holds *and gets better* over 3–4 days

Geyser Peak Cabernet Sauvignon, California

	PC	T	V
	$	23	22

This "textbook Sonoma Cab" "hits all the right notes"—cedar, berry fruit, fine tannins, for a good price.

Kitchen Countertop Survivor™ Grade: B

Your notes: _____

Greg Norman Cabernet/Merlot, Australia

	PC	T	V
	$$	20	20

The dark berry flavors are "nice," but some tasters note they've "had other Aussie Cab/Merlots that are just as good, for less money."

Kitchen Countertop Survivor™ Grade: Avg.

Your notes: _____

Groth Napa Cabernet Sauvignon, California

	PC	T	V
	$$$$	26	20

Although "pricey," this wine remains fairly reasonable for a luxury Cabernet, with plush tannins and deep cassis fruit, elegantly framed with vanilla oak.

Kitchen Countertop Survivor™ Grade: B+

Your notes: _____

Heitz Napa Cabernet Sauvignon, California

	PC	T	V
	$$$$	28	18

The "fabulous earthy-minty qualities," and powerful dark fruit are Heitz signatures.

Kitchen Countertop Survivor™ Grade: B+

Your notes: _____

Hess Collection Mountain Cuvee, California

	PC	T	V
	$$$	24	24

"Nice spice/pepper flavor" in this Syrah-spiked blend. Velvety tannins, ripe cassis, and raspberry.

Kitchen Countertop Survivor™ Grade: B+

Your notes: _____

Hess Select Cabernet Sauvignon, California

	PC	T	V
	$$	21	19

My tasters "love" this "always-reliable" Cabernet's plum and blackberry flavors and touch of earthy spiciness, and you will, too.

Kitchen Countertop Survivor™ Grade: B

Your notes: _____

Hogue Cabernet Sauvignon, PC   T   V
Washington $ X   X

✗ Another "deal for the price" Cab from Washington, with earthy-cocoa scent and blackberry fruit.

Kitchen Countertop Survivor™ Grade: Avg.

Your notes: _____

Jacob's Creek Cabernet Sauvignon, PC   T   V
Australia $ 22   24

The nice minty-berry fruit, soft tannin, and great price make it an "amazing value for the money."

Kitchen Countertop Survivor™ Grade: B

Your notes: _____

J. Lohr 7 Oaks Cabernet Sauvignon, PC   T   V
California $$ 24   24

Always a price/value star with wild exotic berry fruit and luxurious coconut cream scent from American oak.

Kitchen Countertop Survivor™ Grade: B+

Your notes: _____

Jordan Cabernet Sauvignon, PC   T   V
California $$$$ 25   21

Quality can vary by vintage, but the elegant style of this Cab distinguishes it from the huge "fruit and oak bomb" Cabs that critics love. Ages well in top years.

Kitchen Countertop Survivor™ Grade: B+

Your notes: _____

Joseph Phelps Insignia Cabernet PC   T   V
Blend, California $$$$ 24   18

A Napa blockbuster, with potent black fruit, licorice, toasted-coconutty oak, and thick tannins.

Kitchen Countertop Survivor™ Grade: B

Your notes: _____

Price Ranges: **$** = $12 or less; **$$** = $12.01–20; **$$$** = $20.01–35; **$$$$** = > $35

Kitchen Countertop Survivor™ Grades: *Avg.* = a "one-day wine," tastes noticeably less fresh the next day; *B* = holds its freshness for 2–3 days after opening; *B+* = holds *and gets better* over 2–3 days after opening; *A* = a 3- to 4-day "freshness window"; *A+* = holds *and gets better* over 3–4 days

Joseph Phelps Napa Cabernet Sauvignon, California

PC	T	V
$$$$	24	21

Real Napa Cab that is priced fairly for what you get: great structure, mint, cedar, coffee-spice, and blackberry fruit.

Kitchen Countertop Survivor™ Grade: B

Your notes: _____

Justin Isosceles Cabernet Blend, California

PC	T	V
$$$$	24	24

This wine put Paso Robles on the map. Its dark berry, minty, and oaky aromas grow more refined with age.

Kitchen Countertop Survivor™ Grade: Avg.

Your notes: _____

Kendall-Jackson Vintner's Reserve Cabernet Sauvignon, California

PC	T	V
$$	21	22

The Cab character—blackberry flavor, earth, and a tug of tannin—is exemplary for the price.

Kitchen Countertop Survivor™ Grade: B

Your notes: _____

Liberty School Cabernet Sauvignon, California

PC	T	V
$$	21	24

As it has for years, this bottling delivers good Cab character—dark plum fruit and spice—at a value price.

Kitchen Countertop Survivor™ Grade: Avg.

Your notes: _____

Little Boomey Cabernet/Shiraz, Australia

PC	T	V
$	X	X

✗ Cinnamon-spice, juicy berry fruit, great value.

Kitchen Countertop Survivor™ Grade: Avg.

Your notes: _____

The Little Penguin Cabernet Sauvignon, Australia

PC	T	V
$	19	20

A "bargain" Cab at this price that really tastes like Cabernet—blackberry fruit and a touch of cedary spice. Bravo!

Kitchen Countertop Survivor™ Grade: Avg.

Your notes: _____

The Little Penguin Cabernet Sauvignon Shiraz, Australia

PC	T	V
$	24	24

"A little sweet" to some, but "yummy-fruity" to others.

Kitchen Countertop Survivor™ Grade: Avg.

Your notes: _____

Los Vascos Cabernet Sauvignon,   PC   T   V
Chile $ 24   26

One of Chile's best budget Cabernets, with dark cherry fruit, a cedary scent, and smooth tannins.
Kitchen Countertop Survivor™ Grade: B
Your notes: _____

Louis Martini Cabernet Sauvignon   PC   T   V
Reserve, California $$$ 24   23

Tasted blind against Cabs at thrice the price, this bottling blew us away—coconutty-spicy oak, huge but balanced blackberry fruit, mint, and eucalyptus.
Kitchen Countertop Survivor™ Grade: A
Your notes: _____

Louis Martini Napa Cabernet,   PC   T   V
California $ X   X

✗ This Cab master delivers the goods: velvety blackberry, cedar, and mint for a great price.
Kitchen Countertop Survivor™ Grade: B+
Your notes: _____

McWilliams Hanwood Estate   PC   T   V
Cabernet Sauvignon, Australia $ X   X

✗ The Shiraz sells more, but I prefer this. Lots of layers for the price—minty, earthy, ripe berries.
Kitchen Countertop Survivor™ Grade: B
Your notes: _____

Merryvale Profile Cabernet Blend,   PC   T   V
California $$$$ 27   18

Although it's "pricey," tasters "love the jammy cassis" fruit and "lavish vanilla" oak of this "blockbuster" style.
Kitchen Countertop Survivor™ Grade: B
Your notes: _____

Mt. Veeder Napa Cabernet   PC   T   V
Sauvignon, California $$$$ 21   24

☺ One of my favorite Cabs, period—with gripping tannins, dense figlike fruit, and great complexity for the price.

Price Ranges: **$** = $12 or less; **$$** = $12.01–20; **$$$** = $20.01–35; **$$$$** = > $35
Kitchen Countertop Survivor™ Grades: *Avg.* = a "one-day wine," tastes noticeably less fresh the next day; *B* = holds its freshness for 2–3 days after opening; *B+* = holds *and gets better* over 2–3 days after opening; *A* = a 3- to 4-day "freshness window"; *A+* = holds *and gets better* over 3–4 days

Kitchen Countertop Survivor™ *Grade: A*

Your notes: _____

Opus One Cabernet Blend,   PC   T   V
California $$$$ 27   18

A "powerful wine" with classy, toasty-vanilla oak and
blackcurrant-cedar flavors that are "so Napa," plus a
coffee/lead-pencil scent that is Bordeaux-like. Ages
beautifully.

Kitchen Fridge Survivor™ *Grade: B*

Your notes: _____

Ornellaia Super Tuscan,   PC   T   V
Italy $$$$ 26   18

Its fame results in a "high price," but it's distinctive
with sexy vanilla oak and licorice/balsamic/rosemary/
dried-cherry complexity.

Kitchen Countertop Survivor™ *Grade: A+*

Your notes: _____

Pahlmeyer Meritage Napa Valley,   PC   T   V
California $$$$ 26   18

This boutique Cabernet has "great fruit flavors of
wild dark berries," "massive oak," and a "great
finish." Collector-types find the "very high price"
"worth it."

Kitchen Countertop Survivor™ *Grade: B*

Your notes: _____

Penfolds Bin 389 Cabernet   PC   T   V
Sauvignon/Shiraz, Australia $$$ 27   23

☺ This "awesome" wine delivers on all counts:
complexity, the "yum" factor, and value. The vivid
raspberry fruit and pepper/cedar/spice/coconut scent
are delicious young, but the wine also develops great
complexity with age.

Kitchen Countertop Survivor™ *Grade: A*

Your notes: _____

Penfolds Koonunga Hill Cabernet/   PC   T   V
Merlot, Australia $ 21   23

The cedar scent of Cabernet, plus the plummy
softness of Merlot at a good price for the quality.

Kitchen Countertop Survivor™ *Grade: B*

Your notes: _____

Pine Ridge Cabernet Sauvignon   PC   T   V
Stag's Leap District, California $$$$ 27   23

A classic Stag's Leap district Cab style, with earthy-blackberry fruit, and a soft scent of cocoa and forest floor.

Kitchen Countertop Survivor™ Grade: B
Your notes: _____

Pride Mountain Vineyards   PC   T   V
Cabernet Sauvignon, California $$$$ 26   19

Major fans (me included) for this wine's "gorgeous aromas," "dense, incredible dark fruit," and "great quality to price ratio when you compare it against some of the hard-to-find California cult wines."

Kitchen Countertop Survivor™ Grade: B
Your notes: _____

Quintessa Cabernet Blend,   PC   T   V
California $$$$ 26   18

The price has jumped, but it remains elegant, with deep cassis fruit flavor and subtle scents of autumn leaf pile, and soft vanilla.

Kitchen Countertop Survivor™ Grade: A
Your notes: _____

Raymond Napa Cabernet   PC   T   V
Sauvignon, California $$ 24   21

The Raymonds put quality in the bottle for a good price. It's "minty and elegant," balanced, not heavy.

Kitchen Countertop Survivor™ Grade: B
Your notes: _____

R.H. Phillips Toasted Head Cabernet   PC   T   V
Sauvignon, California $$ 23   23

Tasters like the "big Cab flavor for a good price."

Kitchen Countertop Survivor™ Grade: Avg.
Your notes: _____

Price Ranges: **$** = $12 or less; **$$** = $12.01–20; **$$$** = $20.01–35; **$$$$** = > $35

Kitchen Countertop Survivor™ Grades: *Avg.* = a "one-day wine," tastes noticeably less fresh the next day; *B* = holds its freshness for 2–3 days after opening; *B+* = holds *and gets better* over 2–3 days after opening; *A* = a 3- to 4-day "freshness window"; *A+* = holds *and gets better* over 3–4 days

Robert Mondavi Cabernet	PC	T	V
Sauvignon Reserve, California	$$$$	25	21

A Napa blue chip redolent of eucalyptus and bitter-sweet chocolate; delicious young, but it ages well, too.

Kitchen Countertop Survivor™ Grade: B

Your notes: _____

Robert Mondavi Napa Cabernet	PC	T	V
Sauvignon, California	$$	20	23

I've found the quality uneven year to year, but at its best this Cab's deep cassis and licorice flavor and cedary, spicy, minty scent are consistent style signatures and a benchmark for the category.

Kitchen Countertop Survivor™ Grade: Avg.

Your notes: _____

Rodney Strong Sonoma Cabernet	PC	T	V
Sauvignon, California	$$	21	21

My tasters "love" the coconutty oak scent and "huge fruit" that "tastes more expensive than it is."

Kitchen Countertop Survivor™ Grade: Avg.

Your notes: _____

Rosemount Diamond Label	PC	T	V
Cabernet Sauvignon Australia	$	24	24

☺ My tasters rave that this "jammy," "very-well-made" Aussie Cab is "simply one of the best buys in wine."

Kitchen Countertop Survivor™ Grade: Avg.

Your notes: _____

Rust-en-Vrede Estate Red,	PC	T	V
South Africa	$$$	24	24

"Like a good Bordeaux" but there's Shiraz mixed with Cab and Merlot. It's "very characteristic" of South Africa reds, with velvety tannins and heady-meaty notes with the ripe fruit.

Kitchen Countertop Survivor™ Grade: B

Your notes: _____

Santa Rita 120 Cabernet Sauvignon,	PC	T	V
Chile	$	26	28

It is indeed "a price that's hard to believe" for the quality and flavor punch it delivers. The nice tannic grip and meaty-spicy scent and flavor show the rustic Chilean Cabernet character that I love.

Kitchen Countertop Survivor™ Grade: B
Your notes: _____

Sebastiani Sonoma Cabernet	PC	T	V
Sauvignon, California	$$	24	21

☺ I agree with this taster's comment: "This winery is doing things so well at such affordable prices." You just don't expect such complexity of "blackberry," "cassis," and spice at this price.

Kitchen Countertop Survivor™ Grade: B
Your notes: _____

Shafer Hillside Select Cabernet	PC	T	V
Sauvignon, California	$$$$	29	18

"Big and bold, yet balanced and refined," with cedar-autumn leaves and vanilla scent and lush cassis fruit layered with cocoa and licorice.

Kitchen Countertop Survivor™ Grade: A
Your notes: _____

Silverado Napa Cabernet	PC	T	V
Sauvignon, California	$$$$	24	20

The elegant but firm style is classy, with cassis flavor, sweet-vanilla oak, and earthiness.

Kitchen Countertop Survivor™ Grade: B
Your notes: _____

Silver Oak Alexander Valley	PC	T	V
Cabernet Sauvignon, California	$$$$	27	19

This wine's die-hard devotees find its consistency and uniqueness "worth the price." It is known for intense wild berry fruit, velvety tannins, a coconut-dill scent coming from American oak barrels, and ageability.

Kitchen Countertop Survivor™ Grade: B
Your notes: _____

Simi Sonoma Cabernet Sauvignon,	PC	T	V
California	$$$	24	25

Excellent value for the money and classy, true California Cab style: blackberry, earth, spice.

Price Ranges: **$** = $12 or less; **$$** = $12.01–20; **$$$** = $20.01–35; **$$$$** = > $35
Kitchen Countertop Survivor™ Grades: *Avg.* = a "one-day wine," tastes noticeably less fresh the next day; *B* = holds its freshness for 2–3 days after opening; *B+* = holds *and gets better* over 2–3 days after opening; *A* = a 3- to 4-day "freshness window"; *A+* = holds *and gets better* over 3–4 days

Kitchen Countertop Survivor™ Grade: B
Your notes: _____

Smoking Loon Cabernet | PC | T | V
Sauvignon, California | $ | 20 | 26

"Excellent for the money" is this brand's signature, making this Cab "good for every day," yet unique for its "earthy" taste.

Kitchen Countertop Survivor™ Grade: Avg.
Your notes: _____

Staglin Family Cabernet | PC | T | V
Sauvignon, California | $$$$ | 24 | 17

"Just delicious" and, like their Chard, so perfectly pitched between elegance (the texture) and intensity (the dense black fruit and heady vanilla-coffee scent).

Kitchen Countertop Survivor™ Grade: B
Your notes: _____

Stag's Leap Wine Cellars Napa | PC | T | V
Cabernet Sauvignon, California | $$$$ | 26 | 20

"Pricey," with dark spices, mint, and berry.

Kitchen Countertop Survivor™ Grade: B
Your notes: _____

Sterling Cabernet Sauvignon | PC | T | V
Reserve, California | $$$$ | X | X

✗ Opulent vanilla, chocolate, and licorice with huge mouth-coating cassis fruit and plush tannins.

Kitchen Countertop Survivor™ Grade: B+
Your notes: _____

Sterling Vineyards Napa Cabernet | PC | T | V
Sauvignon, California | $$$ | 24 | 22

Although tasters praise this blue-chip Cab's "concentrated" "jammy fruits," I think it is bested by others at the same price.

Kitchen Countertop Survivor™ Grade: B
Your notes: _____

Sterling Vintner's Collection | PC | T | V
Cabernet Sauvignon, California | $ | X | X

✗ Honestly more for the money than the Napa bottling, with soft blackberry fruit and spice.

Kitchen Countertop Survivor™ Grade: Avg.
Your notes: _____

| **Stonestreet Alexander Valley** | PC | T | V |
| Cabernet Sauvignon, California | $$$ | 24 | 18 |

The elegance and scents of vanilla, damp earth, crushed mint, and blackberry are classic Alexander Valley.

Kitchen Countertop Survivor™ Grade: Avg.

Your notes: _____

| **Twin Fin Cabernet Sauvignon,** | PC | T | V |
| California | $ | X | X |

✗ Gulpable, with red berry fruit and soft spice.

Kitchen Countertop Survivor™ Grade: Avg.

Your notes: _____

| **Veramonte Cabernet Sauvignon,** | PC | T | V |
| Chile | $ | 19 | 19 |

A "real value find for consumers," licorice-berry fruit, chewy tannin, and savory spice; tastes like twice the price.

Kitchen Countertop Survivor™ Grade: Avg.

Your notes: _____

| **Viader Napa Valley Cabernet** | PC | T | V |
| Blend, California | $$$$ | 28 | 18 |

This "wonderfully smooth" Napa Cab blend feels like cashmere for the tongue. Its "glorious fruit," sweet complexity are "as good as any of the cult Cabs" but an elegance that's rare in the category.

Kitchen Countertop Survivor™ Grade: A

Your notes: _____

| **Whitehall Lane Cabernet** | PC | T | V |
| Sauvignon Reserve, California | $$$$ | 28 | 19 |

The "chewy, smoky" full black fruit is velvety and delicious now, but ages beautifully, too.

Kitchen Countertop Survivor™ Grade: A

Your notes: _____

Price Ranges: **$** = $12 or less; **$$** = $12.01–20; **$$$** = $20.01–35; **$$$$** = > $35

Kitchen Countertop Survivor™ Grades: *Avg.* = a "one-day wine," tastes noticeably less fresh the next day; *B* = holds its freshness for 2–3 days after opening; *B+* = holds *and gets better* over 2–3 days after opening; *A* = a 3- to 4-day "freshness window"; *A+* = holds *and gets better* over 3–4 days

Rioja, Ribera del Duero, and Other Spanish Reds

Category Profile: Like other classic Euro wines, it's the place—called a Denominación de Origen (DO)—rather than the grape on a Spanish wine label. Spain's signature red grape, used in both the Rioja (*ree-OH-huh*) and the Ribera del Duero (*ree-BEAR-uh dell DWAIR-oh*) DOs, is called Tempranillo (*temp-rah-NEE-oh*). Depending on quality level, the style of Rioja ranges from easy drinking and spicy to seriously rich, leathery/toffee. Ribera del Duero is generally big and tannic. The other Spanish reds here are from Priorat (*pre-oh-RAHT*), known for strong, inky-dark cellar candidates (usually made from Tempranillo, Cabernet, and/or Grenache). Though not represented in the top red wine sellers, Penedes (*pen-eh-DESS*), which is better known for Cava sparkling wines, is also an outstanding source of values in every style and color.

Serve: Cool room temperature; as a rule Spanish reds are exemplary food wines, but basic reds from Penedes and Rioja (with the word *Crianza* on the label), and emerging regions like Navarra, Toro, and Somontano, are good "anytime" wines and tasty on their own.

When: If you dine out often in wine-focused restaurants, Spanish reds are *the* red wine category for world-class drinking that's also affordable.

With: The classic matches are pork and lamb, either roasted or grilled; also amazing with slow-roasted chicken or turkey and hams, sausages, and other cured meats. Finally, try a Spanish Ribera del Duero, Priorat, or Rioja Reserva or Gran Reserva with good-quality cheese. (Spanish Manchego is wonderful and available in supermarkets.)

In: An all-purpose wineglass or larger-bowled red wine stem.

	PC	T	V
Abadia Retuerta Seleccion Especial, Spain	$$$	24	29

"Classy," "herb-tinged" ripe fruit and smokiness.
Kitchen Countertop Survivor™ Grade: A+
Your notes: _____

Alvaro Palacios Les Terrasses (*ALL-vahr-oh puh-LAH-see-os lay tear-AHSS*) **Priorat, Spain**

	PC	T	V
	$$$	23	23

Lush, intense, and inky, with beautiful black cherry flavors, toasty oak, and a long finish.

Kitchen Countertop Survivor™ Grade: B

Your notes: _____

Borsao Grenache/Tempranillo, Spain

	PC	T	V
	$	24	24

"Unexpectedly good" for the price, with soft fruit and nice spiciness that "doesn't overpower food."

Kitchen Countertop Survivor™ Grade: B+

Your notes: _____

El Coto Rioja Reserva, Spain

	PC	T	V
	$$	X	X

✗ Leathery-spicy-raisiny flavor; "old style" but still stylish.

Kitchen Countertop Survivor™ Grade: B+

Your notes: _____

Marques de Arienzo Rioja Reserva, Spain

	PC	T	V
	$$	22	23

A subtle style of Rioja—tobacco, toffee, and dried spice scent, dark berry and raisin fruit flavor.

Kitchen Countertop Survivor™ Grade: B

Your notes: _____

Marques de Caceres (*mahr-KESS deh CAH-sair-ess*) **Rioja Crianza, Spain**

	PC	T	V
	$$	24	22

With "lots of cherry fruit" and "typical toffee-spice," this Rioja Crianza is among my favorite basic Riojas.

Kitchen Countertop Survivor™ Grade: B+

Your notes: _____

Marques de Riscal (*mahr-KESS deh ree-SKALL*) **Rioja Crianza, Spain**

	PC	T	V
	$	20	19

This wine earns praise for its lovely spicy nose, silken texture, and savory-strawberry flavor.

Price Ranges: **$** = $12 or less; **$$** = $12.01–20; **$$$** = $20.01–35; **$$$$** = > $35

Kitchen Countertop Survivor™ Grades: *Avg.* = a "one-day wine," tastes noticeably less fresh the next day; *B* = holds its freshness for 2–3 days after opening; *B+* = holds *and gets better* over 2–3 days after opening; *A* = a 3- to 4-day "freshness window"; *A+* = holds *and gets better* over 3–4 days

Kitchen Countertop Survivor™ *Grade: B+*
Your notes: _____

Marques de Riscal Rioja Gran   PC   T   V
Reserva, Spain $$$ X   X
✗ Date and dried figs; leather, chewy tannins; and great spice, with a long buttery-coconut finish.
Kitchen Countertop Survivor™ *Grade: B+*
Your notes: _____

Marques de Riscal Rioja Reserva,   PC   T   V
Spain $$ 22   19
A "nice upgrade from the Crianza" (the base-level Riscal), with more oak aging that gives toffee/coconut scents to match the raisiny and chocolatey flavor.
Kitchen Countertop Survivor™ *Grade: B*
Your notes: _____

Montecillo (*mohn-teh-SEE-yoh*)   PC   T   V
Rioja Crianza, Spain $ 27   27
Another favorite of wine aficionados, for its Old-World savory spiciness and long finish. Very nice indeed.
Kitchen Countertop Survivor™ *Grade: Avg.*
Your notes: _____

Montecillo Rioja Reserva,   PC   T   V
Spain $$ 21   21
Extra oak aging creates layers of tobacco, toffee, and sweet spice alongside the fig and raisin fruit.
Kitchen Countertop Survivor™ *Grade: B+*
Your notes: _____

Muga (*MOO-guh*) Rioja Reserva,   PC   T   V
Spain $$$ 25   22
A world-class wine and a relative value in that realm, with stunning fig, prune, and dried cherry fruit and dense but suede-smooth tannins.
Kitchen Countertop Survivor™ *Grade: A+*
Your notes: _____

Osborne Solaz Tempranillo,   PC   T   V
Spain $ 24   27
A great way to get to know Spain's signature Tempranillo grape (here blended with Cab). It's got a smoky scent, lots of pretty plum fruit, and soft tannin.
Kitchen Countertop Survivor™ *Grade: Avg.*
Your notes: _____

Pesquera (*pess-CARE-uh*) Ribera del Duero, Spain	PC	T	V
	$$$	24	24

This wine is back on form, with deep cherry fruit, oak, and structure that's "smooth" yet built for aging.

Kitchen Countertop Survivor™ *Grade: B*

Your notes: _____

Vinicola del Priorat Onix (*veen-EE-co-lah dell PREE-oh-raht OH-nix*), Spain	PC	T	V
	$$	20	22

Among Priorat wines, this one's "more affordable than most," with deep berry fruit, tarry scent, and chewy tannins.

Kitchen Countertop Survivor™ *Grade: A*

Your notes: _____

Other Reds

Category Profile: As with the whites, this isn't a cohesive category but rather a spot to put big-selling reds that don't neatly fit a grape or region category—namely, proprietary blends, and uncommon varietals.

Proprietary Blends—These may be tasty, inexpensive blends or ambitious signature blends at luxury prices.

Uncommon Varietals—These are quite exciting. I introduced Malbec and Carmenere in the Merlot section, because I think they are distinctive and delicious alternatives for Merlot lovers. Although the names and even the style (bold and a little peppery) are similar, Petite Sirah and Syrah (Shiraz) are not the same grape.

Serve: Cool room temperature, or even slightly chilled.

When: Anytime you need an interesting, value-priced red.

With: Snacks and everyday meals.

In: An all-purpose wineglass.

Price Ranges: **$** = $12 or less; **$$** = $12.01–20; **$$$** = $20.01–35; **$$$$** = > $35

Kitchen Countertop Survivor™ Grades: *Avg.* = a "one-day wine," tastes noticeably less fresh the next day; *B* = holds its freshness for 2–3 days after opening; *B+* = holds *and gets better* over 2–3 days after opening; *A* = a 3- to 4-day "freshness window"; *A+* = holds *and gets better* over 3–4 days

Alamos by Catena Malbec,   PC   T   V
Argentina $$ 27   28

An Argentina pioneer. The intense blackberry fruit, velvety texture, and vanilla-scented oak are at once sleek and powerful.

Kitchen Fridge Survivor™ Grade: Avg.
Your notes: _____

Bogle Petite Sirah,   PC   T   V
California $ 27   26

It's a black pepper and berries mouthful that my tasters call an "awesome value."

Kitchen Countertop Survivor™ Grade: B
Your notes: _____

Ca'del Solo Big House Red,   PC   T   V
California $ 22   19

This "spicy," juicy red offers "great value" and easy drinkability—a "fun for everyday" wine.

Kitchen Countertop Survivor™ Grade: A
Your notes: _____

Cline Ancient Vines Mourvedre,   PC   T   V
California $$ 24   28

"Very rich" dark berry fruit with "spice and depth."

Kitchen Countertop Survivor™ Grade: B+
Your notes: _____

Concannon Petite Sirah,   PC   T   V
California $ 26   26

Take a black pepper and berry scent, add explode-in-your-mouth fruit-pie flavor, chewy tannins, and a long licorice finish, and you've got this unique, fun wine.

Kitchen Countertop Survivor™ Grade: B+
Your notes: _____

Concha y Toro Casillero del Diablo   PC   T   V
Carmenere, Chile $ 24   22

The wine is spicy, raisiny, and oozing with character, and has a heady scent like molasses-cured bacon. Just try it!

Kitchen Fridge Survivor™ Grade: B
Your notes: _____

Concha y Toro Terrunyo   PC   T   V
Carmenere, Chile $$$ 23   20

Like the concentrated essence of wild berries (huckleberries, raspberries), with a velvety-plush texture and sweet spice-cola scents. Worth a search!

Kitchen Countertop Survivor™ Grade: B

Your notes: _____

Domaine de la Mordoree Cotes-du-   **PC**   **T**   **V**
Rhone Red, France   **$$**   **24**   **24**

"Very nice" spice and pomegranate flavor, without being too intense.

Kitchen Countertop Survivor™ Grade: B

Your notes: _____

Domaine Santa Duc Gigonadas,   **PC**   **T**   **V**
France   **$$$**   **24**   **18**

The "gorgeous berry and cherry fruit" are spiked with the peppery spice typical of the Gigondas region. The gripping tannis and rustic earthiness make it great with smoked fare, bean dishes, and mushroom dishes.

Kitchen Countertop Survivor™ Grade: B+

Your notes: _____

Finca Flichman Malbec Reserva,   **PC**   **T**   **V**
Argentina   **$**   **26**   **26**

Very "smooth," "spicy," and "wow" for the money.

Kitchen Countertop Survivor™ Grade: B

Your notes: _____

Foppiano Petite Sirah,   **PC**   **T**   **V**
California   **$$**   **23**   **21**

A "manly wine" with sturdy tannin and spice to support the dark berry fruit.

Kitchen Fridge Survivor™ Grade: B

Your notes: _____

Montes Malbec,   **PC**   **T**   **V**
Chile   **$**   **27**   **27**

"Incredible" flavor, smooth and plummy, "great value."

Kitchen Countertop Survivor™ Grade: Avg.

Your notes: _____

Price Ranges: **$** = $12 or less; **$$** = $12.01–20; **$$$** = $20.01–35; **$$$$** = > $35

Kitchen Countertop Survivor™ Grades: **Avg.** = a "one-day wine," tastes noticeably less fresh the next day; **B** = holds its freshness for 2–3 days after opening; **B+** = holds *and gets better* over 2–3 days after opening; **A** = a 3- to 4-day "freshness window"; **A+** = holds *and gets better* over 3–4 days

Navarro Correas Malbec,	PC	T	V
Argentina	$	25	25

Rustic but really inviting, with an earthy, leathery, savory spice scent, and silky, subtle plum fruit.

Kitchen Countertop Survivor™ Grade: B

Your notes: _____

Red Truck by Cline Cellars,	PC	T	V
California	$	22	22

Mostly Rhone grapes in this fun blend, so there's lots of savory spice and juicy, "bowl-of-berries" fruit.

Kitchen Countertop Survivor™ Grade: Avg.

Your notes: _____

Silkwood Petite Sirah,	PC	T	V
California	$$$	24	18

"Huge" black fruit, chewy tannins, and a "long finish."

Kitchen Countertop Survivor™ Grade: B+

Your notes: _____

Stags' Leap Winery Petite Sirah,	PC	T	V
California	$$$	25	23

One of "the best" Petite Sirahs available, with licorice and blackberry scents and flavors, chewy tannins.

Kitchen Countertop Survivor™ Grade: B

Your notes: _____

Terrazas Alto Malbec,	PC	T	V
Argentina	$	24	24

This "juicy, plummy, spicy" Malbec gets "great value" marks from my tasters.

Kitchen Countertop Survivor™ Grade: Avg.

Your notes: _____

Veramonte Primus,	PC	T	V
Chile	$$	21	18

This pioneer Carmenere blend is still one of the best, with a lot of exotic berry fruit, both savory and sweet spices, and a smoky-meaty note.

Kitchen Countertop Survivor™ Grade: B

Your notes: _____

Italian Regional Reds

Category Profile: This group includes small Italian regions like Valpolicella and Lambrusco, whose market presence is dominated by a few big-selling, well-known brands.

Serve: Cool room temperature or slightly chilled.

When: As the Italians would, for everyday drinking.

With: Snacks and everyday meals.

In: An all-purpose wineglass.

	PC	T	V
Allegrini Valpolicella (*al-uh-GREE-nee val-pole-uh-CHELL-uh*), Italy	**$**	**22**	**22**

Pros hail this bottling as "*the* classic Valpolicella," with dried cherry flavor, spicy scent, vibrant acidity.
Kitchen Countertop Survivor™ *Grade: B*
Your notes: _____

	PC	T	V
Bolla Valpolicella, Italy	**$**	**17**	**18**

This Valpolicella is fruity and soft but scores poorly compared to other everyday Italians at the price.
Kitchen Countertop Survivor™ *Grade: Avg.*
Your notes: _____

	PC	T	V
Cantina Zaccagnini Montepulciano d'Abruzzo, Italy	**$**	**27**	**27**

Tasters "fell in love" with the soft, food-loving savory spice and sweet strawberry flavors for a "value" price.
Kitchen Countertop Survivor™ *Grade: B*
Your notes: _____

	PC	T	V
Ceretto Barbaresco Asij, Italy	**$$$$.**	**24**	**18**

New to the Nebbiolo grape? This bottle proudly shows off its aromas of dark berries, tar, and smoke. An aged cheese will soften its tannic grip.
Kitchen Countertop Survivor™ *Grade: A+*
Your notes: _____

Price Ranges: **$** = $12 or less; **$$** = $12.01–20; **$$$** = $20.01–35; **$$$$** = > $35
Kitchen Countertop Survivor™ Grades: *Avg.* = a "one-day wine," tastes noticeably less fresh the next day; *B* = holds its freshness for 2–3 days after opening; *B+* = holds *and gets better* over 2–3 days after opening; *A* = a 3- to 4-day "freshness window"; *A+* = holds *and gets better* over 3–4 days

Citra Montepulciano d'Abruzzo   PC   T   V
(*CHEE-truh mon-teh-pool-CHAH-no* $ 18   20
dah-BROOT-so), Italy

A yummy little wine for the money, whose fruity earthy spiciness make almost any dish taste better.

Kitchen Countertop Survivor™ Grade: B

Your notes: _____

Falesco Vitiano (*fuh-LESS-co   PC   T   V
vee-tee-AH-no), Italy** $ 20   21

"There's probably no better wine for the money," say my tasters. It's "spicy," "fruity," "smooth," "just delicious!"

Kitchen Countertop Survivor™ Grade: B

Your notes: _____

Michele Chiarlo Barbera d'Asti,   PC   T   V
Italy $ 24   26

This Barbera is low in tannin, with lively acidity and a flavor of dried cherries, sweet spice, and balsamic.

Kitchen Countertop Survivor™ Grade: B

Your notes: _____

Pio Cesare Barolo,   PC   T   V
Italy $$$$ 23   20

A good price for the quality, with deep plum, cedar, and tar scent, and dusty berry-rhubarb flavor.

Kitchen Countertop Survivor™ Grade: A

Your notes: _____

Taurino Salice Salentino,   PC   T   V
Italy $ 24   24

Tasters love the "rustic, mouth-watering bright berries" and the "great character for the price."

Kitchen Countertop Survivor™ Grade: B+

Your notes: _____

Syrah/Shiraz and Other Rhone-Style Reds

Category Profile: The varietal Shiraz, Australia's signature red, is so hot that most pros say it has unseated Merlot as consumers' go-to grape. Popularity has its price for Shiraz lovers, though, because many of the biggest brands have begun to taste like generic red wine rather than the spunky Shiraz with which we fell in love. I've focused on brands that have stayed true to the Shiraz taste. The same grape, under the French spelling *Syrah,* also forms the backbone for France's revered Rhone Valley reds with centuries-old reputations. These include Cotes-du-Rhone (*coat-duh-ROAN*), Cote-Rotie (*ro-TEE*), Hermitage (*uhr-muh-TAHJ*), and Chateauneuf-du-Pape (*shah-toe-NUFF-duh-POP*). Like Shiraz, Cotes-du-Rhone, with its lovely spicy fruit character, is a one-dollar-sign wonder. The latter three are true French classics and, in my view, currently lead that elite group in quality for the money. They are full-bodied, powerful, peppery, earthy, concentrated, and oak aged. Finally, most major American wineries, and many smaller players, are bottling California or Washington State versions, often labeled with the Aussie spelling *Shiraz* rather than the French *Syrah.*

Serve: Room temperature; aeration enhances the aroma and flavor.

When: Basic Syrah/Shiraz and Cotes-du-Rhone are great everyday drinking wines; in restaurants, these are great go-to categories for relative value.

With: Grilled, barbecued, or roasted anything (including fish and vegetables); outstanding with steaks, fine cheeses, and other dishes that call for a full red wine; I also love these styles with traditional Thanksgiving fare.

In: An all-purpose wineglass or a larger-bowled red wine stem.

	PC	T	V
Alice White Shiraz, Australia	**$**	27	27

"A lot of bang for the buck" thanks to its "spicy scent and wild raspberry fruit."

Kitchen Countertop Survivor™ Grade: B
Your notes: _____

Price Ranges: **$** = $12 or less; **$$** = $12.01–20; **$$$** = $20.01–35; **$$$$** = > $35
Kitchen Countertop Survivor™ Grades: **Avg.** = a "one-day wine," tastes noticeably less fresh the next day; **B** = holds its freshness for 2–3 days after opening; **B+** = holds *and gets better* over 2–3 days after opening; **A** = a 3- to 4-day "freshness window"; **A+** = holds *and gets better* over 3–4 days

Beaulieu Vineyard (BV) Coastal Estates Shiraz, California

PC	T	V
$	X	X

✗ Meaty, juicy dark plum and berries; a yummy steal.

Kitchen Countertop Survivor™ Grade: B

Your notes: _____

Beaulieu Vineyard (BV) Napa Valley Syrah, California

PC	T	V
$	X	X

✗ Dark fig and raspberry, vanilla, licorice, and tobacco.

Kitchen Countertop Survivor™ Grade: B

Your notes: _____

Black Opal Shiraz, Australia

PC	T	V
$	18	19

"Always a great value," with juicy fruit and a soft texture that makes it a great "house red."

Kitchen Countertop Survivor™ Grade: Avg.

Your notes: _____

Blackstone Syrah, California

PC	T	V
$	24	24

"Very rich, dark fruit with a nice spice at the end."

Kitchen Countertop Survivor™ Grade: Avg.

Your notes: _____

Brokenwood Shiraz, Australia

PC	T	V
$$$	24	24

"Soft tannins," a licorice scent, "chocolate and black cherries" on the palate, and good aging potential.

Kitchen Countertop Survivor™ Grade: B+

Your notes: _____

Brown Brothers Shiraz, Australia

PC	T	V
$	28	28

"Great fruit" that's "perfect for summer barbecue."

Kitchen Countertop Survivor™ Grade: B

Your notes: _____

Buckley's Shiraz, Australia

PC	T	V
$	24	29

"Good value" with coconut-raspberry and some pepper.

Kitchen Countertop Survivor™ Grade: B

Your notes: _____

Chapoutier Chateauneuf-du-Pape	PC	T	V
Le Bernardine, France	$$$	24	24

The scent of sun-warmed figs, leather, pepper, and touch of rosemary transports you to the south of France.

Kitchen Countertop Survivor™ Grade: B

Your notes: _____

Chapoutier Cotes-du-Rhone Rouge,	PC	T	V
France	$	24	18

Rustic pepper-cumin scent, silky strawberry-rhubarb flavor, awesome with herbed anything.

Kitchen Countertop Survivor™ Grade: A

Your notes: _____

Chateau de Beaucastel	PC	T	V
Chateauneuf-du-Pape, France	$$$$	24	21

Although it's "expensive," the Asian spice and leather scent and powerful fig and dark berry fruit are fabulous. Cellars beautifully.

Kitchen Countertop Survivor™ Grade: A+

Your notes: _____

Chateau La Nerthe (*shah-TOE lah*	PC	T	V
NAIRT) Chateauneuf-du-Pape,	$$$$	24	23
France			

The pepper/spicy/leathery scents, gripping tannins, and dried cranberry-anise flavors are textbook Chateauneuf, built for rich meats and stews.

Kitchen Countertop Survivor™ Grade: A

Your notes: _____

Cline Syrah,	PC	T	V
California	$	22	23

Cline puts vibrant berry fruit flavor and spicy-zingy scent in the bottle for a great price.

Kitchen Countertop Survivor™ Grade: B+

Your notes: _____

Price Ranges: **$** = $12 or less; **$$** = $12.01–20; **$$$** = $20.01–35; **$$$$** = > $35

Kitchen Countertop Survivor™ Grades: *Avg.* = a "one-day wine," tastes noticeably less fresh the next day; *B* = holds its freshness for 2–3 days after opening; *B+* = holds *and gets better* over 2–3 days after opening; *A* = a 3- to 4-day "freshness window"; *A+* = holds *and gets better* over 3–4 days

Columbia Winery Syrah,   PC   T   V
Washington $$ X   X

✗ Red plum, smoke and anise flavors, very smooth.

Kitchen Countertop Survivor™ Grade: Avg.

Your notes: _____

D'Arenberg The Footbolt Shiraz,   PC   T   V
Australia $$ 28   24

☺ "Intense and well balanced" wine: meaty-smoky, tangy berries, savory and sweet spices, all at a "nice price."

Kitchen Countertop Survivor™ Grade: B

Your notes: _____

Duboeuf (Georges) Cotes-du-Rhone PC   T   V
(*du-BUFF coat-duh-ROAN*), France $ 20   22

Juicy and fresh, with red cherry and spicy pomegranate.

Kitchen Countertop Survivor™ Grade: B

Your notes: _____

E & M Guigal (*ghee-GALL*)   PC   T   V
Cotes-du-Rhone, France $$ 23   23

A value from the famous Guigal name, with cherry fruit and pepper-spice notes.

Kitchen Countertop Survivor™ Grade: A

Your notes: _____

E & M Guigal Cote-Rotie Brune et PC   T   V
Blonde, France $$$$ 26   21

Is it the texture ("liquid velvet"), the scent ("pepper and lavender"), or flavor ("blackberry") that's most compelling? My tasters note: it "will age 20 years."

Kitchen Countertop Survivor™ Grade: B+

Your notes: _____

Gallo Family Vineyards Sonoma   PC   T   V
Reserve Syrah, California $ X   X

✗ The best Syrah at this price—deep berry fruit, with an alluring meaty quality. A meal in a glass!

Kitchen Countertop Survivor™ Grade: B

Your notes: _____

Goats Do Roam Red,   PC   T   V
South Africa $ 18   18

A tongue-in-cheek take on French Cotes-du-Rhone, with a South African flair from Pinotage in the blend. The result is meaty-peppery, dried cranberry flavors.

Kitchen Countertop Survivor™ Grade: Avg.

Your notes: _____

Greg Norman Shiraz,	PC	T	V
Australia	$$	20	20

It wasn't for everyone on my panel, but many liked the "smooth," "spicy" character at a "good price."

Kitchen Countertop Survivor™ Grade: Avg.

Your notes: _____

Hill of Content Grenache/Shiraz,	PC	T	V
Australia	$$	25	25

The raspberry scent, the ripe, jammy berry fruit taste, and juicy texture are de-lish!

Kitchen Countertop Survivor™ Grade: A

Your notes: _____

HRM Rex Goliath Shiraz,	PC	T	V
California	$	18	24

Sweet raspberry-vanilla, smoke, and soft spice.

Kitchen Countertop Survivor™ Grade: Avg.

Your notes: _____

Jaboulet (*jhah-boo-LAY*)	PC	T	V
Parallele 45 Cotes-du-Rhone,	$	24	26
France			

A budget Rhone with earthy red-berry fruit and smoky black pepper scents.

Kitchen Countertop Survivor™ Grade: B

Your notes: _____

Jacob's Creek Shiraz/Cabernet	PC	T	V
Sauvignon, Australia	$	23	26

"Great taste and great value," with exotic raspberry and eucalyptus notes and a plump texture.

Kitchen Countertop Survivor™ Grade: B+

Your notes: _____

Price Ranges: **$** = $12 or less; **$$** = $12.01–20; **$$$** = $20.01–35; **$$$$** = > $35

Kitchen Countertop Survivor™ Grades: *Avg.* = a "one-day wine," tastes noticeably less fresh the next day; *B* = holds its freshness for 2–3 days after opening; *B+* = holds *and gets better* over 2–3 days after opening; *A* = a 3- to 4-day "freshness window"; *A+* = holds *and gets better* over 3–4 days

Jade Mountain Napa Syrah,   PC   T   V
California $$$ 24   24

☺ The best California Syrah for the money, raspberry fruit, pepper-cumin-rosemary scent.

Kitchen Countertop Survivor™ Grade: B+
Your notes: _____

Joseph Phelps Le Mistral,   PC   T   V
California $$$ 26   20

This mainly Grenache-Syrah blend is "excellent," with strawberry-rhubarb fruit and zippy spice.

Kitchen Countertop Survivor™ Grade: B+
Your notes: _____

Joseph Phelps Pastiche (pah-STEESH) PC   T   V
Rouge, California $$ 27   24

A mixture of grapes similar to French Cotes-du-Rhone, with peppery spice and juicy strawberry-pomegranate fruit.

Kitchen Countertop Survivor™ Grade: B
Your notes: _____

La Vieille Ferme (*lah vee-yay*   PC   T   V
***FAIRM;* means "the old farm")** $ 21   26
Cotes-du-Ventoux, France

This raspberry-ripe, lively red is a tasting panel favorite, with "great character" for the price.

Kitchen Countertop Survivor™ Grade: B+
Your notes: _____

Lindemans Bin 50 Shiraz,   PC   T   V
Australia $ 27   26

✓ Ripe raspberry fruit and a black pepper scent; an all-around great drink and great buy.

Kitchen Countertop Survivor™ Grade: B+
Your notes: _____

Marquis Philips Sarah's Blend,   PC   T   V
Australia $$ 26   26

Shiraz, Cab, and Merlot, with "explosive fruit and spiciness" and "velvety" tannins.

Kitchen Countertop Survivor™ Grade: B
Your notes: _____

Penfolds Grange,   PC   T   V
Australia $$$$ 29   22

For most of us, one for the "once in a lifetime" wine list, with coconut-dill-clove-eucalyptus scent, the deepest raspberry fruit you can imagine, endless finish.

Kitchen Countertop Survivor™ Grade: B+

Your notes: _____

Penfolds Kalimna Shiraz Bin 28, Australia

	PC	T	V
	$$$	26	23

☺ Real-deal Aussie Shiraz—it's full of black pepper, plum compote flavors, and thick velvety tannins.

Kitchen Countertop Survivor™ Grade: B

Your notes: _____

Penfolds Koonunga Hill Shiraz Cabernet, Australia

	PC	T	V
	$	23	23

☺ You can't beat this plummy, slightly spicy red for easy drinkability, yet with some nice tannic grip.

Kitchen Countertop Survivor™ Grade: Avg.

Your notes: _____

Peter Lehmann Clancy's Shiraz, Australia

	PC	T	V
	$$	X	X

✗ Amazing cinnamon-clove spice and blackberry fruit.

Kitchen Countertop Survivor™ Grade: B+

Your notes: _____

Red Bicyclette Syrah, France

	PC	T	V
	$	X	X

✗ While the other varietals in this line are subpar, this is peppery and lively with rustic dried fruit flavor.

Kitchen Countertop Survivor™ Grade: Avg.

Your notes: _____

Rosemount Diamond Label Shiraz, Australia

	PC	T	V
	$	22	25

Still a "best buy" that counts legions of devotees to its signature raspberry taste and spice scent.

Kitchen Countertop Survivor™ Grade: B+

Your notes: _____

Price Ranges: **$** = $12 or less; **$$** = $12.01–20; **$$$** = $20.01–35; **$$$$** = > $35

Kitchen Countertop Survivor™ Grades: *Avg.* = a "one-day wine," tastes noticeably less fresh the next day; *B* = holds its freshness for 2–3 days after opening; *B+* = holds *and gets better* over 2–3 days after opening; *A* = a 3- to 4-day "freshness window"; *A+* = holds *and gets better* over 3–4 days

Rosemount Diamond Label Shiraz/ PC   T   V
Cabernet Sauvignon, Australia $ 21   21
Juicy, mouthwatering berry fruit, a touch of mint in
the scent, and a gentle tug of tannin.

Kitchen Countertop Survivor™ Grade: A
Your notes: _____

Rosemount GSM (Grenache-Shiraz- PC   T   V
Mourvedre), Australia $$$ 27   23
☺ This "wow" wine shows all the hallmarks of blends
from these three Rhone red grapes—both savory and
sweet spices; smoky/meaty scent, and rich, jammy
black cherry and blueberry flavors.

Kitchen Countertop Survivor™ Grade: A
Your notes: _____

Sterling Vintner's Collection   PC   T   V
Shiraz, California $ X   X
✗ Balsamic-y fig fruit, vanilla, and licorice.

Kitchen Countertop Survivor™ Grade: Avg.
Your notes: _____

Toasted Head Shiraz,   PC   T   V
California $$ X   X
✗ The meaty-raspberry flavor is like a meal; great value.

Kitchen Countertop Survivor™ Grade: B
Your notes: _____

Val d'Orbieu La Cuvee Mythique,   PC   T   V
France $ 24   24
Balanced, soft fruit, "mild pepper" in the finish.

Kitchen Countertop Survivor™ Grade: Avg.
Your notes: _____

Wolf Blass Yellow Label   PC   T   V
Shiraz, Australia $ 26   20
The black cherry and black pepper complexity make it
among the best for the price.

Kitchen Countertop Survivor™ Grade: Avg.
Your notes: _____

Wyndham Bin 555 Shiraz,   PC   T   V
Australia $ 22   24
This "always reliable" Aussie Shiraz is rich but
balanced and smooth, with "spicy plum" fruit.

Kitchen Countertop Survivor™ Grade: Avg.
Your notes: _____

Yellow Tail Shiraz,	**PC**	**T**	**V**
Australia	**$**	**19**	**23**

I agree it's "not as good as their Chardonnay," but most of my tasters call it a "good quaff" at an "unbeatable price."

Kitchen Countertop Survivor™ Grade: Avg.

Your notes: _____

Red Zinfandel

Category Profile: *Groupie* is the apt moniker for devotees of this California specialty, which ranges in style from medium-bodied, with bright and juicy raspberry flavors, to lush, full-bodied, and high in alcohol with intense blueberry, licorice, and even chocolate scents and flavors. Many of the best vineyards have old vines that produce some amazingly intense, complex wines. Zins usually are oaky—a little or a lot, depending on the intensity of the grapes used. The grape intensity is a function of the vineyard—its age and its location. California's most famous red Zinfandel areas are Sonoma (especially the Dry Creek Valley subdistrict), Napa, Amador, and the Sierra foothills. Lodi, in California's Central Valley, is also a good source.

Serve: Room temperature; aeration enhances the aroma and flavor.

When: Value Zinfandels are excellent for everyday drinking; good restaurant lists usually have a selection worth exploring across the price spectrum.

With: Burgers, pizza, lamb (especially with Indian or Moroccan spices), and quality cheeses are favorites— even dark chocolate!

In: An all-purpose wineglass or a larger-bowled red wine stem.

Price Ranges: **$** = $12 or less; **$$** = $12.01–20; **$$$** = $20.01–35; **$$$$** = > $35

Kitchen Countertop Survivor™ Grades: ***Avg.*** = a "one-day wine," tastes noticeably less fresh the next day; ***B*** = holds its freshness for 2–3 days after opening; ***B+*** = holds *and gets better* over 2–3 days after opening; ***A*** = a 3- to 4-day "freshness window"; ***A+*** = holds *and gets better* over 3–4 days

Beaulieu Vineyard Napa Valley   PC   T   V
Zinfandel, California $$ 20   20

Tasters recommend this wine's "jammy" fruit flavors "with grilled steaks."

Kitchen Countertop Survivor™ Grade: Avg.

Your notes: _____

Blackstone Zinfandel,   PC   T   V
California $$ X   X

✗ "Molasses and fig" scent, with powerful plum jam fruit.

Kitchen Countertop Survivor™ Grade: Avg.

Your notes: _____

Bogle Old Vines Zinfandel,   PC   T   V
California $ 24   26

☺ The "great fruit and berry flavor" and "kind of chewy texture" are typical of old-vines Zinfandel.

Kitchen Countertop Survivor™ Grade: Avg.

Your notes: _____

Cline Zinfandel,   PC   T   V
California $ 21   21

Lots of spice and fruit "for a great price" prompted tasters to describe this as "the perfect house wine."

Kitchen Countertop Survivor™ Grade: Avg.

Your notes: _____

Clos du Bois Sonoma Zinfandel,   PC   T   V
California $$ 19   20

Sweet oak in the scent, raspberry fruit, soft tannins. To me, it tops their more popular Merlot, and it's cheaper.

Kitchen Countertop Survivor™ Grade: B

Your notes: _____

Dancing Bull Zinfandel,   PC   T   V
California $ 24   26

The "nice fruit and spice" are great every day for sipping, and pairing with bold foods.

Kitchen Countertop Survivor™ Grade: Avg.

Your notes: _____

Dashe Cellars Dry Creek Zinfandel,   PC   T   V
California $$$ 24   22

"Phenomenal" inky complexity that "makes you want to crawl inside the glass" of ripe fig, spice, and licorice.

Kitchen Countertop Survivor™ Grade: Avg.
Your notes: _____

Dry Creek Vineyard Reserve   PC   T   V
Zinfandel, California   \$\$\$ 23   22

A perfect introduction to old-vines Zin—"blueberries and chocolate," as one of my sommelier buddies describes the flavor, with thick and velvety tannins.
Kitchen Countertop Survivor™ Grade: A
Your notes: _____

Fetzer Valley Oaks Zinfandel,   PC   T   V
California   \$ 24   21

Juicy, spicy, nice cherry flavors and the consistency you can count on from Fetzer's Valley Oaks line.
Kitchen Countertop Survivor™ Grade: B+
Your notes: _____

Gallo Family Vineyards Zinfandel,   PC   T   V
California   \$ X   X

✗ Probably the most delicious, juicy-jam Zin at this price.
Kitchen Countertop Survivor™ Grade: B+
Your notes: _____

Girard Old Vine Zinfandel,   PC   T   V
California   \$\$\$ 24   18

"Earthy, loaded with pepper" and ripe fig fruit, and a lot better balanced than most big California Zins these days.
Kitchen Countertop Survivor™ Grade: B+
Your notes: _____

Grgich Hills Napa Zinfandel,   PC   T   V
California   \$\$\$ 26   22

This wine's complexity, firm structure, and restraint deliver the power of Zin, with a subtle scent and flavor—cherry fruit, spice, and oak.
Kitchen Countertop Survivor™ Grade: A
Your notes: _____

Price Ranges: **\$** = \$12 or less; **\$\$** = \$12.01–20; **\$\$\$** = \$20.01–35; **\$\$\$\$** = > \$35
Kitchen Countertop Survivor™ Grades: ***Avg.*** = a "one-day wine," tastes noticeably less fresh the next day; ***B*** = holds its freshness for 2–3 days after opening; ***B+*** = holds *and gets better* over 2–3 days after opening; ***A*** = a 3- to 4-day "freshness window"; ***A+*** = holds *and gets better* over 3–4 days

Joel Gott Zinfandel,   PC   T   V
California $$ 22   24

The exotic style—blueberry pie filling and licorice—
might make you think "pricey," but not so. Yay!

Kitchen Countertop Survivor™ Grade: B+
Your notes: _____

Kendall-Jackson Vintner's Reserve   PC   T   V
Zinfandel, California $ 20   19

Some mixed reviews here, but most tasters consider it
"solid," as do I. It drinks nicely by itself and with bold
food, especially anything from the grill.

Kitchen Countertop Survivor™ Grade: B
Your notes: _____

Kenwood Jack London Zinfandel,   PC   T   V
California $$$ 24   18

✗ Big and chewy, with blueberry, licorice, and raisin
flavors.

Kitchen Countertop Survivor™ Grade: Avg.
Your notes: _____

Laurel Glen Reds,   PC   T   V
California $ 22   24

As one taster put it: "Fabulous flavor in a Zin 'field
blend'. Great with food, great alone, great value."

Kitchen Countertop Survivor™ Grade: B
Your notes: _____

Louis Martini Monte Rosso Gnarly   PC   T   V
Vines Zinfandel, California $$$$ X   X

✗ A big Zin for a modest price, with intense spice and
fig fruit but also great balance and structure.

Kitchen Countertop Survivor™ Grade: B
Your notes: _____

Montevina Amador Zinfandel,   PC   T   V
California $ 21   20

Classic Amador Zin: leathery, savory-spice scent
(think cumin and cardamom), prune and licorice
flavors, and a firm tannic grip.

Kitchen Countertop Survivor™ Grade: B+
Your notes: _____

Murphy-Goode Liar's Dice   PC   T   V
Zinfandel, California $$ 27   25

"Dense black cherry" flavor, vanilla oak, and spice that
"blows away" even more expensive Zins.

Kitchen Countertop Survivor™ *Grade: Avg.*
Your notes: _____

Rabbit Ridge Paso Robles | PC | T | V
Zinfandel, California | $$ | 21 | 24

Formerly a Sonoma Zin specialist now in Paso Robles. Look for "gulpable" wild berry fruit, spice, and smooth tannins.

Kitchen Countertop Survivor™ *Grade: Avg.*
Your notes: _____

Rafanelli Zinfandel, | PC | T | V
California | $$$$ | 26 | 24

One of my favorite Zins. The huge chocolate and blueberry flavors and chewy texture are big yet balanced.

Kitchen Countertop Survivor™ *Grade: B+*
Your notes: _____

Rancho Zabaco Dry Creek Valley | PC | T | V
Zinfandel, California | $$ | 27 | 21

This is textbook Dry Creek Zin—blueberry compote flavors, sweet spice, thick and juicy texture.

Kitchen Countertop Survivor™ *Grade: Avg.*
Your notes: _____

Rancho Zabaco Heritage Vines | PC | T | V
Zinfandel, California | $$ | 24 | 21

"The price went up," but it's still rustic and thick with dried-cherry fruit and tobacco.

Kitchen Countertop Survivor™ *Grade: B*
Your notes: _____

Rancho Zabaco Russian River | PC | T | V
Zinfandel, California | $$$ | X | X

✗ A Zin mouthful: raspberry jam, sweet spice, and vanilla.

Kitchen Countertop Survivor™ *Grade: B+*
Your notes: _____

Price Ranges: **$** = $12 or less; **$$** = $12.01–20; **$$$** = $20.01–35; **$$$$** = > $35

Kitchen Countertop Survivor™ Grades: *Avg.* = a "one-day wine," tastes noticeably less fresh the next day; *B* = holds its freshness for 2–3 days after opening; *B+* = holds *and gets better* over 2–3 days after opening; *A* = a 3- to 4-day "freshness window"; *A+* = holds *and gets better* over 3–4 days

Rancho Zabaco Stefani Zinfandel,   PC   T   V
California $$$ X   X

✗ Blueberries and chocolate! Big, juicy, not too pricey.

Kitchen Countertop Survivor™ Grade: B

Your notes: _____

Ravenswood Belloni Zinfandel,   PC   T   V
California $$$ X   X

✗ Chewy and ripe with boysenberry, tobacco, sweet spice.

Kitchen Countertop Survivor™ Grade: B

Your notes: _____

Ravenswood Sonoma Old Vines   PC   T   V
Zinfandel, California $$ 23   23

Chock-full of "spice," "zest," and fig fruit, this is a "can't go wrong" bottling from one of California's best Zin producers.

Kitchen Countertop Survivor™ Grade: B

Your notes: _____

Ravenswood Vintners Blend   PC   T   V
Zinfandel, California $ 22   22

This classic gets high marks for taste and value, with blueberry and spice flavors and a "yummy juiciness."

Kitchen Countertop Survivor™ Grade: A

Your notes: _____

Renwood Sierra Zinfandel,   PC   T   V
California $$ 23   21

The "flavors of raspberry and spice," meaty-leathery scent, and plump tannins are classic Amador Zin.

Kitchen Countertop Survivor™ Grade: Avg.

Your notes: _____

Ridge Geyserville (Zinfandel),   PC   T   V
California $$$ 28   22

☺ ✓ This wine garners raves from my tasters. The scent is complex cedar, savory-sweet spice, and dark fruit that's very intense and velvety.

Kitchen Countertop Survivor™ Grade: A+

Your notes: _____

Robert Mondavi Napa Zinfandel,   PC   T   V
California $$ 24   24

A "chewy" Zin with plush but gripping tannins, plus lots of red cherry fruit and sweet cinnamon spice.

Kitchen Countertop Survivor™ Grade: Avg.
Your notes: _____

Rombauer Zinfandel,   PC   T   V
California $$$ 28   18
A "big fruit forward" Zin with "succulent dark cherry."
Kitchen Countertop Survivor™ Grade: B
Your notes: _____

Rosenblum Zinfandel Vintner's   PC   T   V
Cuvee, California $ 23   23
The luscious blueberry fruit makes this "slurpable"
and a "best under $10 Zin."
Kitchen Fridge Survivor™ Grade: B
Your notes: _____

Seghesio Sonoma Zinfandel,   PC   T   V
California $$ 25   24
"What a great deal," say my tasters because it offers
real Sonoma character—wild-berry fruit, dried
spices—at an affordable price.
Kitchen Countertop Survivor™ Grade: Avg.
Your notes: _____

Talus Zinfandel,   PC   T   V
California $ X   X
✗ Just delish for the money—wild berries, spice, and
licorice.
Kitchen Countertop Survivor™ Grade: Avg.
Your notes: _____

Woodbridge Fish Net Creek Old   PC   T   V
Vine Zinfandel, California $ X   X
✗ For the price, amazingly plush and complex, with
scents of fig preserves, anise, sweet spice, and savory
herbs.
Kitchen Countertop Survivor™ Grade: B
Your notes: _____

Price Ranges: **$** = $12 or less; **$$** = $12.01–20; **$$$** = $20.01–35;
$$$$ = > $35
Kitchen Countertop Survivor™ Grades: ***Avg.*** = a "one-day wine,"
tastes noticeably less fresh the next day; ***B*** = holds its freshness for
2–3 days after opening; ***B+*** = holds *and gets better* over 2–3 days
after opening; ***A*** = a 3- to 4-day "freshness window"; ***A+*** = holds *and
gets better* over 3–4 days

Woodbridge (Robert Mondavi)   PC   T   V
Zinfandel, California $ 24   24

The best varietal in the Woodbridge line, with nice ripe plump fruit.

Kitchen Countertop Survivor™ Grade: Avg.

Your notes: _____

DESSERT WINES

Category Profile: There are plenty of great and available dessert wines to choose from, many of them affordable enough to enjoy often, with or instead of dessert (they're fat free!). These are dessert selections suggested by my tasters and by me. I hope you'll try them, because they will really jazz up your wine and food life.

Serve: Serving temperature depends on the wine, so see the individual entries.

When: With dessert, or as dessert; the lighter ones also make nice aperitifs. If you like to entertain, they're great. Add fruit, cheese, or some cookies, and you have a very classy end to a meal with very low hassle.

With: Blue cheese, chocolate, or simple cookies (like biscotti or shortbread) are classic.

In: An all-purpose wineglass or a smaller wineglass (the standard serving is 3 ounces rather than the traditional 6 for most wines).

Banfi Brachetto d'Acqui,   PC   T   V
Italy $$$ 26   26

This "great for a summer afternoon with chocolate" has delicious juicy-berry flavor that seems to always surprise and delight.

Kitchen Countertop Survivor™ Grade: B

Your notes: _____

Baron Philippe de Rothschild   PC   T   V
Sauternes, France $$$ 22   20

The classic and beautiful honeyed, crème brûlée, and peach scent and flavors of true Sauternes.

Kitchen Countertop Survivor™ Grade: A

Your notes: _____

Blandy's 10-Year-Old Malmsey Madeira, Portugal

	PC	T	V
	$$$$	24	20

Caramel, burnt sugar, toffee, burnt orange, toasted nuts, spice, and a cut of tangy acidity. Pair with chocolate!

Kitchen Countertop Survivor™ Grade: A+

Your notes: _____

Bonny Doon Muscat Vin de Glaciere (*van duh glahss-YAIR*), California

	PC	T	V
	$$$	25	23

Lush passion fruit and peach flavor. Great price.

Kitchen Fridge Survivor™ Grade: A

Your notes: _____

Broadbent 3 Year Fine Rich Madeira, Portugal

	PC	T	V
	$$	20	23

A great starter Madeira, giving you the candied orange peel–toffee-caramel character at an easy price.

Kitchen Fridge Survivor™ Grade: A+

Your notes: _____

Campbell's Rutherglen Muscat, Australia

	PC	T	V
	$$$	24	18

"Liquid Fig Newtons!" Stunning with chocolate.

Kitchen Fridge Survivor™ Grade: A+

Your notes: _____

Chambers Rosewood Vineyards Rutherglen Muscadelle, Australia

	PC	T	V
	$$$	23	23

A deep, viscous flavor of dried figs and toasted nuts.

Kitchen Fridge Survivor™ Grade: A+

Your notes: _____

Chapoutier Muscat de Beaumes de Venise, France

	PC	T	V
	$$	22	20

An alluring candied orange peel and honeysuckle scent and peach flavor.

Kitchen Countertop Survivor™ Grade: B

Your notes: _____

Price Ranges: **$** = $12 or less; **$$** = $12.01–20; **$$$** = $20.01–35; **$$$$** = > $35

Kitchen Countertop Survivor™ Grades: ***Avg.*** = a "one-day wine," tastes noticeably less fresh the next day; ***B*** = holds its freshness for 2–3 days after opening; ***B+*** = holds *and gets better* over 2–3 days after opening; ***A*** = a 3- to 4-day "freshness window"; ***A+*** = holds *and gets better* over 3–4 days

Chateau Rabaud-Promis (*shah-TOE rah-BOW pro-MEE*) Sauternes, France

	PC	T	V
	$$$$	24	20

"Like honey," with the scent of flowers, honey, peach preserves, and a hint of earth.

Kitchen Fridge Survivor™ Grade: B+

Your notes: _____

Cockburn's Fine Ruby Port, Portugal

	PC	T	V
	$	20	22

Enjoy this fig-and-spice-flavored dessert wine over many weeks, as the leftovers hold up well.

Kitchen Fridge Survivor™ Grade: A+

Your notes: _____

Covey Run Semillon Ice Wine, Washington

	PC	T	V
	$$$$	X	X

✗ Pineapple and candied orange peel; zesty acidity.

Kitchen Countertop Survivor™ Grade: B+

Your notes: _____

Dow's Colheita Tawny Port 1992, Portugal

	PC	T	V
	$$$	X	X

✗ Vintage tawny is rare, yet still a steal for the quality; toasted walnuts, caramel, toffee—wow!

Kitchen Countertop Survivor™ Grade: A

Your notes: _____

Emilio Lustau Pedro Ximenez "San Emilio" (*eh-MEE-lee-oh LOO-stau Pedro Hee-MEN-ez san eh-MEE-lee-oh*) Sherry, Spain

	PC	T	V
	$$$	28	24

Redolent with fig flavors and "lovely with all chocolate desserts."

Kitchen Fridge Survivor™ Grade: A+

Your notes: _____

Ferreira Doña Antonia Port, Portugal

	PC	T	V
	$$	24	24

Tawny-style Port—all amber gold color, toasted nut, cinnamon sugar, cappuccino, and maple scents and flavors.

Kitchen Countertop Survivor™ Grade: A+

Your notes: _____

Ficklin Tinta "Port,"   PC   T   V
California $$ 21   23

A very worthy version of the Port style, with chocolate, nuts, dried figs, and sweet spices.

Kitchen Countertop Survivor™ Grade: A+

Your notes: _____

Fonseca Bin 27 Port,   PC   T   V
Portugal $$ 23   23

This is Port in the ruby style, with flavors of ripest figs, licorice, and allspice. Yum!

Kitchen Countertop Survivor™ Grade: A+

Your notes: _____

Hogue Late Harvest Riesling,   PC   T   V
Washington $ 25   25

Lightly sweet with a "hint of malt flavor." Great price and convenient screw-top package.

Kitchen Countertop Survivor™ Grade: Avg.

Your notes: _____

Inniskillin Riesling Ice Wine,   PC   T   V
Canada $$$$ 28   18

"Pricey" but "worth it," with "creamy, rich" fruit.

Kitchen Countertop Survivor™ Grade: A

Your notes: _____

Leacock's Rainwater Madeira,   PC   T   V
Portugal $$ X   X

✗ Toffee and orange zest with a tangy lemon drop finish.

Kitchen Countertop Survivor™ Grade: A

Your notes: _____

Michele Chiarlo Nivole ("Clouds")   PC   T   V
Moscato d'Asti, Italy $$$ 29   23

Honeysuckle-scented, low in alcohol, high in fruit (apricot and tangerine) and refreshment.

Kitchen Countertop Survivor™ Grade: B

Your notes: _____

Price Ranges: **$** = $12 or less; **$$** = $12.01–20; **$$$** = $20.01–35; **$$$$** = > $35

Kitchen Countertop Survivor™ Grades: *Avg.* = a "one-day wine," tastes noticeably less fresh the next day; *B* = holds its freshness for 2–3 days after opening; *B+* = holds *and gets better* over 2–3 days after opening; *A* = a 3- to 4-day "freshness window"; *A+* = holds *and gets better* over 3–4 days

Rivetti Moscato d'Asti La Spinetta,   PC   T   V
Italy $$ 23   24

I agree it's the "gold standard by which all others should be judged" in the category of Moscato d'Asti (the Moscato grape from the town of Asti). The honeysuckle, orange blossom, and apricot scent and flavor are gorgeous, and the light alcohol makes it a "great brunch wine."

Kitchen Countertop Survivor™ *Grade: B+*

Your notes: _____

RL Buller Fine Muscat,   PC   T   V
Australia $$$ 26   27

Syrupy "toffee, coffee, and caramel" makes it "the perfect soak for pound cake."

Kitchen Countertop Survivor™ *Grade: A*

Your notes: _____

St. Supery Moscato,   PC   T   V
California $$ 27   21

"A wonderful dessert wine" with the scent of honeysuckles and the flavor of spiced apricots.

Kitchen Fridge Survivor™ *Grade: B+*

Your notes: _____

Smith Woodhouse Lodge Reserve   PC   T   V
Port, Portugal $$$ X   X

✗ Dried figs, dates, and berry syrup; long finish.

Kitchen Countertop Survivor™ *Grade: A*

Your notes: _____

Taylor Fladgate 20 Year Tawny   PC   T   V
Port, Portugal $$$$ 24   19

"Pricey" due to the decades of aging, but complex—toasted walnuts, streusel, and caramel.

Kitchen Fridge Survivor™ *Grade: Avg.*

Your notes: _____

Warre 10-Year-Old Otima Tawny   PC   T   V
Port, Portugal $$$ 22   16

The "nut flavor" and "smooth, warming texture" are classic to tawny Port; a touch sweet but not at all cloying.

Kitchen Fridge Survivor™ *Grade: A+*

Your notes: _____

THE GREAT WINE MADE SIMPLE MINI-COURSE: A WINE CLASS IN A GLASS

How do you go about choosing wine? The best way to ensure you'll be happy with your wine choices is to learn your taste.

Here are two quick wine lessons, adapted from my book *Great Wine Made Simple,* that will let you do exactly that. You're probably thinking, Will there be a test? In a way, every pulled cork is a test, but for the *wine:* Are you happy with what you got for the price you paid, and would you buy it again? This mini-course will teach you to pick wines that pass muster by helping you learn what styles and tastes you like in a wine and how to use the label to help you find them.

If you want, you can complete each lesson in a matter of minutes. As with food, tasting impressions form quickly with wine. Then you can get dinner on the table, accompanied by your wine picks. Start by doing the first lesson, "White Wine Made Simple," one evening, and then Lesson 2, "Red Wine Made Simple," another time. Or you can invite friends over and make it a party. Everyone will learn a little bit about wine, while having fun.

Setup

Glassware: You will need three glasses per taster. A simple all-purpose wineglass is ideal, but clear disposables are fine, too.

Pouring: Start with a tasting portion (about an ounce of each wine). Tasters can repour more of their favorite to enjoy with hors d'oeuvres or dinner.

Flights: Taste the Lesson 1 whites first and then the Lesson 2 reds (pros call each sequence of wine a *flight*). There is no need to wash or rinse the glasses.

To Taste It Is to Know It

Tasting is the fastest way to learn about wine. My restaurant guests tell me this all the time: They know what wines they like when they try them. The trick is in understanding the style and knowing how to ask for it and get it again: "I'd like a Chardonnay with lots of buttery, toasty oak and gobs of creamy, tropical fruit flavors." If you don't know what it means, you might feel silly offering a description like that when wine shopping. But those words really are in the glass, and these easy-to-follow tasting lessons will help you recognize the styles and learn which ones are your favorites.

The Lessons

What You'll Do:

For Lesson 1, "White Wine Made Simple," you will comparison-taste three major white wine grapes: Riesling, Sauvignon Blanc, and Chardonnay. For Lesson 2, "Red Wine Made Simple," you will compare three major reds: Pinot Noir, Merlot, and Cabernet Sauvignon. Follow these easy steps:

1. Buy your wines. Make your choice from the varietal sections of this book. It's best to choose wines in the same price category—for example, all one-dollar-sign wines. To make the most of the lesson, choose wines from the region(s) suggested in each grape's "tasting notes."
2. Chill (whites only), pour, and taste the wines in the order of body, light to full, as shown in the tasting notes.
3. Use the tasting notes as a guide, and record your own if you want.

What You'll Learn:

Body styles of the major grapes—light, medium, or full. You'll see that Riesling is lighter (less heavy) than Chardonnay, in the same way that, for example, skim milk is lighter than heavy cream.

What the major grapes taste like—When tasted side by side, the grapes are quite distinctive, just as a pear tastes different from an apple, a strawberry tastes different from a blueberry, and so on.

What other wine flavor words taste like—Specifically, you'll experience these tastes: oaky, tannic, crisp, and fruity. Knowing them is helpful because they're used a lot in this book, on wine bottle labels, and by sellers of wine—merchants, waiters, and so on.

Getting comfortable with these basics will equip you to describe the wine styles you like to a waiter or wine merchant and to use the information on a bottle label to find those styles on your own. In the "Buying Lingo" section that follows, I've defined lots of other style words and listed some wine types you can try to experience them.

Tasting Lesson 1
WHITE WINE MADE SIMPLE

Instructions: Taste the wines in numbered order. Note your impressions of:

Color: Which is lightest and which is darkest? Whites can range from pale straw to deep yellow-gold. The darker the color, the fuller the body.

Scent: While they all smell like white wine, the aromas differ, from delicate and tangy to rich and fruity.

Taste and Body: In the same way that fruits range from crisp and tart (like apples) to ripe and lush (like mangoes), the wine tastes will vary along with the body styles of the grapes, from light to full.

Which grape and style do you like best? If you like more than one style, that's great, too!

The White Wines

Grape 1: Riesling (any region)—light bodied

Description: Crisp and refreshing, with vibrant fruit flavor ranging from apple to peach.

Brand name:_____

Your notes: _____

_____

Grape 2: Sauvignon Blanc (France or New Zealand)—medium bodied

Description: Very distinctive! The smell is exotically pungent, the taste tangy and mouthwatering, like citrus fruit (lime and grapefruit).

Brand name:_____

Your notes: _____

_____

Grape 3: Chardonnay (California)—full bodied

Description: The richest scent and taste, with fruit flavor ranging from ripe apples to peaches to tropical fruits. You can feel the full-bodied texture, too. "Oaky" scents come through as a sweet, buttery, or toasty impression.

Brand name: _____

Your notes: _____

_____

Tasting Lesson 2
RED WINE MADE SIMPLE

Instructions: Again, taste the wines in numbered order and note your impressions.

Color: Red wines range in color from transparent ruby, like the Pinot Noir, to inky dark purple—the darker the color, the fuller the body.

Scent: In addition to the smell of "red wine," you'll get the cherrylike smell of Pinot Noir, perhaps plum character in the Merlot, and a rich dark-berry smell in the Cabernet. There are other scents, too, so enjoy them. You can also compare your impressions with those included in the reviews section of the book.

Taste and Body: Like white wines, red wines range from light and delicate to rich and intense. You'll note the differences in body from light to full and the distinctive taste character of each grape. As you can see, tasting them side by side makes it easy to detect and compare the differences.

The Red Wines

Grape 1: Pinot Noir (any region)—light bodied

Description: Delicate cherrylike fruit flavor, silky-smooth texture, mouthwatering acidity, all of which make Pinot Noir a versatile wine for most types of food.

Brand name: _____

Your notes: _____

_____

Grape 2: Merlot (California, Chile, or Washington)—medium bodied

Description: More intense than Pinot Noir: rich "red wine" flavor, yet not too heavy. That's probably why it's so popular!

Brand name:_____

Your notes:_____

_____

Grape 3: Cabernet Sauvignon (Chile or California)—full bodied

Description: The fullest-bodied, most intense taste. Notice the drying sensation it leaves on your tongue? That's tannin, a natural grape component that, like color, comes from the skin. As you can see, more color and more tannin come together. Tasting high-tannin wines with fat or protein counters that drying sensation (that's why Cabernet and red meat are considered classic partners). In reds, an "oaky" character comes through as one or more of these scents: spice, cedar, smoke, toastiness, vanilla, and coconut. No wonder buyers love it!

Brand name:_____

Your notes:_____

_____

Buying Lingo

Here are the meanings of other major wine style words that you see in this book and on wine bottles.

Acidity—The tangy, tart, crisp, mouthwatering component in wine. It's a prominent characteristic of Riesling, Sauvignon Blanc, and Pinot Grigio whites and Pinot Noir and Chianti/Sangiovese reds.

Bag-in-a-Box—A box with a wine-filled bag inside that deflates as the wine is consumed, preventing oxidation.

Balance—The harmony of all the wine's main components: fruit, alcohol, and acidity, plus sweetness (if any), oak (if used in the wine making), and tannin (in reds). As with food, balance in the wine is important to your enjoyment, and a sign of quality. But it's also a matter of taste—the dish may taste "too salty" and the wine "too oaky" for one person but be fine to another.

Barrel aged / barrel fermented—The wine was aged or fermented (or both) in oak barrels. The barrels give fuller body as well as an "oaky" character to the wine's scent and flavor, making it seem richer. "Oaky" scents are often in the sweet family—but *not* sugary. Rather, *toasty, spicy, vanilla, buttery,* and *coconut* are the common wine words to describe "oaky" character. Other label signals that mean "oaky": Barrel Fermented, Barrel Select, Barrel Cuvee, Cask Fermented.

Bouquet—All of the wine's scents, which come from the grape(s) used, the techniques (like oak aging), the age of the wine, and the vineyard characteristics (like soil and climate).

Bright—Vivid and vibrant. Usually used as a modifier, like "bright fruit" or "bright acidity."

Buttery—Literally, the creamy-sweet smell of butter. One by-product of fermentation is an ester that mimics the butter smell, so you may well notice this in some wines, especially barrel-fermented Chardonnays.

Corked, corky—Refers to a wine whose scent or taste has been tainted by corks or wine-making equipment infected with a bacteria called TCA. While not harmful to health, TCA gives wines a musty smell and taste.

Creamy—Can mean a smell similar to fresh cream or a smooth and lush texture. In sparkling wines, it's a textural delicacy and smoothness of the bubbles.

Crisp—See ACIDITY.

Dry—A wine without sweetness (though not without fruit; see FRUITY for more on this).

Earthy—As with cheeses, potatoes, mushrooms, and other good consumables, wines can have scents and flavors reminiscent of, or owing to, the soil. The "earth" terms commonly attributed to wine include *mushrooms, truffles, flint, dusty, gravelly, wet leaves,* and even *barnyard.*

Exotic—Just as it applies to other things, this description suggests unusual and alluring characteristics in wine. Quite often refers to wines with a floral or spicy style or flavors beyond your typical fruit bowl, such as tropical fruits or rare berries.

Floral—Having scents that mimic flower scents, whether fresh (as in the honeysuckle scent of some Rieslings) or dried (as in the wilted rose petal scent of some Gewurztraminers).

Food friendly—Food-friendly wines have taste characteristics that pair well with a wide variety of foods without clashing or overpowering— namely, good acidity and moderate (not too heavy) body. The food-friendly whites include Riesling and Sauvignon Blanc; the reds include Chianti, Spanish Rioja, red Rhone, and Pinot Noir wines.

Fruity—Marked by a prominent smell and taste of fruit. In whites the fruit tastes can range from lean and tangy (like lemons and crisp apples) to medium (like melons and peaches) to lush (like mangoes and pineapples). In reds, think cranberries and cherries, plums and blueberries, figs and prunes. Note that *fruity* doesn't mean "sweet." The taste and smell of ripe fruit are perceived as sweet, but they're not sugary. Most wines on the market are at once dry (meaning not sweet) and fruity, with lots of fruit flavor.

Grassy—Describes a wine marked with scents of fresh-cut grass or herbs or even green vegetables (like green pepper and asparagus). It's a signature of Sauvignon Blanc wines, especially those grown in New Zealand and France. *Herbal* and *herbaceous* are close synonyms.

Herbal, herbaceous—See GRASSY.

Legs—The drips running down the inside of the wineglass after you swirl it. Not a sign of quality (as in "good legs") but of viscosity. Fast-running legs indicate a low-viscosity wine and slow legs a high-viscosity wine. The higher the viscosity, the richer and fuller the wine feels in your mouth.

Nose—The smell of the wine. Isn't it interesting how wines have a nose, legs, and body? As you've no doubt discovered, they have personalities, too!

Oaky—See BARREL AGED.

Off-dry—A lightly sweet wine.

Old vines—Refers to wine from vines significantly older than average, usually at least 30 years old and sometimes far older. Older vines yield a smaller, but often more intensely flavored, crop of grapes.

Regional wine—A wine named for the region where the grapes are grown, such as Champagne, Chianti, and Pouilly-Fuisse.

Spicy—A wine with scents and flavors reminiscent of spices, both sweet (cinnamon, ginger, cardamom, clove) and savory (pepper, cumin, curry).

Sweet—A wine that has perceptible sugar, called *residual sugar* because it is left over from fermentation and not converted to alcohol. A wine can be lightly sweet like a Moscato or very sweet like a Port or Sauternes.

Tannic—A red wine whose tannin is noticeable— a little or a lot—as a drying sensation on your tongue ranging from gentle (lightly tannic) to velvety (richly tannic) to harsh (too tannic).

Terroir—The distinctive flavors, scents, and character of a wine owing to its vineyard source. For example, the terroir of French red Burgundies is sometimes described as *earthy*.

Toasty—Wines with a toasty, roasted, caramelized, or smoky scent reminiscent of coffee beans, toasted nuts or spices, or burnt sugar.

Unfiltered—A wine that has not been filtered before bottling (which is common practice). Some say filtering the wine strips out flavor, but not every-one agrees. I think most tasters cannot tell the difference.

Varietal wine—A wine named for the grape used to make it, such as Chardonnay or Merlot.

Handling Wine Leftovers

I developed the Kitchen Countertop Survivor™ and Kitchen Fridge Survivor™ grades to give you an idea of how long each wine stays in good drinking condi-tion if you don't finish the bottle. In the same way that resealing the cereal box or wrapping and refriger-ating leftovers will extend their freshness window, you can do the same for wine by handling the left-overs as follows:

Still Wines

Recork—At a minimum, close the bottle with its orig-inal cork. Most wines will stay fresh a day or two at normal room temperature. To extend that freshness-window, purchase a vacuum-sealer (available in kitchen-ware shops and wine shops). You simply cork the bottle with the purchased rubber stopper, which has a one-way valve. The accompanying plastic vacuum pump is then placed on top of the stopper; you pump the handle repeatedly until the resistance tightens, indicating the air has been pumped out of the bottle. (Note: A few wine experts don't think rubber stoppers work, but I have used them for years. In my restaurants, I have found they extended the life of bottles opened for by-the-glass service at least two days longer than just sealing with the original cork.)

Refrigerate stoppered (and vacuum-sealed) bottles, whether white, pink, or red. Refrigeration of anything slows the spoilage, and your red wine, once removed from the fridge and poured in the glass, will quickly come to serving temperature.

For even longer shelf-life, you can preserve partial bottles with inert gas. I recommend this especially for more expensive wines. Wine Life and Private Preserve are two brands that I have used (sold in wine shops and accessories catalogs). They come in a can that feels light, as if it were empty. Inside is an inert gas mixture that is heavier than air. The can's spray nozzle is inserted into the bottle. A one-second spray fills the empty bottle space with the inert gas, displacing the air inside, which is the key because no air in contact with the wine means no oxidation. Then you quickly replace the cork (make sure the fit is tight). My experience in restaurants using gas systems for very upscale wines by the glass is that they keep well for a week or more.

Sparkling Wines
Your best bet is to purchase "clam shell" Champagne stoppers, with one or two hinged metal clamps attached to a stopper top that has a rubber or plastic gasket for a tight seal. You place the stopper on top, press down, and then anchor the clamps to the bottle lip. If you open your sparkler carefully and don't "pop" the cork, losing precious carbonation, a stoppered partial bottle will keep its effervescence for at least a few days, and sometimes much longer.

SAVVY SHOPPER: RETAIL WINE BUYING

Supermarkets, pharmacies, price clubs, catalogs, state stores, megastores, dot.coms, and boutiques . . . where you shop for wine depends a lot on the state where you live, because selling wine requires a state license. What many people don't realize is how much the wine laws vary from one state to the next.

In most states, the regulations affect the prices you pay for wine, what wines are available, and how you get your hands on them (ideally, they are delivered to your door or poured at your table, but this isn't always legal). Here is a quick summary of the retail scene to help you make the most of your buying power wherever you live.

Wine Availability The single biggest frustration for every wine buyer and winery is bureaucracy. To ensure the collection of excise taxes, in nearly all states every single wine must be registered and approved in some way before it can be sold. If a wine you're seeking isn't available in your area, this is probably the reason. For many small boutique wineries, it just isn't worth the bother and expense to get legal approval for the few cases of wine they would sell in a particular state. One extreme example is Pennsylvania, a "control state" where wine is sold exclusively by a state-run monopoly that, without competition, has little incentive to source a lot of boutique wines. By contrast, California, New York, and Chicago, with high demand and competition, are good markets for wine availability.

Wine Prices and Discounts Wine prices can vary from one state to the next due to different tax rates. And in general, prices are lower in competitive markets, where stores can use discounts, sale prices, and so on to vie for your business.

Where they are legal, case discounts of 10% to 15% are a great way to get the best possible prices for your favorite wines. On the more expensive wines, many people I know coordinate their buying with friends and family so they can buy full cases and get these discounts.

Delivery and Wine-by-Mail In many states, it is not legal for stores or other retailers to deliver wine to the purchaser.

Many catalogs and Web sites sell wine by mail. Some are affiliated with retail stores or wineries, whereas others are strictly virtual stores. The conveniences include shopping on your own time and terms, from home or office, helpful buying recommendations and information, and usually home delivery. Keep in mind that the laws governing such shipping are complex, and vary from state to state (in some states it is completely prohibited).

Mail-order wine clubs are an interesting option when you are looking for new wines to try. For information on my own wine club, Andrea's A-List,™ visit my Web site, www.andreawine.com.

Where Should I Shop? That depends on what you're buying. If you know what you want, then price is your main consideration, and you'll get your best deals at venues that concentrate on volume sales— discount stores, price clubs, and so on. If you want buying advice, or are buying rare wines, you're better off in a wine shop or merchant specializing in collectible wines. These stores have trained buyers who taste and know their inventory well; they can help you with your decision. The better stores also have temperature-controlled storage for their rare wines, which is critical to ensure you get a product in good condition. There are also Web-based fine and rare wine specialists, but that is a fairly new market. I suggest you purchase fine and rare wines only through sources with a good track record of customer service. In that way, if you have problems with a shipment, you will have some recourse.

Can I Take That Bottle on the Wine List Home with Me? In most states, restaurants' wine licenses allow for sale and consumption "on-premise" only, meaning they cannot sell you a bottle to take home.

Burgundy Buyers, Beware With the exception of volume categories such as Beaujolais, Macon, and Pouilly-Fuissé, buyers of French white and red Burgundy should shop only at fine wine merchants, preferably those that specialize in Burgundy, for two reasons. First, Burgundy is simply too fragile to handle the storage conditions in most stores. Burgundy specialists ensure temperature-controlled storage. Second, selection is a major factor, because quality varies a lot from one winery to the next, and from one vintage to the next. Specialist stores have the needed buying expertise to ensure the quality of their offerings.

Is That a Deal or a Disaster? Floor stacks, "end caps," private labels, and bin ends can be a boon for the buyer, or a bust, depending on where you are shopping. Here's what you need to know about them:

"Floor Stacks" of large-volume categories and brands (e.g., branded varietal wines)—These are a best bet in supermarkets and other volume-based venues, where they're used to draw your attention to a price markdown. Take advantage of it to stock up for everyday or party wines.

"End Cap" wine displays featured at the ends of aisles—A good bet, especially in fine wine shops. You may not have heard of the wine, but they're usually "hidden gems" that the buyer discovered and bought in volume, to offer you quality and uniqueness at a savings.

"Bin Ends"—Retailers often clear out the last few bottles of something by discounting the price. In reputable retail stores, they are usually still good quality, and thus a good bet. Otherwise, steer clear.

Private labels—These are wines blended and bottled exclusively for the retailer—again, good bets in reputable stores, who stake their reputation on your satisfaction with their private labels.

"Shelf-talkers"—Written signs, reviews, and ratings. Good shops offer their own recommendations in lieu of, or along with, critics' scores. If the only information is a critic's score, check to be sure that the vintage being sold matches that of the wine that was reviewed.

BUYING WINE IN RESTAURANTS

Wine List Strategy Session

A lot of us have a love–hate relationship with the wine list. On the one hand, we know it holds the potential to enhance the evening, impress the date or client, broaden our horizons, or all three. But it also makes us feel intimidated, inadequate, overwhelmed, and . . .

Panicked by prices—That goes for both the cheapest wines *and* the most expensive ones; we're leery of extremes.

Pressured by pairing—Will this wine "go with" our food?

Overwhelmed by options—Can this wine I've never heard of possibly be any good? Does my selection measure up? (Remember, the restaurant is supposed to impress *you,* not the other way around.) This "phone book" wine list makes me want to dial 911.

Stumped by Styles—Food menus are easy because we understand the key terms: appetizer, entree, dessert, salad, soup, fish, meat, and so on. But after *white* and *red,* most of us get lost pretty quickly with wine categories. (Burgundy . . . is that a style, a color, a place, or all three?)

Let's deal with the first three above. For the lowdown on wine list terms, use the decoder that follows to pinpoint the grapes and styles behind all the major wine names.

Wine List Prices

The prices on wine lists reflect three things:

- *The dining-out experience*—The restaurant wine markup is higher than in retail stores because the decor is (usually) nicer, and you get to stay a while, during which time they open the wine, serve it in a nice glass, and clean up afterward.

They also may have invested in the cost and expertise to select and store the wine properly. Consequently those who enjoy drinking wine in restaurants are accustomed to being charged more for the wine than you would pay to drink the same bottle at home. That said, exorbitant markups are, in my opinion, the biggest deterrent to more guests enjoying wine in restaurants (which is both good for the guests and good for business). You can always vote with your wallet and dine in restaurants with guest-friendly wine pricing.

- *Location*—Restaurants in exclusive resorts, in urban centers with a business clientele, or with a star chef behind them, tend toward higher wine markups, because they can get away with it. The logic, so to speak, is that if you're on vacation, it's on the company, or it's just the "in" place, high markups (on everything) are part of the price of admission. However, I don't really think that's right, and I do think these places would sell more wine with lower markups.

- *The rarity of the wine*—Often, the rarer the wine (either because it's in high demand due to critics' hype or because it's old and just a few bottles remain), the higher the markup. It's a form of rationing in the face of high demand/low supply. Food can be the same way (lobsters, truffles, caviar, etc.).

Getting the Most Restaurant Wine for Your Money

Seeking value doesn't make you a cheapskate. Here are the best strategies to keep in mind:

1. Take the road less traveled—Chardonnay and Cabernet Sauvignon are what I call "comfort wines" because they're so well known. But their prices often reflect a "comfort premium" (in the same way that a name-brand toothpaste costs more than the store brand). These spectacular wine styles often give better value for the money, because they're less widely known:

   Whites
   Riesling
   Sauvignon Blanc and Fume Blanc

Sancerre (a French Loire Valley wine made
from the Sauvignon Blanc grape)
Anything from Washington State or New
Zealand

Reds
Cotes-du-Rhone and other French Rhone
Valley reds
Red Zinfandel from California
Spanish Rioja and other reds from Spain
Cabernet Sauvignon from Chile

2. Savvy Splurging—There's no doubt about it:
nothing commemorates, celebrates, or im-
presses better than a special wine. Since splurging on wine in a restaurant can mean especially
big bucks, here are the "trophy" wine styles that
give you the most for your money on wine lists:

French Champagne—I think that Champagne (the real stuff from France's Champagne region) is among the most affordable
luxuries on the planet, and its wine list
prices are often among the best of all the
"badge" wine categories (such as French
Bordeaux and Burgundy, cult California
Cabernets, and boutique Italian wines).

California's Blue Chip Cabernets—I don't
mean the tiny-production cult-movement
Cabernets but rather the classics that have
been around for decades, and still make
world-class wine at a fair price. Names
like Beringer, BV, Franciscan, Mt. Veeder,
Robert Mondavi, Silver Oak, Simi, and
Stag's Leap all made the survey, and for
good reason: they're excellent and available.

Italian Chianti Classico Riserva—This
recommendation may surprise you, but I
include it because the quality for the price
is better than ever, and recent vintages
have been great. I also think that across the
country a lot of people celebrate and do
business in steak houses and Italian restaurants, which tend to carry this wine category because it complements their food.

3. The Midprice/Midstyle "Safety Zone"—This is a strategy I first developed not for dining guests but for our *waiters* trying to help diners choose a bottle, usually with very little to go on (many people aren't comfortable describing their taste preference, and they rarely broadcast their budget for fear of looking cheap). The midprice/midstyle strategy is this: in any wine list category (e.g., Chardonnays and Italian reds), if you go for the midprice range in that section, odds are good the wine will be midstyle. Midstyle is my shorthand for the most typical, crowd-pleasing version, likely to satisfy a high proportion of guests and to be sticker shock free. The fact is that the more expensive the wine is, the more distinctive and even unusual its style is likely to be. If it's not to your taste *and* you've spent a lot, you're doubly disappointed.

4. Ask—With wine more popular than ever, restaurants are the most proactive they've ever been in seeking to put quality and value on their wine lists. So ask for it: "What's the best red wine deal on your list right now?" Or, if you have a style preference, say something like "We want to spend $XX. Which of these Chardonnays do you think is the best for the money?"

Pairing Wine and Food

Worrying a lot about this is a big waste of time, because most wines complement most foods, regardless of wine color, center-of-the-plate protein, and all that other stuff. How well? Their affinity can range from "fine" to "Omigod." You can pretty much expect at least a nice combination every time you have wine with food and great matches from time to time (of course, frequent experimentation ups your odds). The point is, your style preference is a lot more important than the pairing, per se, because if you hate the dish or the wine, you're hardly likely to enjoy the pairing. That said, here is a list of wine styles that are especially favored by sommeliers and chefs for their exceptional food affinity and versatility, along with a few best-bet food recommendations:

Favorite "Food Wines"	Best-Bet Food Matches
White	
Champagne and Sparkling Wine—So many people save bubbly just for toasts, but it's an amazing "food wine"	Sushi All shellfish Cheeses (even stinky ones) Omelets and other egg dishes Mushroom sauces (on risotto, pasta or whatever)
Riesling from Germany, Alsace (France), America, Australia	Mexican, southwestern, and other spicy foods Shellfish Cured meats and sausages
Alsace (France) White Wines—Riesling, Pinot Gris, and Gewurztraminer	Pacific Rim foods—Japanese, Thai, Korean, Chinese Indian food Smoked meats and charcuterie Meat stews (really!)
Sauvignon Blanc and wines made from it (French Sancerre, Pouilly-Fume, and white Bordeaux)	Goat cheese Salads Herbed sauces (like pesto) Tomato dishes (salads, soups, sauces)
Red	
Beaujolais (from France)	Mushroom dishes
Pinot Noir	Fish (especially rich ones like tuna, salmon, and cod) Smoked meats Grilled vegetables Duck
Chianti, Rosso di Montalcino, and other Italian reds made from the Sangiovese grape	Pizza, eggplant parmigiana (and other Italian-American–inspired tastes) Cheesy dishes Spicy sausages
Rioja from Spain	Roasted and grilled meats

Choosing from the Wine List

You've got the wine list. Unless you know a lot about wine, you now face at least one of these dilemmas:

- You've never heard of any of the wines listed or at least none of those in your price range. (Okay, maybe you've heard of Dom Pérignon, but let's be real.) Or the names you do recognize don't interest you.

- You have no idea how much a decent selection should cost. But you *do* know you want to keep to your budget, without broadcasting it to your guests and the entire dining room.
- The wine list is so huge you don't even want to open it.

Wine List Playbook

Remember, you're the buyer. Good restaurants want you to enjoy wine and to feel comfortable with the list, your budget, and so on. As far as the wine-snobby ones go, what are you doing there anyway? (Okay, if you took a gamble on a new place or somebody else picked it, the strategies here can help.)

The basics:

1. *Don't worry if you haven't heard of the names.* There are literally thousands of worthy wines beyond the big brand names, and many restaurants feature them to spice up their selection.
2. *Determine what you want to spend.* I think most people want the best deal they can get. With that in mind, here are some price/value rules of thumb. In most restaurants the wine prices tend to relate to the food prices, as follows:
   - Wines by-the-glass: The price window for good-quality wines that please a high percentage of diners usually parallels the restaurant's mid- to top-priced appetizers. So if the Caesar salad (or wings or whatever) is $5.95, expect to spend that, plus or minus a dollar or two, for a good glass of wine. This goes for dessert wine, too. Champagne and sparkling wines can be more, due to the cost of the product and greater waste because it goes flat.
   - Bottles: This is far more variable, but in general most restaurants try to offer an ample selection of good-quality bottles priced in what I call a "selling zone" that's benchmarked to their highest entree price, plus a margin. That's the variable part. It can range from $5–10 on average in national chain restaurants and their peers to at least $10–20 in luxury and destination restaurants. So if

the casual chain's steak-and-shrimp-scampi combo costs $17.95, the $20–30 zone on their wine list will likely hold plenty of good bottle choices. In an urban restaurant where the star chef's signature herb-crusted lamb costs $28, you could expect a cluster of worthy bottles in the $35–55 range.

We in the trade find it funny, and nearly universal, that guests shy away from the least expensive wines on our lists, suspicious that there's something "wrong" with the wine. But any restaurant that's committed to wine, whether casual chain or destination eatery, puts extra effort into finding top-quality wines at the lowest price points. They may come from grapes or regions you don't know, but my advice is to muster your sense of adventure and try them. In the worst-case scenario, you'll be underwhelmed, but since tastes vary, this can happen with wine at any price. I think the odds are better that you'll enjoy one of the best deals on the wine list.

The wine list transaction: You've set your budget. Now it's time to zero in on a selection. You've got two choices—go it alone or ask for help. In either case, here's what to do:

1. Ask for the wine list right away. It's a pet peeve of mine that guests even *need* to ask (rather than getting the list automatically with the food menus), because that can cause both service delays and anxiety. Many people are scared to request the list for fear it "commits" them to a purchase, before they can determine whether they'll be comfortable with the prices and choices available. As you're being handed the menus, say "We'll take a look at the wine list, too" to indicate you want a copy to review, not a pushy sales job. *Tip:* I always ask that the wine-by-the-glass list be brought, too. Since many places change them often, they may be on a separate card or a specials board. (I think verbal listings are the worst, because often key information, like the price or winery, can get lost in translation.)

2. Determine any style particulars you're in the mood for:

- White or red?
- A particular grape, region, or body style?

If the table can't reach a consensus, look at wine-by-the-glass and half-bottle options. This can happen when preferences differ or food choices are all over the map ("I'm having the oysters, he's having the wild boar, we want one wine . . ." is a stumper I've actually faced!).

3. Find your style zone in the list. Turn to the section that represents your chosen category—e.g., whites, the wine-by-the-glass section, Chardonnays, Italian reds, or whatever—or let the server know what style particulars you have in mind.

4. Match your budget. Pick a wine priced accordingly, keeping in mind these "safety zones":
   - The wines recommended in this book
   - Winery or region names that you remember liking or hearing good things about (e.g., Chianti in Italy or a different offering from your favorite white Zinfandel producer)
   - The midprice/midstyle zone (as I explained earlier, many lists have this "sweet spot" of well-made, moderately priced offerings)
   - Featured wine specials, if they meet your price parameters

You can communicate your budget while keeping your dignity with this easy trick I teach waiters:
   - Find your style zone—e.g., Pinot Grigios—in the wine list.
   - With both you and the server looking at the list, *point to the price* of a wine that's close to what you want to spend and then say, "We were looking at this one. What do you think?"
   - Keep pointing long enough for the server to see the price, and you'll be understood without having to say (in front of your date or client), "No more than thirty bucks, okay?"

I ask my waiters to point to the price, starting at a moderate level, with their first wine suggestion. From there the guest's reaction shows his or her intentions, without the embarrassment of having to talk price.

There's no formula, but the bottom line is this: whether glass or bottle, it's hard to go wrong with popular grapes and styles, moderate prices, the "signature" or featured wine(s) of the restaurant, and/or the waiter's enthusiastic recommendation. If you don't like it, chalk it up to experience—the same could happen with a first-time food choice, right? Most of the time, experimentation pays off. So enjoy!

Wine List Decoder

Wine is like food—it's easy to choose from among the styles with which you're familiar. That's why wines like Pinot Grigio, Chardonnay, Chianti, and Merlot are such big sellers. But when navigating other parts of the list, namely less-common grape varieties and the classic European regional wines, I think many of us get lost pretty quickly. And yet these are major players in the wine world, without which buyers miss out on a whole array of delicious options, from classic to cutting edge.

This decoder gives you the tools you need to explore them. It reveals:

> *The grapes used* to make the classic wines—If it's a grape you've tried, then you'll have an idea of what the wine tastes like.
> *The body styles from light to full* of every major wine category—The waiters and wine students with whom I work always find this extremely helpful, because it breaks up the wine world into broad, logical categories that are easy to understand and similar to the way we classify other things. With food, for example, we have vegetables, meat, fish, and so on.
> *The taste profile,* in simple terms—The exact taste of any wine is subjective (I say apple, you say pear), but knowing how the tastes *compare* is a great tool to help you identify your preferred style.

The names are set up just as you might see them on a wine list, under the key country and region headings, and in each section they are arranged by body style from light to full. (For whites, Italy comes before France in body style, overall. Their order is reversed for reds.) Finally, where applicable I've highlighted the major grapes in italics in the column on the left to help you quickly see just how widely used these grapes are and thus how much you already know about these heretofore mystifying wine names.

Sparkling Wines

- **Italy**

Asti Spumante	Muscat (Moscato)	Light; floral, hint of sweetness
Prosecco	Prosecco	Delicate; crisp, tangy, the wine used in Bellini cocktails

- **Spain**

Cava	Locals: Xarel-lo, Parellada, Macabeo plus Chardonnay	Light; crisp, refreshing

- **France**

Champagne	The red (yes!) grapes Pinot Noir and Pinot Meunier, plus Chardonnay	To me, all are heavenly, but check the style on the label: Blanc de Blancs—delicate and tangy Brut NV, vintage and luxury—range from soft and creamy to rich and toasty

White Wines

- **Italy**

Frascati	Trebbiano, Malvasia	As you've noticed, mostly local grapes are used in Italy's whites. But the style of all these is easy to remember: light, tangy, and refreshing. Pinot Grigio, the best known, is also more distinctive—pleasant pear and lemon flavors, tasty but not heavy. The less common Pinot Bianco is similar.
Soave	Garganega, Trebbiano	
Orvieto	Grechetto, Procanico, and many others	
Gavi	Cortese	
Vernaccia	Vernaccia	
Pinot Grigio		

- **Germany**

Riesling	Riesling rules Germany's quality wine scene	Feather-light but flavor-packed: fruit salad in a glass

- **France**
  - *Alsace—Grape names are on the label:*

	Pinot Blanc	Light; tangy, pleasant
Riesling	Riesling	Fuller than German Riesling but not heavy; citrus, apples, subtle but layered
	Pinot Gris	Smooth, richer texture; fruit compote flavors
	Gewurztraminer	Sweet spices, apricots, lychee fruit

- **Loire Valley**

Vouvray	Chenin Blanc	Look for the style name: Sec—dry and tangy; Demi-sec—baked apple, hint of sweetness; Moelleux—honeyed dessert style

Sauvignon Blanc

Sancerre and Pouilly-Fume	Sauvignon Blanc	Light to medium; subtle fruit, racy acidity

- **White Bordeaux**

Sauvignon Blanc & Semillon

Entre-Deux-Mers	Sauvignon Blanc and Semillon	Tangy, crisp, light
Graves Pessac-Leognan		Medium to full; ranging from creamy lemon-lime to lush fig flavors; pricey ones are usually oaky

- **Burgundy White**

Chardonnay

Macon St.-Veran Pouilly-Fuisse	Every Chardonnay in the world is modeled on white French Burgundy	Light; refreshing, citrus-apple flavors
Chablis		Subtle, mineral, green apple

St. Aubin		
Meursault		Medium; pear, dried apple, nutty; complexity ranging from simple to sublime
Puligny-Montrachet		
Chassagne-Montrachet		
Corton-Charlemagne		

Red Wines

- **France**
  - *Red Burgundy*

Beaujolais	Gamay	Uncomplicated, light; fruity, pleasant
Beaujolais-Villages		
Beaujolais Cru:		More complex, plum-berry taste, smooth (the wines are named for their village)
Morgon,		
Moulin-a-Vent, etc.		

Pinot Noir

Cote de Beaune	Pinot Noir	Ranging from light body, pretty cherry taste to extraordinary complexity: captivating spice, berry and earth scents, silky texture, berries and plums flavor
Santenay		
Volnay		
Pommard		
Nuits-St.-Georges		
Vosne-Romanee		
Gevrey-Chambertin		
Clos de Vougeot, etc.		

  - *Red Bordeaux*

Merlot

Pomerol	Merlot, plus Cabernet Franc and Cabernet Sauvignon	Medium to full; oaky-vanilla scent, plum flavor
St. Emilion		

Cabernet Sauvignon

Medoc	Cabernet Sauvignon, plus Merlot, Cabernet Franc, and Petit Verdot	Full; chunky-velvety texture; cedar-spice-toasty scent; dark berry flavor
Margaux		
Pauillac		
St-Estephe		

- **Rhone Red**

Syrah, aka Shiraz

Cotes-du-Rhone	Mainly Grenache, Syrah, Cinsault, Mourvedre	Medium to full; juicy texture; spicy raspberry scent and taste
Cote-Rotie	Syrah, plus a splash of white Viognier	Full; brawny texture; peppery scent; plum and dark berry taste
Hermitage	Syrah, plus a touch of the white grapes Marsanne and Roussane	Similar to Cote-Rotie
Chateauneuf-du-Pape	Mainly Syrah, Grenache, Cinsault, Mourvedre	Full; exotic leathery-spicy scent; spiced fig and berry compote taste

(Red Zinfandel is here in the light-to-full body spectrum)

- **Spain**
  - **Rioja**

Rioja Crianza, Reserva and Gran Reserva	Tempranillo, plus Garnacha, aka Grenache, and other local grapes	Ranging from soft and smooth, juicy strawberry character (Crianza); to full, caramel-leather scent, spicy-dried fruit taste (Reserva and Gran Reserva)

  - **Ribera del Duero**

	Mostly Tempranillo	Full; mouth-filling texture; toasty-spice scent; anise and plum taste

  - **Priorat**

Sometimes Cabernet Sauvignon

Priorat	Varied blends may include Cabernet Sauvignon, Garnacha, and other local grapes	Full; gripping texture; meaty-leathery-fig scent; superconcentrated plum and dark berry taste

- **Italy**

As you'll notice from the left column, Italy's classic regions mostly march to their own *bellissimo* beat.

  - **Veneto**

Valpolicella	Corvina plus other local grapes	Light; mouthwatering, tangy cherry taste and scent

Amarone della Valpolicella	Corvina; same vineyards as Valpolicella	Full; rich, velvety texture; toasted almond/prune scent; intense dark raisin and dried fig taste (think Fig Newtons)

- ### *Piedmont*

Dolcetto d'Alba (the best known of the Dolcettos, but others are good, too)	Dolcetto	Light; zesty, spicy, cranberry-sour cherry taste
Barbera d'Alba (look for Barbera d'Asti and others)	Barbera	Medium; licorice-spice-berry scent; earth and berry taste
Barolo Barbaresco	Nebbiolo	Full; "chewy" texture; exotic earth, licorice, tar scent; strawberry-spice taste

- ### *Tuscany*

Chianti/ Chianti Classico	Sangiovese	Ranges from light, easy, lip-smacking strawberry-spice character to intense, gripping texture; plum, licorice, and earth scent and taste
Vino Nobile di Monte-pulciano	Prugnolo (a type of Sangiovese)	Medium-to-full; velvety texture, earth-spice, stewed plum taste
Brunello di Montalcino	Brunello (a type of Sangiovese)	Very full; "chewy" in the mouth; powerful dark-fruit flavor

Sometimes Cabernet Sauvignon

"Super Tuscans"— not a region but an important category	Usually a blend of Sangiovese and Cabernet Sauvignon	Modeled to be a classy cross between French red Bordeaux and Italian Chianti; usually full, spicy, and intense, with deep plum and berry flavors

The bottom line on restaurant wine lists: In my opinion, it's not the size of the list that matters but rather the restaurant's effort to make enjoying wine as easy as possible for its guests. How? As always, it comes down to the basics:

Top Ten Tip-Offs You're in a Wine-Wise Restaurant

1. You're *never* made to feel you have to spend a lot to get something good.
2. Wine by the glass is taken as seriously as bottles, with a good range of styles and prices, listed prominently so you don't have to "hunt" to find them.
3. The wine list is presented automatically, so you don't have to ask for it (and wait while the waiter searches for a copy).
4. There are lots of quality bottle choices in the moderate price zone.
5. Wine service, whether glass or bottle, is helpful, speedy, and proficient.
6. Waiters draw your attention to "great values" rather than just the expensive stuff.
7. *Affordable* wine pairings are offered for the signature dishes—either on the menu or by servers.
8. You can ask for a taste before you choose a wine by the glass if you're not sure which you want.
9. It's no problem to split a glass, or get just a half-glass, of by-the-glass offerings. (Great for situations when you want only a little wine or want to try a range of different wines.)
10. There's no such thing as no-name "house white and red." (House-featured wines are fine, but they, and you, merit a name or grape and a region.)

ROBINSON RECOMMENDS . . .

Tear out this page, fold it, and put it into your wallet. These are my picks for the best wines in the book. They are go-to wines that you can always count on to deliver outstanding quality for the price.

Best of the Big Brands—In supermarkets, chain restaurants, and hotels.

Alice White—Much better than Yellowtail in the same price point.

Beaulieu Vineyard (BV)—In my opinion, *the best;* from their basic Coastal Estates line to their top-of-the-line, amazing quality for the money. They've been around so long you might have forgotten about them. If so, you are missing out.

Columbia Crest—Across-the-board quality for cheap.

Blackstone—Nice reds but everything they make is good for the price.

Gallo Family Vineyards—Used to be Gallo of Sonoma. I don't know how they do it for the price, but just excellent across the board.

Kendall-Jackson Vintner's Reserve—Excellent quality and varietal character across the whole line.

Lindemans—Their value-priced bin series is fantastic for the money.

Sterling Vintner's Collection—Better and cheaper than their Napa line.

Twin Fin—A fantastic value newcomer.

Specialists—These are worth the search.

Sparkling—Iron Horse, Domaine Carneros

Riesling—Eroica, Trimbach

Sauvignon Blanc—Frog's Leap, Ferrari-Carano, St. Supery

Chardonnay—Chalone, Chateau St. Jean, Cuvaison

Pinot Noir—Au Bon Climat, Etude, MacMurray Ranch

Merlot—Franciscan, St. Francis

Cabernet Sauvignon and Blends—Estancia, Franciscan, Mt. Veeder

Syrah/Shiraz—Penfolds, D'Arenberg

Zinfandel—Ridge, Ravenswood, Rafanelli

Italy and Tuscan Reds—Brolio, Castello di Gabbiano (the best Chiantis for the money)

Spanish Reds—Montecillo, Marques de Riscal Riojas

Worth the Splurge—For a special occasion or for cellaring, these are the wines that repay the investment in pleasure, ageability (for the reds), and wow factor.

Brut NV Champagne

Charles Heidsieck—decadent and toasty

Moët & Chandon—outstanding, medium-bodied

Perrier-Jouët—elegant, long finish

Luxury Champagne

Bollinger RD—toasty-nutty, extraordinary

Dom Perignon—better than ever

Krug Grand Cuvee—like you've died and awoken in heaven's croissant bakery

Riesling

Trimbach Cuvee Frederic Emile—mineral complexity, incredible length

Sauvignon Blanc

Duckhorn—truly special, complex melon flavors and great concentration

Chardonnay

Kistler—very toasty, rich, decadent

Leflaive (Domaine) Puligny-Montrachet—baked apple, marzipan, very classy

Pinot Noir

Au Bon Climat single vineyards—sexy, meaty, silky, good agers

Williams-Selyem—deep, pure spiced cherry, long finish, great ageability

Merlot

Duckhorn—opulent, lush, intense

Shafer—gorgeous succulent fruit, licorice, chocolate

Cabernet Sauvignon and Blends

BV George de Latour Private Reserve—thick, rich, classy, ages great

Caymus—powerful, rich, like-no-other coconut scent

Opus One—opulent, classy, the best-aging CA Cab blend I know of

Spain

Muga Rioja—leather, tobacco, great intensity

Pesquera Ribera del Duero—spice, concentrated fruit, good ageability

Overlooked and Underrated—That means the prices are great for the quality.

Bogle—especially the Petite Sirah

Chateau Souverain—amazing wines in the $15–25 range

Cline—Zins and Syrahs

Los Vascos and Veramonte—two of Chile's best at great budget prices

Spanish Rioja Reds—look for Marques de Riscal, Marques de Caceres, and Montecillo; don't be afraid to try other brands because this region offers a lot for the money

Wolf-Blass and Jacob's Creek—so much more character for the money in Aussie varietals than most of the competition

Woodbridge single vineyard series—small lots of vineyard-designated wines that are only slightly more expensive, but dramatically more exciting, than the base Woodbridge line

Andrea's Best Bets: Wines for Every Occasion

Best "House" Wines for Every Day—Sparkling, White, and Red

(*House* means *your* house.) These are great go-to wines to keep around for every day and company, too, because they're tasty, *very* inexpensive, and go with everything from takeout to Sunday dinner. They're also wines that got high Kitchen Fridge/Countertop Survivor™ grades, so you don't have to worry if you don't finish the bottle right away. (Selections are listed by body style—lightest to fullest.)

Sparkling

Segura Viudas Aria Cava Extra Dry Sparkling, Spain

Domaine Ste. Michelle Blanc de Noirs Brut
  Sparkling, Washington

House Whites

Ca' del Solo Big House White, California

Columbia Winery Cellarmaster's Reserve Riesling,
  Washington

Lindemans Bin 65 Chardonnay, Australia

Gallo Family Vineyards Sonoma Reserve
  Chardonnay, California

Dry Creek Fume Blanc, California

Reds

Echelon Central Coast Pinot Noir, California

Duboeuf (Georges) Cotes-du-Rhone, France

Montecillo Rioja Crianza, Spain

Wolf Blass Yellow Label Shiraz, Australia

Los Vascos Cabernet Sauvignon, Chile

Columbia Crest Grand Estates Merlot, Washington

Impress the Date—Hip Wines

White

Bonny Doon Pacific Rim Riesling, USA/Germany

Frog's Leap Sauvignon Blanc, California

Monkey Bay Sauvignon Blanc, New Zealand

R.H. Phillips Toasted Head Chardonnay,
  California

Smoking Loon Viognier, California

Red

Firesteed Pinot Noir, Oregon

Joel Gott Zinfandel, California

Baron Philippe de Rothschild, Escudo Rojo
  Cabernet Blend, Chile

Alamos by Catena Malbec, Argentina

D'Arenberg The Footbolt Shiraz, Australia

Impress the Client—Blue Chip Wines

Sparkling/White

Veuve Clicquot Yellow Label Champagne, France

Cloudy Bay Sauvignon Blanc, New Zealand

Ferrari-Carano Fume Blanc, California
Robert Mondavi Napa Fume Blanc, California
Sonoma-Cutrer Russian River Ranches Chardonnay, California
Talbott (Robert) Sleepy Hollow Vineyard Chardonnay, California

Red

Etude Carneros Pinot Noir, California
Domaine Drouhin Willamette Valley Pinot Noir, Oregon
Duckhorn Napa Merlot, California
Ridge Geyserville (Zinfandel), California
Stag's Leap Wine Cellars Napa Cabernet Sauvignon, California
Silver Oak Alexander Valley Cabernet Sauvignon, California

You're Invited—Unimpeachable Bottles to Bring to Dinner

(You *do* still have to send a note the next day.)

Trimbach Riesling, Alsace, France
Simi Sauvignon Blanc, California
St. Supery Sauvignon Blanc, California
Louis Jadot Pouilly-Fuisse, France
Beringer Napa Chardonnay, California
Calera Santa Barbara Pinot Noir, California
Ruffino Chianti Classico Riserva Ducale Gold Label, Italy
Penfolds Bin 389 Cabernet Sauvignon/Shiraz, Australia
St. Francis Sonoma Merlot, California
Franciscan Oakville Estate Cabernet Sauvignon, California
Mt. Veeder Napa Cabernet Sauvignon, California

Cellar Candidates

These wines have consistently proven age worthy throughout my restaurant career. The time window shown for each is the number of years' aging in reasonably cool cellar conditions to reach peak drinking condition. But this "peak" is in terms of *my* taste—namely when the wine's texture has softened and enriched, the aromas have become more layered, but the fruit remains vibrant. You may need to adjust your cellar regimen according to your taste. Generally, longer aging gradually trades youthful fruit and acidity for a whole new spectrum of aromas, many of which you might not instantly associate with grapes or wine. In whites, aging commonly leads to softened acidity and a nutty/caramel character; in reds, softened tannins and a leathery/spicy character.

White

Trimbach Riesling, France (3–4 yr)
Trimbach Pinot Gris Reserve, France (4–5 yr)
Grgich Hills Chardonnay, California (5–7 yr)
Chateau Montelena Chardonnay, California (5–7 yr)
Kistler Durrell Chardonnay, California (5–7 yr)
Leflaive (Domaine) Puligny-Montrachet, France (7–9 yr)
Leflaive (Olivier) Puligny-Montrachet, France (2–4 yr)

Red

Merry Edwards Russian River Pinot Noir, California (3–4 yr)
Etude Carneros Pinot Noir, California (5–6 yr)
Williams-Selyem Hirsch Vineyard Pinot Noir, California (5–7 yr)
Felsina Chianti Classico, Italy (5–7 yr)
Frescobaldi Chianti Rufina Riserva, Italy (5–7 yr)
Ruffino Chianti Classico Riserva Ducale Gold Label, Italy (5–7 yr)
Banfi Brunello di Montalcino, Italy (8–10 yr)
Duckhorn Napa Merlot, California (5–7 yr)
Shafer Merlot, California (4–5 yr)
Chateau Lynch-Bages Bordeaux, France (7–9 yr)
Cakebread Napa Cabernet Sauvignon, California (5–7 yr)
Chateau Gruaud-Larose Bordeaux, France (7–9 yr)
Groth Napa Cabernet Sauvignon, California (5–7 yr)
Heitz Napa Cabernet Sauvignon, California (5–7 yr)
Mt. Veeder Napa Cabernet Sauvignon, California (6–8 yr)
Penfolds Bin 389 Cabernet Sauvignon/Shiraz, Australia (6–8 yr)
Silver Oak Alexander Valley Cabernet Sauvignon, California (6–8 yr)

Stag's Leap Wine Cellars Napa Cabernet Sauvignon, California (5–7 yr)

Muga Rioja Reserva, Spain (7–9 yr)

Pesquera Ribera del Duero, Spain (7–9 yr)

Chateau de Beaucastel Chateauneuf-du-Pape Rouge, France (6–8 yr)

Grgich Hills Napa Zinfandel, California (4–5 yr)

Ridge Geyserville (Zinfandel), California (5–7 yr)

CUISINE COMPLEMENTS

Whether you're dining out, ordering in, or whipping it up yourself, the following wine recommendations will help you choose a wine to flatter the food in question. If your store doesn't carry that specific wine bottle, ask for a similar selection.

Thanksgiving Wines

More than any other meal, the traditional Thanksgiving lineup features a pretty schizo range of flavors—from gooey-sweet yams to spicy stuffing to tangy cranberry sauce and everything in between. These wines are like a group hug for all the flavors at the table and the guests around it. My tip: choose a white and a red, put them on the table, and let the diners taste and help themselves to whichever they care to drink. (Selections are listed by body style—lightest to fullest.)

	White	Red
S T E A L	Cavit Pinot Grigio, Italy Bonny Doon Pacific Rim Riesling (USA/Germany) Geyser Peak Sauvignon Blanc, California Pierre Sparr Alsace-One, France Fetzer Valley Oaks Gewurztraminer, California Gallo Family Vineyards Reserve Chardonnay, California	Louis Jadot Beaujolais-Villages, France Falesco Vitiano, Italy Duboeuf Cotes-du-Rhone, France Marques de Caceres Rioja Crianza, Spain Cline Zinfandel, California Rosemount Diamond Label Shiraz/Cabernet Sauvignon, Australia
S P L U R G E	Martin Codax Albarino, Spain Trimbach Riesling, France Robert Mondavi Napa Fume Blanc, California Hugel Gewurztraminer, France Cuvaison Napa Valley Chardonnay, California	Morgan 12 Clones Pinot Noir, California Chateau de Beaucastel Chateauneuf-du-Pape, France Penfolds Bin 389 Cabernet Sauvignon/Shiraz, Australia Pesquera Ribera del Duero, Spain Ridge Geyserville (Zinfandel), California

Barbecue
Rose Menage a Trois, California
Ca' del Solo Big House White, California
Dry Creek Fume Blanc, California
Black Opal Shiraz, Australia
Hill of Content Grenache/Shiraz, Australia
Jaboulet Parallele 45 Cotes-du-Rhone, France
Montevina Amador Zinfandel, California

Chinese Food
Hugel Pinot Blanc, France
Jolivet Sancerre, France
Navarro Gewurztraminer, California
Echelon Central Coast Pinot Noir, California
Marques de Caceres Rioja Crianza, Spain
Ravenswood Vintners Blend Zinfandel, California
Louis Jadot Beaujolais-Villages, France
Allegrini Valpolicella, Italy

Nuevo Latino (Cuban, Caribbean, South American)
Freixenet Brut de Noirs Cava Rose, Spain
Robert Mondavi Private Selection Pinot Grigio,
   California
Marques de Riscal White Rueda, Spain
Dallas Conte Merlot, Chile
Los Vascos Cabernet Sauvignon, Chile
Woodbridge (Robert Mondavi) Zinfandel, California

Picnics
Cavit Pinot Grigio, Italy
Domaine Ste. Michelle Blanc de Noirs Sparkling,
   Washington
Beringer White Zinfandel, California
Lindemans Bin 65 Chardonnay, Australia
Citra Montepulciano d'Abruzzo, Italy
Duboeuf (Georges) Beaujolais-Villages, France

Sushi
Moët & Chandon White Star Champagne, France
Trimbach Riesling, France
Burgans Albarino, Spain
Jolivet Sancerre, France
Monkey Bay Sauvignon Blanc, New Zealand
Frog's Leap Sauvignon Blanc, California

Louis Jadot Pouilly-Fuisse, France
Duboeuf Beaujolais-Villages, France
Twin Fin Pinot Noir, California
Calera Santa Barbara Pinot Noir, California

Clambake/Lobster Bake

Murphy-Goode Fume Blanc, California
Gallo Family Vineyards Reserve Chardonnay,
 California
Beringer Napa Chardonnay, California
Cambria Katherine's Vineyard Chardonnay,
 California
Louis Jadot Beaujolais-Villages, France
Firesteed Pinot Noir, Oregon

Mexican Food

Pierre Sparr Alsace-One, France
Veramonte Sauvignon Blanc, Chile
Hugel Gewurztraminer, France
Beringer White Zinfandel, California
Dry Creek Fume Blanc, California
Duboeuf (Georges) Cotes-du-Rhone, France
Cline Zinfandel, California
Ravenswood Vintners Blend Zinfandel, California

Pizza

Citra Montepulciano d'Abruzzo, Italy
Cantina Zaccagnini Montepulciano, Italy
Montecillo Rioja Crianza, Spain
D'Arenberg The Footbolt Shiraz, Australia
Montevina Amador Zinfandel, California
Woodbridge (Robert Mondavi) Zinfandel, California
Penfolds Koonunga Hill Shiraz Cabernet Sauvignon,
 Australia

The Cheese Course

Frescobaldi Nippozano Chianti Rufina Riserva, Italy
Penfolds Bin 389 Cabernet Sauvignon/Shiraz,
 Australia
Chateau de Beaucastel Chateauneuf-du-Pape,
 France
Muga Rioja Reserva, Spain
Pesquera Ribera del Duero, Spain
Ridge Geyserville (Zinfandel), California
Rosemount GSM (Grenache-Shiraz-Mourvedre),
 Australia

Grgich Hills Napa Zinfandel, California
Mt. Veeder Napa Cabernet Sauvignon, California
Chateau Gruaud-Larose Bordeaux, France
Banfi Brunello di Montalcino, Italy
Alvaro Palacios Les Terrasses Priorat, Spain

Steak

Ferrari-Carano Carneros Chardonnay, California
Talbott (Robert) Sleepy Hollow Vineyard
 Chardonnay, California
Archery Summit Arcus Estate Pinot Noir,
 Willamette Valley, Oregon
Domaine Drouhin Willamette Valley Pinot Noir,
 Oregon
Ruffino Chianti Classico Riserva Ducale Gold
 Label, Italy
Pio Cesare Barolo, Italy
Shafer Merlot, California
Cakebread Napa Cabernet Sauvignon, California
Beringer Knights Valley Cabernet Sauvignon,
 California
Robert Mondavi Cabernet Sauvignon Reserve,
 California
Groth Napa Cabernet Sauvignon, California
Stag's Leap Wine Cellars Napa Cabernet Sauvignon,
 California
Joseph Phelps Napa Cabernet Sauvignon,
 California
Rancho Zabaco Dry Creek Valley Zinfandel,
 California

Salad

Ruffino Orvieto, Italy
Hugel Pinot Blanc, France
Trimbach Riesling, France
Henri Bourgeois Pouilly Fume, France
Louis Jadot Macon-Villages Chardonnay, France
Allegrini Valpolicella, Italy
Calera Santa Barbara Pinot Noir, California

Vegetarian

Gallo Family Vineyards Reserve Pinot Gris, California
Hess Select Chardonnay, California
Estancia Pinnacles Pinot Noir, California
Castello di Gabbiano Chianti, Italy
Jaboulet Parallele 45 Cotes-du-Rhone, France

WINERY INDEX

Au Bon Climat, California
Rincon and Rosemary's Pinot Noir $$$$ 81
Santa Barbara Chardonnay $$$ 54
Santa Barbara Pinot Noir $$ 81
Talley Vineyard Pinot Noir $$$$ 81

Babcock, California
11 Oaks Sauvignon Blanc $$$ 43

Babich Marlborough, New Zealand
Sauvignon Blanc $ 43

Ballatore, California
Gran Spumante $ 23

Banfi, Italy
Brachetto d'Acqui $$$ 152
Brunello di Montalcino $$$$ 95
Chianti Classico Riserva $$ 95
Le Rime Pinot Grigio/Chardonnay $ 31

Banrock Station, Australia
Riesling $ 37

Baron Philippe de Rothschild, Chile
Escudo Rojo Cabernet Blend $$ 115

Baron Philippe de Rothschild, France
Sauternes $$$ 152

Beaulieu Vineyard (BV), California
Carneros Pinot Noir $$ 81
Coastal Estates Cabernet Sauvignon $ 108
Coastal Estates Chardonnay $ 54
Coastal Estates Merlot $ 99
Coastal Estates Pinot Noir $ 82
Coastal Estates Sauvignon Blanc $ 44
Coastal Estates Shiraz $ 138
George de Latour Private Reserve Cabernet 109
  Sauvignon $$$$
Napa Valley Cabernet Sauvignon $$ 109
Napa Valley Syrah $ 138
Napa Valley Zinfandel $$ 146
Reserve Pinot Noir $$ 82
Rutherford Cabernet Sauvignon $$$ 109

Becker, Texas
Viognier $$ 68

Benton Lane, Oregon
Pinot Noir $$ 82

Benziger, California
Sauvignon Blanc $$ 44

Beringer, California
Chenin Blanc $ 68
Gewurztraminer $ 68
Johannisberg Riesling $ 37
Knights Valley Cabernet Sauvignon $$$ 109

Napa Chardonnay **$**   54
Napa Merlot **$$$**   99
Private Reserve Cabernet Sauvignon **$$$$**   110
White Zinfandel **$**   76

Black Box 3L, California
Napa Chardonnay **$**   54
Napa Merlot **$**   99

Black Opal, Australia
Cabernet Sauvignon **$**   110
Shiraz **$**   138

Blackstone, California
Cabernet Sauvignon **$**   110
Monterey Chardonnay **$$**   54
Merlot **$$**   100
Syrah **$**   138
Zinfandel **$**   146

Blandy's, Portugal
10-Year-Old Malmsey Madeira **$$$$**   153

Bodegas Ochoa, Spain
Garnacha Rosado **$**   76

Bogle, California
Merlot **$**   100
Old Vines Zinfandel **$**   146
Petite Sirah **$**   132

Bolla, Italy
Pinot Grigio **$**   32
Valpolicella **$**   135

Bollinger, Champagne, France
RD **$$$$**   23
Special Cuvee Brut **$$$$**   23

Bonny Doon, California
Big House Pink **$**   76
Muscat Vin de Glaciere **$$$**   153
Pacific Rim Riesling (USA/Germany) **$**   37
Vin Gris de Cigare Pink Wine **$$**   76

Borsao, Spain
Grenache/Tempranillo **$**   129

Bouvet, Loire Valley, France
Brut Sparkling **$$**   24

Brancott, New Zealand
Marlborough Reserve Pinot Noir **$$**   82
Reserve Sauvignon Blanc **$$**   44
Sauvignon Blanc **$**   44

Broadbent, Portugal
3 Year Fine Rich Madeira **$$**   153

Brokenwood, Australia
Shiraz **$$$**   138

Brown Brothers, Australia
Shiraz $ 138

Buckeley's, Australia
Shiraz $ 138

Buena Vista, California
Carneros Chardonnay $$ 54
Carneros Pinot Noir $$ 82

Burgans (Bodegas Vilarino-Cambados), Spain
Albarino $$ 68

Ca'del Solo, California
Big House Red $ 132
Big House White $ 69

Cain, California
Cain Cuvee Bordeaux Style Red $$$ 110

Cakebread, California
Napa Cabernet Sauvignon $$$$ 110
Napa Chardonnay $$$$ 55
Sauvignon Blanc $$$ 44

Calera, California
Santa Barbara Pinot Noir $$$ 82

Cambria, California
Julia's Vineyard Pinot Noir $$ 82
Katherine's Vineyard Chardonnay $$ 55

Campbell's, Australia
Rutherglen Muscat $$$ 153

Cantina Zaccagnini, Italy
Montepulciano d'Abruzzo $ 135

Casa Lapostolle, Chile
Cuvee Alexandre Cabernet Sauvignon $$ 110
Cuvee Alexandre Chardonnay $$ 55
Cuvee Alexandre Merlot $$ 100
Sauvignon Blanc $ 44

Castello di Brolio, Italy
Chianti Classico $$$ 95

Castello di Gabbiano, Italy
Chianti Classico $ 96
Chianti Classico Riserva $$ 96

Castle Rock, California
Pinot Noir $ 83

Catena, Argentina
Chardonnay $$ 55

Cavit, Italy
Pinot Grigio $ 32

Caymus, California
Napa Cabernet Sauvignon $$$$ 111

Chateau Prieure-Lichine, France
Bordeaux **$$$** — 113

Chateau Rabaud-Promis, France
Sauternes **$$$$** — 154

Chateau Souverain, California
Alexander Valley Cabernet Sauvignon **$$$** — 113
Alexander Valley Merlot **$$** — 100

Chateau Ste. Michelle, Washington
Columbia Valley Cabernet Sauvignon **$$** — 113
Columbia Valley Chardonnay **$** — 56
Columbia Valley Merlot **$$** — 100
Columbia Valley Sauvignon Blanc **$** — 45
Gewurztraminer **$** — 69
Johannisberg Riesling **$** — 37

Chateau St. Jean, California
Cinq Cepages Cabernet Blend **$$$$** — 113
Fume Blanc **$** — 45
Robert Young Chardonnay **$$$** — 56
Sonoma Chardonnay **$** — 56
Pinot Noir **$$** — 83

Chehalem, Oregon
Pinot Gris **$$** — 32

Christian Moueix, France
Merlot **$** — 100

Citra, Italy
Montepulciano d'Abruzzo **$** — 136

Cline, California
Ancient Vines Mourvedre **$$** — 132
Red Truck **$** — 134
Syrah **$** — 139
Zinfandel **$** — 146

Clos du Bois, California
Alexander Valley Reserve Merlot **$$$** — 101
Marlstone **$$$$** — 113
Pinot Grigio **$** — 32
Sonoma Cabernet Sauvignon **$$** — 114
Sonoma Chardonnay **$** — 56
Sonoma Merlot **$$** — 101
Sonoma Pinot Noir **$$$** — 83
Sonoma Zinfandel **$$** — 146

Cloudline, Oregon
Pinot Noir **$$** — 83

Cloudy Bay, New Zealand
Sauvignon Blanc **$$$** — 45

Cockburn's, Portugal
Fine Ruby Port **$** — 154

Codorniu, Spain
Cava Rose **$$** — 24

Dashe Cellars, California
Dry Creek Zinfandel $$$ 146

David Bruce, California
Santa Cruz Pinot Noir $$$ 84

Dehlinger, California
Pinot Noir $$$$ 84

Deloach, California
Pinot Noir $$ 84

Domaine Carneros, California
Brut $$$ 24
Le Reve $$$$ 24
Pinot Noir $$$ 84

Domaine Chandon, California
Blanc de Noirs $$ 24
Brut Classic $$ 25
Riche $$ 25

Domaine de la Mordoree, France
Cotes-du-Rhone Red $$ 133

Domaine Drouhin, Oregon
Willamette Valley Pinot Noir $$$$ 84

Domaine Ott, France
Bandol Rose $$ 76

Domaine Santa Duc, France
Gigondas $$$ 000

Domaine Ste. Michelle, Washington
Blanc de Noir $ 25

Domaine Vincent Delaporte, France
Sancerre $$$ 45

Domaine Weinbach, France
Gewurztraminer Cuvee Theo $$$$ 70

Dom Perignon, Champagne, France
Brut $$$$ 25

Dr. Konstantin Frank, New York
Dry Riesling $$ 38

Dr. Loosen, Germany
Riesling Kabinett Estate $$$ 38

Dow's Colheita, Portugal
Tawny Port 1992 $$$ 154

Dry Creek, California
Cabernet Sauvignon $$ 114
Chenin Blanc $ 70
Fume Blanc $$ 46
Reserve Zinfandel $$$ 147

Drylands, New Zealand
Sauvignon Blanc $$ 46

Duboeuf (Georges), France
Beaujolais Nouveau **$** 79
Beaujolais-Villages **$** 79
Cotes-du-Rhone **$** 140

Duckhorn, California
Napa Merlot **$$$$** 102
Sauvignon Blanc **$$$** 46

Duck Pond, Oregon
Pinot Noir **$$** 84

Dyed in the Wool, New Zealand
Sauvignon Blanc **$** 46

E & M Guigal, France
Cote-Rotie Brune et Blonde **$$$$** 140
Cotes-du-Rhone **$$** 140

Ecco Domani, Italy
Pinot Grigio **$** 32

Echelon, California
Central Coast Pinot Noir **$** 85

Edna Valley Vineyard, California
Pinot Noir **$$** 85

El Coto, Spain
Rioja Reserva **$$** 129

Elk Cove, Oregon
Pinot Noir **$$** 85

Emilio Lustau, Spain
Pedro Ximenez "San Emilio" Sherry **$$$** 154

Erath, Oregon
Pinot Gris **$$** 32

Eroica, Washington
Riesling **$$$** 38

Estancia, California
Alexander Valley Red Meritage **$$$** 115
Cabernet Sauvignon **$$** 115
Pinnacles Chardonnay **$** 57
Pinnacles Pinot Noir **$$** 85

Etude, California
Carneros Pinot Noir **$$$$** 85

Faiveley, France
Mercurey Clos Rochette **$$$** 57

Falesco, Italy
Montiano **$$$$** 102
Vitiano **$** 136

Fall Creek, Texas
Chenin Blanc **$** 70
Merlot **$$** 102

Far Niente, California
Cabernet Sauvignon **$$$$**   115
Chardonnay **$$$$**   57

Fat Bastard, France
Chardonnay **$**   58

Felsina, Italy
Chianti Classico **$$$**   96

Felton Road, New Zealand
Pinot Noir **$$$$**   85
Riesling **$$$**   38

Ferrari-Carano, California
Carneros Chardonnay **$$$**   58
Fume Blanc **$$**   46
Siena Sonoma County **$$$**   115

Ferreira, Portugal
Doña Antonia Port **$$**   154

Fess Parker, California
Santa Barbara Pinot Noir **$$**   86

Fetzer, California
Valley Oaks Cabernet Sauvignon **$**   116
Valley Oaks Chardonnay **$**   58
Valley Oaks Gewurztraminer **$**   70
Valley Oaks Johannisberg Riesling **$**   38
Valley Oaks Merlot **$**   102
Valley Oaks Zinfandel **$**   147

Ficklin, California
Tinta "Port" **$$**   155

Finca Flichman, Argentina
Malbec Reserva **$**   133

Firesteed, Oregon
Pinot Noir **$**   86

Fisher Vineyards, California
Coach Insignia **$$$$**   116

Five Rivers Ranch, California
Pinot Noir **$**   86

Flora Springs, California
Barrel Fermented Chardonnay **$$$**   58
Pinot Grigio **$$**   33
Triology **$$$$**   116

Flowers, California
Pinot Noir **$$$$**   86

Folonari, Italy
Pinot Grigio **$**   33

Fonseca, Portugal
Bin 27 Port **$$**   155

Foppiano, California
  Petite Sirah **$$**   133

Franciscan, California
  Magnificat Meritage **$$$$**   116
  Oakville Chardonnay **$$**   58
  Oakville Estate Cabernet Sauvignon **$$$**   117
  Oakville Estate Merlot **$$$**   102

Francis Coppola
  See Coppola

Frank Family, California
  Chardonnay **$$$**   58

Frei Brothers Redwood Creek, California
  Sauvignon Blanc **$**   46

Frei Brothers Reserve, California
  Cabernet Sauvignon **$$**   117
  Merlot **$$**   103
  Pinot Noir **$$**   86
  Russian River Chardonnay **$$**   59

Freixenet, Spain
  Brut de Noirs Cava Rose **$**   25

Frescobaldi Nippozano, Italy
  Chianti Rufina Riserva **$$**   96

Frog's Leap, California
  Cabernet Sauvignon **$$$**   117
  Merlot **$$$$**   103
  Sauvignon Blanc **$$**   47

Gallo Family Vineyards, California
  Barelli Creek Cabernet Sauvignon **$$$**   117
  Reserve Cabernet Sauvignon **$$**   117
  Reserve Pinot Gris **$**   33
  Reserve Pinot Noir **$**   86
  Sonoma Reserve Chardonnay **$**   59
  Sonoma Reserve Merlot **$**   103
  Sonoma Reserve Syrah **$**   140
  Zinfandel **$**   147

Geyser Peak, California
  Cabernet Sauvignon **$**   118
  Chardonnay **$**   59
  Sauvignon Blanc **$**   47

Girard, California
  Old Vine Zinfandel **$$$**   147

Goats Do Roam, South Africa
  Red **$**   77
  Rose **$**   140

Gosset, France
  Brut Rose **$$$$**   26

Jaboulet, France
    Parallele 45 Cotes-du-Rhone **$**   141

Jacob's Creek, Australia
    Cabernet Sauvignon **$**   119
    Chardonnay **$**   60
    Shiraz/Cabernet **$**   141

Jade Mountain, California
    Napa Syrah **$$**   142

Jekel, California
    Riesling **$**   39

J.J. Prum, Germany
    Kabinett Wehlener Sonnenuhr Riesling **$$**   39

J. Lohr, California
    7 Oaks Cabernet Sauvignon **$$**   119
    Bay Mist Riesling **$**   39
    Riverstone Chardonnay **$**   60

Joel Gott, California
    Sauvignon Blanc **$**   48
    Zinfandel **$$**   148

Jolivet (Pascal), France
    Sancerre **$$**   48

Jordan, California
    Cabernet Sauvignon **$$$$**   119

Joseph Drouhin, France
    Pouilly-Fuisse **$$**   60

Joseph Phelps, California
    Insignia Cabernet Blend **$$$$**   119
    Le Mistral **$$$**   142
    Napa Cabernet Sauvignon **$$$$**   119
    Pastiche Rouge **$$**   142
    Sauvignon Blanc **$$$**   48

Justin, California
    Isosceles Cabernet Blend **$$$$**   120

J Wine Company, California
    Russian River Pinot Noir **$$$**   87
    Vintage Brut **$$$**   26

Ken Wright, Oregon
    Pinot Noir **$$$$**   87

Kendall-Jackson, California
    Vintner's Reserve Cabernet Sauvignon **$$**   120
    Vintner's Reserve Chardonnay **$**   60
    Vintner's Reserve Merlot **$$**   103
    Vintner's Reserve Pinot Noir **$$**   87
    Vintner's Reserve Riesling **$**   40
    Vintner's Reserve Zinfandel **$**   148

Kenwood, California
    Jack London Zinfandel **$$$**   148
    Sauvignon Blanc **$**   48

Kim Crawford, New Zealand
  Sauvignon Blanc **$$** 48
  Unoaked Chardonnay **$$** 60

King Estate, Oregon
  Pinot Gris **$$** 33
  Pinot Noir **$$$** 87

Kistler, California
  Durell Chardonnay **$$$$** 60

Knoll, Austria
  Gruner-Veltliner Smaragd Trocken Wachau **$$** 72

Korbel, California
  Brut **$** 26

Kris, Italy
  Pinot Grigio **$** 33

Krug, France
  Grande Cuvee Multivintage **$$$$** 27

Kurt Darting, Germany
  Riesling Kabinett **$$** 40

L'Ecole No. 41, Washington
  Walla Walla Valley Merlot **$$$$** 103

Laboure-Roi, France
  Macon Villages **$$** 61

La Crema, California
  Chardonnay **$$** 61
  Sonoma Pinot Noir **$$** 87

Landmark Vineyards, California
  Overlook Chardonnay **$$$** 61

Laurel Glen, California
  Reds **$** 148

Laurent-Perrier, Champagne, France
  Brut LP **$$$$** 27

La Vieille Ferme, France
  Cotes-du-Ventoux Rose **$** 77
  Cotes-du-Ventoux Rouge **$** 142

Leacock's, Portugal
  Rainwater Madeira **$$** 155

Leasingham, Australia
  Bin 7 Riesling **$$** 40

Leflaive (Domaine), France
  Puligny-Montrachet **$$$$** 61

Leflaive (Olivier), France
  St. Aubin **$$$** 61

Leitz, Germany
  Dragonstone Riesling **$$** 40

Liberty School, California
    Cabernet Sauvignon **$$** 120

Lindemans, Australia
    Bin 40 Merlot **$** 104
    Bin 50 Shiraz **$** 142
    Bin 65 Chardonnay **$** 61
    Bin 99 Pinot Noir **$** 88

Lingenfelder, Germany
    Bird Label Riesling **$$** 40

Little Boomey, Australia
    Cabernet/Shiraz **$** 120

The Little Penguin, Australia
    Cabernet Sauvignon **$** 120
    Cabernet Sauvignon Shiraz **$** 120
    Merlot **$** 104

Livio Felluga, Italy
    Pinot Grigio **$$$** 34

Los Vascos, Chile
    Cabernet Sauvignon **$** 121

Louis Jadot, France
    Beaujolais-Villages **$** 79
    Macon-Villages Chardonnay **$** 62
    Pouilly-Fuisse **$$$** 62

Louis Martini, California
    Cabernet Reserve **$$$** 121
    Monte Rosso Gnarly Vines Zinfandel **$$$$** 148
    Napa Cabernet **$** 000

Luce, Italy
    Super Tuscan **$$$$** 96

Lucien Crochet, France
    Sancerre **$$$** 49

MacMurray Ranch, California
    Pinot Gris **$$** 34
    Sonoma Coast Pinot Noir **$$** 000
    Russian River Valley Pinot Noir **$$$** 88

Markham, California
    Merlot **$$$** 104

Mark West, California
    Central Coast Pinot Noir **$** 88

Marques de Arienzo, Spain
    Rioja Reserva **$$** 129

Marques de Caceres, Spain
    Rioja Crianza **$$** 129
    Rioja Rosado **$** 77

Marques de Riscal, Spain
Rioja Crianza **$** 129
Rioja Gran Reserva **$$$** 130
Rioja Reserva **$$** 130
Rueda White **$** 72

Marquis Philips, Australia
Sarah's Blend **$$** 142

Martin Codax, Spain
Albarino **$** 72

Martinsancho, Spain
Verdejo **$** 72

Mason, California
Sauvignon Blanc **$$** 49

Matanzas Creek, California
Chardonnay **$$$** 62

McWilliams Hanwood Estate, Australia
Cabernet Sauvignon **$** 121
Chardonnay **$** 62
Riesling **$** 40

Menage a Trois, California
Rose **$** 77
White Blend **$** 72

Meridian, California
Pinot Noir **$** 88

Merry Edwards, California
Russian River Valley Pinot Noir **$$$$** 88

Merryvale, California
Profile Cabernet Blend **$$$$** 121
Sauvignon Blanc **$$** 49

Mer Soleil, California
Chardonnay **$$$$** 62

Michele Chiarlo, Italy
Barbera d'Asti **$** 136
Nivole ("Clouds") Moscato d'Asti **$$$** 155

Michel Laroche, Burgundy, France
Chablis St. Martin **$$$** 62

Miner, California
Pinot Noir **$$$$** 88

Mionetto, Italy
DOC Prosecco Brut **$$** 27

Mirassou, California
Chardonnay **$** 63
Pinot Noir **$** 89
Riesling **$** 41

Moët & Chandon, Champagne, France
Brut Imperial **$$$$** 27
Nectar Imperial Rose **$$$$** 28
White Star **$$$$** 28

Mondavi (Robert), California
See Robert Mondavi

Monkey Bay, New Zealand
Sauvignon Blanc **$**   49

Monte Antico, Italy
Toscana **$**   97

Montecillo, Spain
Rioja Crianza **$**   130
Rioja Reserva **$$**   130

Montes, Chile
Alpha "M" **$$$$**   104
Malbec **$**   133
Merlot **$**   104

Montevina, California
Amador Zinfandel **$**   148

Morgan, California
12 Clones Pinot Noir **$$$**   89

Mt. Veeder, California
Napa Cabernet Sauvignon **$$$$**   121

Muga, Spain
Rioja Reserva **$$$**   130

Mumm, Napa, California
Brut Cuvee **$$**   28
Cuvee M **$$**   28

Muros Antiguos, Portugal
Albarino Vinho Verde **$$**   72

Murphy-Goode, California
Fume Blanc **$**   49
Liar's Dice Zinfandel **$$**   148

Navarro, California
Gewurztraminer **$$$**   72

Navarro Correas, Argentina
Malbec **$**   134

Nobilo, New Zealand
Sauvignon Blanc **$**   50

Nozzole, Italy
Chianto Classico Riserva **$$**   97

Opus One, California
Cabernet Blend **$$$$**   122

Ornellaia, Italy
Super Tuscan **$$$$**   122

Orrin Swift, California
Sauvignon Blanc **$$**   50

Osborne, Spain
Solaz Tempranillo **$**   130

Pahlmeyer, California
  Meritage Napa Valley **$$$$**   122

Paul Blanck, France
  Gewurztraminer Classique **$$**   73

Pavillon Blanc du Chateau Margaux, France
  Bordeaux **$$$$**   50

Penfolds, Australia
  Bin 389 Cabernet Sauvignon/Shiraz **$$$**   122
  Grange **$$$$**   142
  Kalimna Shiraz Bin 28 **$$$**   143
  Koonunga Hill Cabernet/Merlot **$**   122
  Koonunga Hill Chardonnay **$**   63
  Koonunga Hill Semillon/Chardonnay **$**   73
  Koonunga Hill Shiraz Cabernet **$**   143

Pepperwood Grove, California
  Pinot Noir **$**   89
  Viognier **$**   73

Perrier-Jouët, Champagne, France
  Flower Bottle **$$$$**   28
  Grand Brut **$$$$**   28

Pesquera, Spain
  Ribera del Duero **$$$**   131

Peter Lehmann, Australia
  Clancy's Shiraz **$$**   143

Pierre Sparr, France
  Alsace-One **$**   73
  Carte d'Or Riesling **$**   41
  Pinot Blanc **$**   73

Pine Ridge, California
  Cabernet Sauvignon Stag's Leap
    District **$$$$**   123

Pio Cesare, Italy
  Barolo **$$$$**   136

Piper-Heidsieck, Champagne, France
  Brut Cuvee **$$$**   29

Piper-Sonoma, California
  Brut **$$**   29

Pol Roger, Champagne, France
  Brut Reserve **$$$**   29

Pommery, Champagne, France
  Brut Royal **$$$$**   29

Ponzi, Oregon
  Pinot Gris **$$**   34
  Pinot Noir **$$$**   89

Pride Mountain Vineyards, California
  Cabernet Sauvignon **$$$$**   123

Quintessa, California
  Cabernet Blend **$$$$**   123

Rabbit Ridge, California
  Paso Robles Zinfandel **$$**   149

Rafanelli, California
  Zinfandel **$$$$**   149

Ramsay, California
  Pinot Noir **$$**   89

Rancho Zabaco, California
  Dry Creek Valley Zinfandel **$$**   149
  Heritage Vines Zinfandel **$$**   149
  Russian River Zinfandel **$$$**   149
  Stefani Zinfandel **$$$**   150

Ravenswood, California
  Belloni Zinfandel **$$$**   150
  Sonoma Old Vines Zinfandel **$$**   150
  Vintners Blend Merlot **$**   104
  Vintners Blend Zinfandel **$**   150

Raymond Estates, California
  Napa Cabernet Sauvignon **$$**   123

Red Bicyclette, France
  Syrah **$**   143

Reichsgraf von Kesselstatt, Germany
  Piesporter Goldtropfchen Riesling Kabinett **$$$**   41

Renwood, California
  Sierra Zinfandel **$$**   150

Rex Goliath, California
  Merlot **$**   103
  Shiraz **$**   141

Rex Hill, Oregon
  Willamette Valley Pinot Noir **$$**   90

R.H. Phillips, California
  Dunnigan Hills Chardonnay **$**   63
  Toasted Head Cabernet Sauvignon **$$**   123
  Toasted Head Chardonnay **$$**   63

Ridge, California
  Geyserville (Zinfandel) **$$$**   150

Rivetti, Italy
  Moscato d'Asti La Spinetta **$$**   156

RL Buller, Australia
  Fine Muscat **$$$**   156

Robert Mondavi, California
  Cabernet Sauvignon Reserve **$$$$**   124
  Carneros Pinot Noir **$$$**   90
  Napa Cabernet Sauvignon **$$**   124
  Napa Chardonnay **$$**   63

Napa Fume Blanc **\$\$** 50
Napa Zinfandel **\$\$** 150
Private Selection Pinot Grigio **\$** 34
Private Selection Pinot Noir **\$** 90
Private Selection Riesling **\$** 41

Robert Sinskey, California
Los Carneros Pinot Noir **\$\$\$** 90

Rocca della Macie, Italy
Chianti Classico **\$\$** 97

Rochioli, California
Pinot Noir **\$\$\$\$** 90

Rodney Strong, California
Sonoma Cabernet Sauvignon **\$\$** 124
Sonoma Chardonnay **\$** 64
Sonoma Merlot **\$\$** 105

Roederer Estate, California
Brut **\$\$\$** 29

Rombauer, California
Chardonnay **\$\$\$** 64
Merlot **\$\$\$** 105
Zinfandel **\$\$\$** 151

Rosemount, Australia
Diamond Label Cabernet Sauvignon **\$** 124
Diamond Label Chardonnay **\$** 64
Diamond Label Shiraz **\$** 143
Diamond Label Shiraz/Cabernet Sauvignon **\$** 144
GSM (Grenache-Shiraz-Mourvedre) **\$\$\$** 144
Traminer Riesling **\$** 73

Rosenblum, California
Vintner's Cuvee Zinfandel **\$** 151

Ruffino, Italy
Chianti Classico Riserva Ducale Gold 97
Label **\$\$\$\$**
Chianti Classico Riserva Ducale Tan 97
Label **\$\$\$**
Lumina Pinot Grigio **\$** 34
Orvieto **\$** 74

Rust-en-Vrede, South Africa
Estate Red **\$\$\$** 124

St. Francis, California
Sonoma Chardonnay **\$** 65
Sonoma Merlot **\$\$** 105

Saintsbury, California
Carneros Pinot Noir **\$\$\$** 91

St. Supery, California
Moscato **\$\$** 156
Sauvignon Blanc **\$\$** 50

Sanford, California
Pinot Noir **$$$** 91

Santa Cristina Sangiovese, Antinori, Italy
See Antinori

Santa Margherita, Italy
Pinot Grigio **$$$** 34

Santa Rita, Chile
120 Cabernet Sauvignon **$** 124

Sea Smoke, California
Botella Pinot Noir **$$$** 91

Sebastiani, California
Sonoma County Cabernet Sauvignon **$$** 125
Sonoma County Merlot **$$** 105
Sonoma County Pinot Noir **$$** 91

Seghesio, California
Sonoma Zinfandel **$$** 151

Segura Viudas, Spain
Aria Estate Cava Brut **$$** 30

Selbach-Oster, Germany
"Fish Label" Riesling **$** 41

Sella & Mosca, Italy
Vermentino **$$** 74

Shafer, California
Hillside Select Cabernet Sauvignon **$$$$** 125
Merlot **$$$$** 105

Siduri, California
Pinot Noir **$$$** 91

Silkwood, California
Petite Sirah **$$$** 134

Silverado, California
Chardonnay **$$$** 64
Napa Cabernet Sauvignon **$$$$** 125
Sauvignon Blanc **$$** 50

Silver Oak, California
Alexander Valley Cabernet Sauvignon **$$$$** 125

Simi, California
Merlot **$$$** 105
Russian River Reserve Chardonnay **$$$** 64
Sauvignon Blanc **$$** 51
Sonoma Cabernet Sauvignon **$$$** 125

Smith Woodhouse, Portugal
Lodge Reserve Port **$$$** 156

Smoking Loon, California
Cabernet Sauvignon **$** 126
Chardonnay **$** 64
Pinot Noir **$** 92

Sauvignon Blanc **$**   51
Viognier **$**   74

Sofia, California
Blanc de Blancs **$$**   30

Sokol Blosser, Oregon
Evolution **$$**   74
Willamette Pinot Noir **$$$**   92

Solaris, California
Pinot Noir **$**   92

Solorosa, California
Rose **$$**   77

Sonoma-Cutrer, California
Russian River Ranches Chardonnay **$$$**   64

Spy Valley, New Zealand
Sauvignon Blanc **$**   51

Staglin Family, California
Cabernet Sauvignon **$$$$**   126

Stag's Leap Wine Cellars, California
Napa Cabernet Sauvignon **$$$$**   126
Napa Merlot **$$$$**   106

Stag's Leap Winery, California
Petite Sirah **$$$**   134

Sterling Vineyards, California
Cabernet Sauvignon Reserve **$$$$**   126
Napa Cabernet Sauvignon **$$$**   126
Napa Chardonnay **$$**   65
Napa Merlot **$$$**   106
Napa Sauvignon Blanc **$$**   51
Vintner's Collection Cabernet Sauvignon **$**   126
Vintner's Collection Chardonnay **$**   65
Vintner's Collection Sauvignon Blanc **$**   51
Vintner's Collection Shiraz **$**   144

Stonestreet, California
Alexander Valley Cabernet Sauvignon **$$$**   127

Straccali, Italy
Chianti **$**   98

Strub, Germany
Niersteiner Paterberg Riesling Spatlese **$$**   42

Sutter Home, California
Gewurztraminer **$**   74
Merlot **$**   106
White Zinfandel **$**   77

Swanson Vineyards, California
Merlot **$$$**   106

Taittinger, Champagne, France
Brut La Française **$$$$**   30

Talbott (Robert), California
  Sleepy Hollow Vineyard Chardonnay **$$$$** 65

Talus, California
  Chardonnay **$** 65
  Pinot Noir **$** 92
  Zinfandel **$** 151

Taurino Salice, Italy
  Salentino **$** 136

Taylor Fladgate, Portugal
  20 Year Tawny Port **$$$$** 156

Terrazas Alto, Argentina
  Malbec **$** 134

Three Blind Moose, California
  Chardonnay **$** 66
  Merlot **$** 106

Toad Hollow, California
  Eye of the Toad Pinot Noir Dry Rose **$** 78

Toasted Head, California
  Shiraz **$$** 144

Traminer, France
  Roncier Pinot Noir **$** 92

Trefethen, California
  Estate Chardonnay **$$$** 66

Trimbach, Alsace, France
  Pinot Gris Reserve **$$** 35
  Riesling **$$** 42
  Riesling Cuvee Frederic Emile **$$$$** 42

Trinchero Family Estates, California
  Pinot Noir **$$$** 92

Truchard, California
  Pinot Noir **$$$** 92

Twin Fin, California
  Cabernet Sauvignon **$** 127
  Chardonnay **$** 66
  Merlot **$** 106
  Pinot Grigio **$** 35
  Pinot Noir **$** 93

Val d'Orbieu, France
  La Cuvee Mythique **$** 144

Veramonte, Chile
  Cabernet Sauvignon **$** 127
  Chardonnay **$** 66
  Primus **$$** 134
  Sauvignon Blanc **$** 52

Veuve Clicquot, Champagne, France
  La Grande Dame **$$$$** 30
  Yellow Label **$$$$** 30

Viader, California
  Napa Valley Cabernet Blend **$$$$**   127

Villa Maria, New Zealand
  Private Bin Sauvignon Blanc **$$**   52

Vinicola del Priorat, Spain
  Onix **$$**   131

Voss, California
  Sauvignon Blanc **$$**   52

Walter Glatzer, Austria
  Gruner-Veltliner Kabinett **$**   74

Warre, Portugal
  10-Year-Old Otima Tawny Port **$$$**   156

Weingartner, Austria
  Gruner-Veltliner Federspiel **$**   74

Whitehall Lane, California
  Cabernet Sauvignon Reserve **$$$$**   127

Whitehaven, New Zealand
  Pinot Noir **$$$**   93
  Sauvignon Blanc **$$**   52

WillaKenzie, Oregon
  Pinot Gris **$$**   35
  Willamette Valley Pinot Noir **$$$**   93

Willamette Valley Vineyards, Oregon
  Pinot Gris **$$**   35
  Whole Berry Pinot Noir **$$**   93

Williams-Selyem, California
  Hirsch Vineyard Pinot Noir **$$$$**   93
  Sonoma Coast Pinot Noir **$$$$**   94

Wolf Blass, Australia
  Yellow Label Chardonnay **$**   66
  Yellow Label Shiraz **$**   144

Wollersheim, Wisconsin
  Prairie Fume **$**   75

Woodbridge (Robert Mondavi), California
  Fish Net Creek Old Vine Zinfandel **$**   151
  Pinot Grigio **$**   35
  Zinfandel **$**   152

Wyndham, Australia
  Bin 555 Shiraz **$**   144

Yellow Tail, Australia
  Chardonnay **$**   66
  Shiraz **$**   145

Zemmer, Italy
  Pinot Grigio **$$**   35

Zind-Humbrecht, France
  Wintzenheim Gewurztraminer **$$**   75

THANKS TO . . .

The tasting panel! You've made buying and drinking wine better and more fun for everyone who picks up this book. Thanks for sharing your hidden gems, and for telling it like it is. Keep tasting!

Cindy Renzi, for Web site help, and Katie McManus, Melissa Manners, and Rachel Soszynski, for all the number-crunching.

Broadway Books, especially Jennifer Josephy and Steve Rubin, for believing in the book.

DEDICATED TO . . .

My husband, John Robinson, and my children, Lucas and Jesse.

And in loving tribute to the memory of the missing from Windows on the World, where wine really was for everyone.

PLEASE JOIN MY TASTING PANEL

To share your comments on wines you like (or dislike), visit www.andreawine.com. While you're there, you can get wine and food pairings, download delicious wine-worthy recipes, and check out my new *Complete Wine Course* DVD, and my wine club:

The A-List™ is my wine club of discoveries that are limited and really amazing for the price. These are wines you won't find in most stores (or buying guides!), delivered to your door (where legal) and paired with recipes I've created to perfectly showcase the wines. Visit www.andreawine.com for more info.

YOUR WINE NOTES

_____

_____

_____

_____

_____

_____

_____

_____

_____

_____

_____

_____

_____

_____

_____

_____

_____

_____

_____

_____

_____

_____

_____

Wine Notes

Wine Notes

Wine Notes

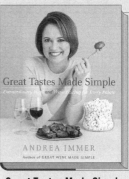